The Reminiscences

of

Dr. WALDO K. LYON
Director,
Arctic Marine Environmental Laboratory
San Diego, California

U. S. Naval Institute
Annapolis, Maryland
1972

Preface

This manuscript is the result of a series of tape recorded interviews given by Dr. Waldo K. Lyon, Director of the Arctic Marine Environmental Laboratory in San Diego, California. The interviews were conducted by Commander Etta Belle Kitchen, USN (Ret.), for the Oral History Office in the U. S. Naval Institute and were held during a period from January to March, 1971, at the home of Dr. Lyon in San Diego.

Dr. Lyon's account of the various scientific journeys to Arctic and Antarctic waters in submarines of the U. S. Navy is indeed an unique story and should prove of great value. He has read the original transcript from the tapes and has made only minor corrections. The reader is asked to bear in mind the fact that this is a transcript of the spoken word rather than the written one.

An alphabetized index of names, places and subjects is included in this volume for greater facility in using the material.

DECLARATION OF TRUST

The undersigned does hereby appoint and designate as his (her) Trustee herein, the Secretary-Treasurer and Publisher of the United States Naval Institute to perform and discharge the following duties, powers, and privileges in connection with the possession and use of a certain taped interview between the undersigned and the Oral History Department of the United States Naval Institute.

1. Classification of Transcript.

(X) a. If classified OPEN, the transcript(s) may be read or the recording(s) audited by the qualified personnel upon presentation of proper credentials, as determined by the Secretary-Treasurer of the U. S. Naval Institute.

( ) b. If classified PERMISSION REQUIRED TO CITE OR QUOTE, the user will be required to obtain permission in writing from the interviewee prior to quoting or citing from either the transcript(s) or the recording(s).

( ) c. If classified PERMISSION REQUIRED, permission must be obtained in writing from the interviewee before the transcribed interview(s) can be examined or the tape recording(s) audited.

( ) d. If classified CLOSED, the transcribed interview(s) and the tape recording(s) will be sealed until a time specified by the interviewee. This may be until the death of the interviewee or for any specified number of years.

2. It is expressly understood that in giving this authorization, I am in no way precluded from placing such restrictions as I may desire upon use of the interview at any time during my lifetime, nor does this authorization in any way affect my rights to the copyright of my literary expressions that may be contained in the interview.

Witness my hand and seal this _tenth_ day of _April_ 1977.

I hereby accept and consent to the foregoing Declaration of Trust and the powers therein conferred upon me as Trustee:

Interview No. 1. with Dr. Waldo K. Lyon

Date: 30 January 1971

Place: His home, 1330 Alexandria Drive, San Diego

Subject: Biography

By: Etta Belle Kitchen

Q: This is the first in a series of interviews with Dr. Lyon, who is the director of the Arctic Submarine Laboratory, Naval Undersea Research and Development Center in San Diego.

I appreciate, Dr. Lyon, and I know the Institute will appreciate your taking the time to set your experiences on tape, and I want to thank you for it.

I would like to approach the interview with the thought of your telling your story of polar exploration, and the story also of the submarine laboratory, and the Navy's work in research and development in that field that automatically parallel each other, if that's satisfactory with you?

Dr. L.: I'll try to do that, if I can think of the parts and the pieces as we go along, year by year, and also some of the individuals who have been involved in this history.

Q: They're certainly part of the story. I would like to begin at the beginning and have a short resume of your background, your vital statistics, and what brought you to this program.

Dr. L.: I would think that should start with why I came to San Diego in early 1941.

Lyon # 1 - 2

Q: Can't we start with the date you were born and the place?

Dr. L.: I thought, maybe, that was already on the record!

Q: Not on this tape.

Dr. L.: Okay, I see. That would be May 19, 1914, in Los Angeles, California, and all of my education was in Los Angeles, through high school and UCLA, starting at UCLA in 1932. I completed my bachelor and master's degree in 1936 and 1937, in the physics department there. Then, I continued on because at that period it was impossible to find a job anyway, so I continued on in graduate school to get my doctor's degree, which was completed in May of 1941, and at that time I had an offer to go to Stanford University, their physics department. However, in the summer of 1940 or thereabouts, when the draft was brought in, in registering for the draft I was one of the very low numbers and was called up in December of 1940, and was able after much help from the university to get a deferment until May of 1941 to get my degree. So, then, realizing what was ahead, and also what should be done, and the fact that the UCLA physics department was becoming involved in acoustics efforts of the military, I came down to San Diego and interviewed what was then the U. S. Navy Radio and Sound Laboratory, a very small organization of about 40 or 50 people.

Q: Located at the same place?

Dr. L.: Located out there on Point Loma where the present Navy Electronics Laboratory Center and the Undersea R and D Center are located.

Q: May I ask one question about your work academically? Was

it on the same line that the Navy was then attempting?

Dr. L.: No.

Q: What was your undergraduate and your graduate work?

Dr. L.: My undergraduate and all my graduate work was in optics and early infrared spectroscopy, not related to acoustics at all. But at that time UCLA was very strong in two fields. One was spectroscopy, and the other was acoustics. I had had courses in acoustics but I had not actually specialized in that at all, just general education. However, the individual that I was really involved with was Lieutenant Commander Delsasso, who was a member of the physics department at UCLA.

Q: A naval officer?

Dr. L.: Yes, but he was reserve, and he was in the physics department, acoustics, at UCLA, and he was called up to active duty as of January 1941, and he reported to the Radio and Sound Laboratory at San Diego. It was his influence, of course, because I needed to do something about my service and because of his interest and we knew each other very well - that was my link to come to this particular locality. So I came to work, then, in May of 1941 under Delsasso here at San Diego. Then all during the war period I was working here at the Radio and Sound Laboratory, really learning acoustics in submarines and working on problems of sonar and submarine detection. But from the submarine's point of view, right from the start, I was not really antisubmarine warfare. I was pro-submarine warfare to begin with.

Lyon #1 - 4

Q: Can you tell me some of the developments that you worked on or towards? During that period?

Dr. L.: A great part of it was submarines going through harbor defenses. Remember that the Pacific was really the pro-submarine warfare, much more than antisubmarine warfare, so for about two and a half or three years of it was on how to get through harbor-defense systems, and naturally we learned about harbor-defense systems of all types and then what submarines could do using the currents, temperature profiles, and what not, of a particular place to avoid being detected getting into harbors.

Of course, I was also involved in some of the harbor defense, because you're on both sides at the same time. And we made a number of experiments in harbor-defense systems up at Seattle, Los Angeles, and, of course, San Diego, just for trials on how to get through the system and how to make the system even better. So it was really that part of it - the submarine versus the harbor-defense system - for a good share of the period.

In addition to that, there was some development in some devices to go on the submarine to detect torpedo attacks. Let me see what else. This was a long time ago.

Q: Did you help develop sonar?

Dr. L.: Sonar's for particular jobs. I was north one of the major sonar developers but I did not play a part with the sonar for going through minefields. This is the sonar which we used later for the under-ice work, but it was developed by the group here at San Diego, but I was not involved in that one. I was more involved in the development of acoustics devices for currents at the bottom – that is, just plain echo-sounding systems and their various uses, and also looking upward for measuring the waves above and the size of wakes – tracking the wakes under ships by what we called acoustical devices. We used the same techniques under ice.

Then, towards the end of the war period ...

Q: I want to ask you if you were ever aware that the things you developed achieved the purpose you developed them for, or whether you felt that your accomplishments had bettered the war effort?

Dr. L.: These were strictly problems that were continually arising in war efforts. Right from the start, here at this laboratory, I was involved directly with the fleet operating forces, and we were solving the problems that were arising day by day. They were not long-term, futuristic kind of problems at all.

Q: But you helped them?

Dr. L.: We probably did. I meant there was one of these continual interchanges with the fleet operators. I was on board during many of the operations, not in the fighting zone, though, all in this area. So there was a continual interchange of their problems and how we could help out, knowing a little bit about the ocean.

Q: Did you do any work on fathometers at that time?

Dr. L.: Yes, a good share of it was.

Q: When you say looking up, are you referring to a fathometer?

Lyon # 1 - 6

Dr. L.: Echo-sounders or fathometers. It doesn't matter whether you're looking up or looking down in the type of technique.

Because of this work on harbor-defense systems and how to get submarines through them took up up into the Seattle area and there we became acquainted with a different set of problems, which arise from going up amongst the islands north of Seattle.

Are you familiar with the area?

Q: Yes, I am.

Dr. L.: When you get up into that area, you get into very different temperatures, water conditions, sound transmission under water than one has out in the Central Pacific or the South Pacific, areas where temperatures are much higher. This also got me in touch with the Canadian people who were engaged in the cold water problem, and this got me and a couple of others of my people interested in an entirely new set of problems that had to do with cold water, not Arctic water but just cold water, and very different sonar conditions under such situations. That was just a new experience. It also got us in contact with some very key individuals who were in Canada, and they've always been very interesting to me, these particular individuals, because they've done a great deal with less facilities. There was a very different point of view in Canada from the U. S., particularly at that time, because they just didn't have the wherewithal they neede to do many of the things that we did, and often, I think, did a little better thinking than we did just because they had less to do it with.

Q: I read a reference to a man - Commander Robertson?

Dr. L.: Well, at this time it was Jack Tully and Bill Cameron who were at the oceanographic group in Nanaimo, British Columbia. Later in this story they become a very important part of the developments because of the joint effort a decade later. But this is when I met these people and became well acquainted with them when we were working on this harbor-defense problem and submarines going through harbor defenses and that type of water that you find up in Seattle and north of there, which is quite different from the southern –

Q: How far north of Seattle did you go at that time?

Dr. L.: At that time only to the top end of Georgia Strait and up into the channels above that. Of course, there had been some submarine activity up along the Aleutians and thereabouts, but in the Pacific area there was really not too much submarine activity in cold water. Quite different from the Atlantic. Really, what we were doing was also attempting to understand some of the problems that the east coast of Canada was facing with the German submarines in the Gulf of St. Lawrence because that is the same cold-water situation where a submarine can hide underneath temperature layers that are formed by these cold waters. It's a very different situation than one normally meets in southern waters. It means that a submarine can lie near the surface or just below a temperature layer and cannot be detected by surface craft.

Q: Even without being under the ice?

Dr. L.: No, no ice, just cold water. These are the problems, and the Germans made very effective use of this layer in their attacks on the shipping that came out of the St. Lawrence. Now Canada or Halifax - Canada - faced this problem in the war and had a very difficult time. Because they didn't have the fighting problem over on the Pacific side, but they still had somewhat similar water conditions in 1944 and 1945, working with the Canadians we were attempting to understand some of these problems, but we didn't have to worry about being shot at.

This was really a Canadian problem instead of the U. S. The U. S. really didn't get involved, but is what sort of drew me and a couple of fellows that were with me into the problem by this sort of roundabout way. Then, realizing that there was an entirely different set of problems in cold water that we just didn't ever experience in the normal areas where the U. S. Navy forces were operating.

Q: Did the German U-boats use the protection of the ice pack ever, or just the cold water?

Dr. L.: On occasions they did. Now the Gulf of St. Lawrence does have ice at a particular time of the year, and it's not too clear now whether at times they used it, but there were a few instances during the war of the German U-boats using ice cover definitely around Greenland, and at that time they made an attack - I don't remember the year, 1942 maybe - from under the ice against the Coast Guard breaker, Northland, I think her name was. I think Thomas, the icebreaker's skipper, had the ship at the time, and one attack was made by a U-boat firing a torpedo from under the ice, and fortunately the torpedo hit the ice and didn't strike the ship. And there were other occasions that apparently the U-boats were using the edge of the ice cover to their advantage, and they definitely did for two years - the 1942-1943 period - work in the Barents Sea and into the Kara Sea against the Russian shipping. That's pretty well documented - Operation Wonderland, or something like that. Not only cruisers were taken in there, but there were submarines operating too. They were not specifically equipped for the problem. They were just taking open sea U-boats and they worked under the ice by periscope, no special sonar equipment. And there were some "very hairy" stories about using the bow of the submarine to feel for the ice and the periscope in a sense of feeling whether they had ice or not. But they did operate under ice cover.

Q: And long before this, Wilkins had attempted to do work under the ice pack also.

Dr. L.: Right. That was in 1931, really before sonar was actually developed at all, or at the period when it was just beginning. So he had to make his attempts with no help.

Now, let's see, we return to the story of 1944-1945 and the end of the war - that's when we were working with the Canadians on this cold-water problem up north of the Seattle area.

The break comes at the end of the war. I'm trying to keep the chronology. Of course, things get kind of mixed up. All during the war there had been two organizations here on Point Loma. One was the University of California Division of War Research, which was organized after I came to the laboratory. I was in the U. S. Navy Radio and Sound Laboratory, but then joined with it later in 1941, the University of California Division of War Research, which became a very large organization due to the buildup of the war, and trying to bring in many people it had a very quick expansion and organization that would take care of the war period, but would not be a permanent long-term organization. Of course, various divisions were organized all over the country for radar, sonar, etc.

Q: Civilian?

Dr. L.: Civilian organizations. That was all under the Office of Scientific Research and Development under Vannevar Bush during that period. I don't know if you need all that history. There was a whole national organization at that time set up under Vannevar Bush, and the whole story is given somewhere else, anyway, but we had the Division of War Research here, and there was a very large sonar organization where many of the acoustical devices and research on sound propagation in the sea, and so on and so forth, was done by that organization. It made very litttle difference which organization one was in because they were joined together. However, I was under the Navy Laboratory at the time. I bring this up because after the war it was necessary to reorganize it again, because the temporary organization, the Division of War Research of the University of California, had to be joined together with a permanent Navy laboratory, and so that's what became then the U. S. Navy Electronics Laboratory in 1946.

Then, at the same time, what happened for me was that in late 1945, remembering that there was an atomic bomb fired in 1945, was

Lyon # 1 - 11

when Operation Crossroads came into being to carry out the tests in the Pacific on further work on atomic bombs, so I became a part of that.

Q: I'd like to have you tell me that story.

Dr. L.: In late 1945 a group that I had at that time got drawn into Operation Crossroads through Roger Revelle, who was then still in uniform. He had been an instructor at Scripps in 1941. He came to the Navy Radio and Sound Laboratory. He was a lieutenant, j.g., was called up into uniform, and was on the Sound Laboratory staff for a number of years, and that's where I got acquainted with him. He was an oceanographer, of course. Then by 1945, he was in Washington, in the Bureau of Ships, and he had been designated to carry out the ocean-measurement side of the Crossroads Operation.

Q: Will you amplify that a bit? What does that mean?

Dr. L.: That means, prior to the bomb, measuring the entire environment out at Bikini from all the biology to what the conditions were in topography, the geology of the area, the water structure, to measure what happens to the water structure, and particularly what I was concerned with for him, the measurement of the waves generated by the explosion on Bikini Atoll.

Q: Comparing all these factors before and after?

Dr. L.: Before and what happened after. So you had to see the environment before to know what happened after. What happened to

Lyon # 1 - 12

the animals before and after. This was the entire picture that he was involved in. If something would happen to the geology of the Bikini Atoll by the explosion, all of this. So it was a very complete story of the entire environment prior to the explosion, and the whole thing repeated again after the explosion. Then, of course, the measurements of what took place at the explosion with regard to the atmosphere and the water, the waves generated.

Q: And your particular part of it?

Dr. L.: My particular part, the group that I had, was to measure the waves generated by the explosion.

Q: What were your conclusions?

Dr. L.: What I had to do with my group was to instrument the whole series of ships - you know, there was a large number of ships involved with the underwater explosion and with the air explosion. There were two explosions. One was detonated in the air above the ships, and the other one was detonated in the water. We instrumented for the wave by using primarily the echo-sounder system. An echo-sounder was put on the ship and if the ship went up and down, you measure it going up and down to get a picture of the waves or the picture of what the ship was doing, and it had to be translated back into the waves. And other devices as to how high the waves were on the beach. It seems to me those were the primary instruments.

So, setting these instruments on board the ship, getting them to work, and going around just a few hours before the shot and turning them all on, then getting in a small boat and getting out of that place, and getting on one of the ships and going off and waiting for the explosion. Then coming back in as soon as we could and getting the records off the echo-sounders.

Q: How long was it before you could return?

Dr. L.: I don't remember now. Two days, three days, something like that.

Q: Did you have a personal reaction to the bomb test itself? Was it bad?

Dr. L.: No, not in that case. It had to do with the more we learned the more we would know about how to use it, or not to use it. At that period it was a question of knowing what the bomb would do, and certainly it was a demonstration of its power and what it did to the environment. That was very important and very useful at that time, and that's what we were working on. I think everyone who witnessed it was certainly impressed - that's a very weak word in this case - by the magnitude of the energy released by the bomb and the destruction that could be wrought. Until one witnessed this, I don't think one really grasped the power that was involved.

Q: I wouldn't imagine a person could possibly grasp it without seeing it. Did you have a conclusion as to whether it should or should not ever be used again after you saw the experiment?

Dr. L.: Yes, certainly after that - after witnessing that I never wanted to see them ever used. I certainly would not want to see them used militarily, except as what's being done, as a deterrent for a balance of power, well and good. Of course, no one would ever wish to see them actually used. But really I'm still very much involved in high explosives. Being involved in the use of submarines, and the use of submarines brings in deterrents, and the use of deterrents is definitely nuclear warfare. But as everyone does, we hope we talk about these things but never use them.

Q: I agree.

Dr. L.: Strange paradox.

Q: How long were you out there for prior —

Dr. L.: Oh, that was from February 1946 until September 1946, because it took us from February 1946 until June to prepare the equipment. The first explosion which was the air shot was some time in July. Then after that we had to go back and set up the ships again, take care of the data from the air shot, which didn't create much of a wave, for the underwater shot, which took place some time in August, the latter part of August, to gather all the data. We all came back from Operation Crossroads in August, and I picked up my family and went immediately up to Canada to work up the data with the Canadians that we had taken the year before on this business of submarines in cold water. And so my wife and two children — we were living up there in Nanaimo, British Columbia, working up the information with Jack Tully and Bill Cameron, the Canadians at the Pacific Oceanographic group. We were at Nanaimo during the period from September through October, and it was at that time the Arctic submarines started because the Navy, through

through Admiral Byrd's pushing, got interested in an operation down in Antarctica - lots of ships, lots of people, lots of everything - after the war period, and so that was when the task force and Operation High Jump was organized in the fall of 1946. I remember the letter coming through, just a routine letter, to the Electronics Laboratory saying we're going to have an operation down in Antarctica, is there anything the laboratory is interested in?

Well, from the experience of working with submarines in just cold water, it seemed the logical thing, how about putting in a submarine that can learn by going down to Antarctica.

Q: What was your position in the facility at that time?

Dr. L.: As head of the Marine Sciences Division, maybe it was Marine Research. Anyway, it had to do with the sea research side of the combined laboratory, the Navy Electronics Laboratory. We had people from the old University Division of War Research and from the Radio and Sound Laboratory who were very interested in the research side of the sea. It had to do with sound propagation work in the sea, studying the sea itself, both biology and its currents and temperatures, structures, and so forth. There was a combined group of about 150 people, as I recall.

Q: And you were the head of that?

Dr. L.: I was the head of that division. We were just organizing the division, which was under the Research Department of the Navy Electronics Laboratory. It was being organized that year.

Q: I didn't ask your position during the war years?

Dr. L.: During the war years I was head of the Sound Division of the Radio and Sound Laboratory. It was a very small laboratory. I came there in 1941 under Delsasso, who was in uniform, to start the Sound Division because there was a Radio and Sound Laboratory and what they had was radio work, radar work, and sound work. It was just starting organization of the Sound Division of the laboratory. It was just building up. And then before the buildup of the war period started, and that's when the University of California's Division of War Research came in and it became the entire acoustics part of that laboratory complex. Keep in mind that, at that time, the Radio and Sound Laboratory had to work under the rules of the Civil Service, which was a very slow process, particularly when you could not hire and add - very slowly, and that just did not fit a war - a coming war - situation. That was one of the main reasons why we had to go through contractual arrangements, like giving work to the California Division of War Research, to gather people together quickly and not be concerned with all the processing that's required, especially during the peacetime Civil Service arrangements. So what happened is that what few people we did get on the Civil Service side, we just sort of married them together with the big body that got put together in the Division of War Research. After the war, then you had to reorganize everything again under peacetime procedural processes and so on of Civil Service.

Q: Then it became NEL?

Lyon # 1 - 17

Dr. L.: Then it became NEL, and we could take these people who had all the experience in War Research and bring them slowly into the Civil Service and fill up -

Q: And that's when you became head of -

Dr. L.: That's when I became head of the Research Division for the undersea.

Q: So any questions relating to High Jump or anything of that nature that was acoustical or the research into the sound of the ocean were put into -

Dr. L.: Yes, normally if it was on the research side, the very experimental side.

Q: Were you excited with the idea of sending a submarine down into the Antarctic operation?

Dr. L.: It just seemed like I didn't have any good reason other than let's try it and see what happens.

Q: Who authorized sending the submarine?

Dr. L.: We wrote a letter then from the Navy Electronics Laboratory to the Chief of Naval Operations suggesting that a submarine be put in, and back came the word - granted. Keeping in mind, remember, at that time there were lots of submarines, lots of ships, and people were looking for things to do, and there was no good reason not to, and no one knew just exactly what would happen either. So the Sennet was then assigned from the Atlantic forces to join the operation.

I joined the Sennet late that year, so the year 1946 I was really gone the whole year, except for the month or two that we were together - the family was together - in Canada. Went off in the Sennet then and was gone from November to March in Antarctica.

Q: Where did you join her?

Dr. L.: I joined her by riding a surface ship, one of the cargo ships that left from Port Hueneme because the Sennet came from the Atlantic. So I rode the USS Merrick actually, a cargo ship, AKA, from Port Hueneme and then met the Sennet somewhere down off the tip of South America and transferred to the Sennet.

Q: How did you transfer?

Dr. L.: By small boat - I don't remember - or rubber boat.

Q: Can you describe the type of submarine it was?

Dr. L.: That was one of the regular so-called fleet types of the war period, and a diesel submarine obviously. It was well equipped with the sonar of the period. The primary interest was the searchlight sonar system, which is a long-range pulsing sonar - it sent out a pulse and got the echo back. But it also had the QLA scanning system which was developed by the Division of War Research in California here at Point Loma and was used by the submarines in the war period for transiting minefields - a type of sonar which presented targets on a screen like a radar screen and permitted the submarines to see a number of targets and avoid them in transiting minefields. These were used successfully in the Pacific during that period.

Q: And this was equipment that you had been instrumental in developing?

Dr. L.: No, I had not been instrumental in developing it, but it was equipment developed here at the Sound complex here on Point Loma for the Pacific Fleet. I'd only been an onlooker for that part, other than using it on occasions on submarines in getting through harbor defenses. I was not involved in its development.

Q: Did they put any special equipment on the Sennet for the Antarctic?

Dr. L.: No, we took the submarine as it came with the standard equipment of the searchlight sonar equipment and the sonar scanning system, because at that time I had no feel for what I was going to run into, the ice cover, I knew nothing about it. I'd never seen a piece of ice on the sea. I was only familiar with working with the open sea and some cold water experiences in Canada, but I had no concept whatsoever of ice or what the problems might be, and that was the real reason for taking the submarine down to Antarctica because of these materials I had read and also heard about from the Canadians and the east coast situation and the Gulf of St. Lawrence, and I knew a little about what the Germans had been doing during the war period in the north Atlantic, but I had no personal experience whatsoever. So we were just taking a standard fleet class submarine with sonar systems into Antarctica to see what would happen.

Q: I'd like to have you describe that experience, how long it was — ?

Dr. L.: The Sennet became part of a task group to go into Little America, which included the Mount Olympus as the flagship, the communications ship, and two AKAs, as I recall, the Yancey and the Merrick, then the Sennet, all escorted by one icebreaker, the Northwind. The Northwind was under the command of Captain Thomas, Coast Guard. This was in January 1947 when we tried to make the approach to Little America. Normally in the Ross Sea at that time of the year the ice would be fairly open and there wouldn't be too much difficulty, but that particular year of 1947 the ice did not break up, as it had in some previous years, and it was very difficult going, and the one icebreaker just had too big a job to handle in trying to get a column of the Mount Olympus, which was a large ship, followed by two AKAs, which are large ships, and followed by a submarine. She had to break ice and these ships would follow in column. And in such a situation, the submarine coming last had a lot of difficulty trying to work its way through the ice on the surface following the icebreaker. Many a time we suddenly got closed in with ice all around, and it was a very difficult situation, as well as the other ships, because of the heavy ice, heavy going. I don't remember all of the details now unless I get out the journal and do it day by day, but I don't think that is of importance. The main point is that we on board learned what it was like to get into sea ice. The submarine did get closed off with ice all around, so we met that situatio

Lyon # 1 - 21

Q: On the surface?

Dr. L.: On the surface. We didn't dare submerge because we were not visualizing the problem, but I did realize that we were not equipped to know the clearances and know what the story of the ice cover was once we got underneath. I had sonar systems looking ahead of me, but I had nothing to tell me what was going to stop me if trying to surface while under ice.

Q: Even if you had submerged right in the ice cover following the <u>Mount Olympus</u> -

Dr. L.: We couldn't dare to do this because there was ice for hundreds of miles in all directions, and I knew nothing about its thickness, other than just guessing. There were icebergs all over the place, and they were huge, running miles in dimensions and depths to the order of 1,200 feet or more in draft. So these were enormous obstacles and having had no experience, no background, no experiments, one doesn't start an experiment in such a situation. So all the operations were on the surface, and we had expected that the ice cover would be such that we could go right in to Little America, and then do some experiments in open water and gradually go under the ice and that kind of thing, where we would be doing a controlled experiment. However, that was not possible just because of the type of ice that we ran into. And then it became pretty obvious that the submarine was not going to play a part of the main objective, which was to establish a camp at Little America on the ice, which included the cargo carriers and the communications ship. So after maybe a week of trying to get through the ice with all these ships, it was decided by Admiral Cruzen, who was the task force commander, and it was obvious to everyone, that we should take the Sennet out of the column so that we could take the cargo-carriers into Little America and set up the camp from where they were going to have flights for the mapping of Little America by aircraft, and take the Sennet out of the ice. So the Northwind then proceeded to lead the cargo ships wherever they could see an opening in the ice, and just take the Sennet separately if they could back out of the ice to the open part of the Antarctic Ocean.

Q: Had you gone in on your own, or were you towed?

Dr. L.: We were not towed in. We were just following, on our own. Now, to get out and do it quickly, we tried various things. We followed the icebreaker, but that became difficult in heavy ice because the icebreaker is very short in length but broad in beam and of such a nature that she'll turn very easily and not necessarily make a nice straight, easy path for a submarine to follow. So the submarine can get hung up on pieces of ice kicked out from the sides by the icebreaker. Then we tried towing, which worked very well, after breaking the cable a few times, but getting heavy enough cable that the icebreaker towed the Sennet by bringing the Sennet right up in the stern of the icebreaker where the towing notch is, so the bow of the Sennet was in the notch in the stern of the icebreaker and she was towed through the ice in that manner. I guess this was one of the most harrowing experiences that one has on a submarine just because of the noise, not because of danger, but when you're being dragged through the ice at the end of an icebreaker and the ice is scraping along the side of the hull and making a shrieking, screeching sound, something like fingernails across a blackboard, only a thousand times worse. And the ship is careening about much like riding on a train when you're going at high speed through a freight yard through switches and crossing "frogs," and you're just being banged and rattled and thrown. I had that sensation on top of all this noise and screeching of ice against the hull.

Q: How long did that last?

Dr. L.: Probably three days or something like that.

Q: Continuous?

DR. L.: Pretty much so.

Q: Day and night?

Dr. L.: Day and night. You can't sleep very well because you'd be sleeping next to the hull, and the ice is scraping along the hull. A good indication is that when the Sennet got out in open water, we looked at the hull, and the hull was bright and shiny steel. All of the paint had been scraped off and it was a bright shiny hull.

Q: Wasn't it dangerous? Could not the ice at some time tear the hull?

Dr. L.: Oh, no. Keep in mind that it works at great pressure, and they're one of the most rugged ships. There was not a danger of that sort, just plain noisy and rough. It was a new experience, that kind of thing. The only real danger would be that - if the cable broke or if the icebreaker hit ice and suddenly stopped and the submarine would sort of bang up into the stern of the icebreaker. The prow of the *Sennet* was pretty well damaged. I remember it was broken by these towing procedures and the propellers had bent and that kind of thing from being dragged through the ice. Other than that, the submarine was in good shape.

Q: Was the propulsion of the submarine on all the time, or was she just being dragged?

Dr. L.: She was just being dragged.

Q: Without any power at all?

Dr. L.: Just dragged, towed right through, for some of the time. Of course, the *Sennet* was under her own power in following the icebreaker or doing her own breaking.

Q: But during the towing period?

Dr. L.: During the towing period, she was just being pulled.

Q: That must have been a harrowing experience. I guess you used that word already.

Dr. L.: Yes. There was really not any danger in being pulled, but it was not comfortable.

Q: What was the condition of everyone's nerves by the end of that three-day period?

Dr. L.: I don't recall now. We got accustomed to it easily enough, except when the screeching and screaming of the ice would take place. You didn't really ever get used to that.

Q: It prepared you for later experiences, I would guess?

Dr. L.: I think that that probably was the most noisy experience and one that kind of irritates the nerves more than some that may occur later. Flooding or fire and things of that sort, of course, put you in much greater danger. You get shock at the time, but that's taken care of pretty quick, as soon as it's solved, and it's not the type of thing - where this just continued and it was just irritating. You were just irritated more than anything else by this noise more than a sense of fear.

Q: It was a first for everyone?

Dr. L.: Right, the first experience that any of these people had ever seen ice or had any experience with it or what it was all about. But then after we did get out in the open sea, we spent the next three weeks or more doing probing experiments where we could submerge. We were all on our own now, we didn't have to worry about anybody else. We were in the open sea. We could make approaches on icebergs and see what we could do with them with sonar equipment, go under the edges of the ice and know that we were near open water. We could probe around and get a feel for what we could do.

For instance, our first experiences were just what the whole problem was about, and about all it did was intrigue us into trying to solve it. One could see that there was much that one could do with a submarine. There wasn't any problem to be solved, and so that was the beginning when you just began to visualize what a submarine under ice cover meant.

Q: Is the Antarctic more forbidding than the Arctic?

Dr. L.: Not really. I think it's less forbidding as far as a submarine is concerned, primarily because of the deep water. Maybe it's more forbidding because it's bigger,, everything's on a bigger scale. However, the ice cover is around the land mass and it extends out into the open sea, and it's much easier to guess and know what's going to happen. You're not under the forces that take place in the Arctic, where it's inside a closed land mass and you can't get out. More unpredictable than learning to - as far as the ice conditions are concerned. The two areas are very different, just because one has the ice surrounding the land mass and expanding into open sea, and the other has the ice confined in a closed sea and it works out through entrances.

So we came back from Antarctica just knowing that we had a nice interesting problem. We had some feel for what the problems were. By the spring of 1947 we were becoming fully intrigued then with the problem. We wrote another request from the Navy Electronics Laboratory, this time to Commander, Submarines, Pacific, because it was understood that the then force commander who was Admiral McCann had expressed a real interest in Arctic affairs because the year before he had taken a group of submarines in his own interests up into the Bering Sea. Later we found out that his interests really stemmed from the time he was a junior officer in 1930 or thereabouts, he was I think in the Philadelphia Navy Yard and was involved in the transfer of the submarine O-12 which was sold to

Hubert Wilkins for a dollar, or whatever he paid for it, was going to be scrapped. Hubert Wilkins modified it with Simon Lake to the Nautilus. He named it the Nautilus, and they sailed into the Arctic Ocean after much trial and tribulation. It's a long story of their own, and I don't know all the details. But they made the attempt to go under the ice in the North Atlantic, north of Spitzbergen, in 1931. And that particular cruise is of interest because the chief scientist on board with Sir Hubert Wilkins was Harald Sverdrup, the Norwegian oceanographer of world fame. He was one of the founders of modern oceanography, and in the late 1930s he came to San Diego to become the director of Scripps Institute of Oceanography, and during the war period he was at Scripps Institute. He was involved during the war in wave predictions for the Navy, and in 1946, 1947, that period, was back as the director of Scripps Institute. He was the scientist on board Wilkins' Nautilus, and in 1947 we had this connection of McCann being on the military side with the submarine that was given to Wilkins, and he was watching Wilkins at that time trying to use a submarine, before sonar was available for submarines. McCann had always kept in his mind and was disturbed by the method that Wilkins was attempting to use, which was to use the submarine as an upside down sled. Wilkins' idea was to go under the ice, and then become positive buoyant and slide around under the ice. Well, that didn't seem just the way to do things after sonar came into being, and so McCann of the Sub Force figured he ought to do something about it. He was already intrigued by it, and so it was in the summer of 1946 that he took the submarines north into the Bering Sea, but they didn't do too much other than find out it was cold and miserable on a submarine because they didn't come prepared for the problem. Again, there was no connection with the science side. So then, when 1947 came around, and I had my experience in the south, and knowing what the problem was, and then asking McCann, it was a natural for us to get together, and so we could prepare one of the submarines to go under the ice with the proper equipment.

Q: Were you able to make your own choice of interest, your own feel of interest? You say you thought you had found the problem. Were you permitted to say, I want to work on this problem?

Dr. L.: Really because I was head of the marine sciences research, or whatever it was, so I did have some freedom, considerable freedom in fact, particularly at the close of the war period when things were a little bit trying to find something. We were closing out a lot of information that had been gathered during the war. People were working on that, and we were also trying to see what the new problems would be. At that time I should say that the commanding officer of the Navy Electronics Laboratory was Captain Rawson Bennett, who later became the Chief of Naval Research, and he's an important point to the story because he had been, way back at the start of the war, one of the main towers or forces to get sonar throughout the Navy properly oriented with the conditions of the sea. All during the war period in the Bureau of Ships he held a key position in electronics and sonar, and had recognized the continual need for research and exploratory work on the sea, and its importance to expanding the capabilities of the Navy so far as sonar is concerned. So he, coming to NEL as the commanding officer, had very open viewpoint on going into anything new to explore it out.

Lyon # 1 - 29

Q: So it had its fortunate aspect!

Dr. L.: It had its fortunate aspect for me because he supported very strongly then anything that we would do working with the fleet people to push their horizons out, so there was no difficulty whatsoever in getting his backing and making the contact with the submarine force commander and using whatever facilities they had right there at the laboratory to get a boat ready. That's when Admiral McCann assigned the Boarfish for the experimental submarine. That was another fleet-class boat, to go and make the first attempt to go underneath the ice cover.

Q: That sounds dramatic, just sitting here and hearing the words said.

Dr. L.: I should point out there was one other attempt to go under the ice by a U. S. submarine. That was the Atule the previous summer, in 1946. This was the Atlantic up in Baffin Bay, but again it was done just like the submarines that made the approach by SubPac in the Bering Sea in 1946 by not having the science side aboard - just by a fleet operator going ahead with whatever he had. The Atule went under the ice for a way, but did not have the instruments required to avoid ice, and went under and struck ice by periscope and came out. The main point is that the submarine force itself was interested in doing things. It was a natural, then, in 1947, why we were successful, because we combined the equipment and ideas from the scientists with the operators on board the ship, and the combination together is very powerful in doing things.

So with the Boarfish we equipped her and made sure that she had the QLA scanning system, so we could tell what was ahead, and this time we took with us Art Roshon and his assistant here at the San Diego Lab under the University's Division of War Research. He was one of the originators of the QLA system.

Q: Can you explain it in layman's terms? Or is it too complex?

Dr. L.: It's a sonar system that is continually transmitting sound and getting the reflections back, but the presentation is put on a screen so that you get a vision - a visual picture - of whatever objects are in front of you. And it has a forward-looking beam so it's telling you what objects or what targets or whatever are ahead of you. Then you know what bearing and how far the objects are, and that gives you a guiding method to avoid them.

Q: Does it give you a picture much like an electrocardiogram does on a piece of paper?

Dr. L.: No, it gives you a motion picture like a radar or TV screen would be. It's not like a photograph, but the object is a bright spot on the screen, like on radar. It gives you the same feeling as a radar - an object is a bright spot. The position on the screen, an angle is the angle relative to the bow, the distance out from the center of the screen would be how far away it is. It gives you a plot of objects in front of you. How far they are, and what angle they are to you just in front.

Lyon # 1 - 31

Q: But not at what depth?

Dr. L.: No. At that time the beam was going out as a cone in the vertical, so you see any objects that lie in this cone. It becomes important to keep in mind because since it's a cone going out from the ship means that farther and farther away, the bigger and bigger the object can stay in there. You don't have any judgment of what depth it may be until you get real close to it.

Q: You must know something is out there?

Dr. L.: You just know something is out there, and it may be at your depth or it may not. But, as you approach it, since it is a cone looking out, and there's an edge to that cone as it approaches you, and you're at a certain depth if that thing is above you, then your cone finally goes under it. So you do get some judgment by when you lose it on your screen as you approach it, as to how deep it is.

Q: What does QLA mean?

Dr. L.: Oh, any of those letters were just designators put on to various equipments during the war period and they don't have any special meaning. At that time, we had all kinds of letters -- QBS and QCS. They were just equipment numbers and the letters themselves do not mean anything. Except there were some codes that you could work to find out what company the equipment was built by, whether it was an active sonar, or whether it was a listening sonar, etc.

Q: But this was new equipment put on the Boarfish, was it?

Lyon # 1 - 32

Dr. L.: It was really not new equipment because many of the submarines had this QLA scanning system all during the war period for going through minefields, so all that we did was to be sure that the system was on Boarfish, we did insist that we have a submarine with such a system so that we would have this capability of looking at what was ahead of us and a picture of up ahead, and then took Art Roshon on board so that it would be in operating condition, and also had somebody to give us an interpretation of what we saw — not knowing what we would see, if we did it. Why we wanted to get Art Rashon? He also became highly interested in the problem, of course. There was the new challenge of using the equipment for other than minefields.

Q: It occurred to me that there were two parts to the problem. First, you had to make the equipment, then, you had to have a person to interpret it and know what it's telling you.

Dr. L.: Interpretation in this case was the major part, in that interpretation gets involved with what the water does to it. It's like looking through the atmosphere on days over a hot pavement, and you will see an image wandering around. Well, the ocean does the same thing for you, too. You must understand the ocean, and what the temperature and density layers do to what you're seeing. The picture that you may see ahead of you may not be directly ahead of you. It may be off here somewhere by bending.

Q: Then you have to learn by trial and error.

DR. L.: You learn by trial and error, by measuring the sea, or just by trying.

Well, the Boarfish, then, was equipped with QLA, but the thing that we did add, that we realized we must have, and the Boarfish normally would not carry, was an echo-sounder or fathometer on the deck, looking up. We had them looking down, so we knew how far we were above the bottom, but we didn't have anything to tell us what we were under. We put an echo-sounder on the Boarfish, plus a recording thermometer and other devices to try to measure what the ocean was as we went through it.

Q: Was this the first time a fathometer had ever been put topside?

Dr. L.: That's right. The first one for this particular purpose, for going under ice, or making a try at it.

Q: Were you in charge of this installation of the equipment and selection of the kind of equipment, and selection of the man to interpret?

Dr. L.: Correct. I was the scientist to do this. I was trying to do it so I made the contact with the sub forces. We had Boarfish right here in San Diego, and Art Roshon and I and the people helping us put the equipment on board. Then, we went with her up to the Chukchi Sea, north of the Bering Strait, in August of 1947. Admiral McCann always did things up in a good way. He meant that we make a study and so he said - well, we'll put everything on and I'll even go myself. So he went along and took the Nereus, a submarine tender, and four other submarines. We had quite a task group, but the Boarfish was the only one that we intended to go under ice.

However, with the Nereus and Gene LaFond, who was at that time the head of the oceanographic section in my division - we had a number of people. He took a group of people and they went on the Nereus and tried to measure the ocean to see what it was all about, for temperature, animals, salinity, everything. It was all new to us. We'd never been in any of this. So a number of people were on board who have now made their names in all kinds of places. Some of them were young kids, students, at that time. For example, one is Walter Munk, today a well known name in geophysics at the University of California, Scripps Institute. It seems to be that Don Pritchard, now the head of Johns Hopkins marine sciences, was on board, too, and other people have gone various places from that original group. But this was all a new experience to everybody, so they were all up there to see what they could learn.

Q: Was it exciting?

DR. L.: I think to everyone it was because of the new experience. They could do any experiment they wanted, and they were going to learn something new, that was all there was to it. I was the only one with some experience, just from the Sennet.

Q: You were the expert!

Dr. L.: In a sense, I suppose, but I didn't know much either. It was the first time for me, other than the Sennet experience.

We got up into the Chukchi Sea in August, then came the decision are we going to do this or not - that is, go under the ice. And I recall that we decided to have a good look at it, so we got the *Nereus* to lower their whale boat. Gene LaFond, Art Roshon, Admiral McCann, and some of the others — we took the small boat and wandered around the ice, just to see what it was all about before going under in the submarine.

Q: Could you penetrate it to any distance?

Dr. L.: Oh, probably, yes. It's all open towards the outer edge, and at that time of the year it's melting, so you can work your way in among the ice floes and probably could go in 20 miles or more, wandering in and out. But that gave us some idea, by seeing what the thickness of the ice was above the water, and trying to guess how much it was below the water — we could get a picture of what it looked like. Having done that, and Admiral McCann was there, too, plus the commanding officer of the *Boarfish* —

Q: In the boat?

Dr. L.: In the boat. We all had a look. Based on that, then, it gave us some picture of the ice and it looked like we should try it. The first trial, then, was with the admiral on board the *Boarfish* and a couple of his staff, Art Roshon, and his helper, and I, and Leighton Morse was with me from my group. We were living on *Boarfish* anyway, so we all made this first trial, which went successfully — no problems.

Q: Can you describe it to me? The excitement, the feeling, the atmosphere on the *Boarfish*?

Dr. L.: I think that is not quite possible because it was very calm and collected. Nothing happened. So, you have the feeling of something new all the time but I don't know how one describes that. We didn;t have any real fear because on that particular cruise we knew the bottom of the sea. We did have information on that, and it was extremely flat. It's the flattest area there is in the world. We had had this look at the ice cover from above, but we did not know how it would look on the screen of the sonar system. Well, we approached and got a feel of what it looked like on the sonars, and Art Rashon could interpret. But we started by still being near the surface and looking with the periscope and seeing what things looked like on the sonar - the impression of what am I seeing, what does it look like under water.

Q: You related what you actually saw to the picture?

Dr. L.: From the periscope to the sonar screen. Then, as we went under pieces and then submerging and going under pieces we could see what it looked like with the echo-sounding system looking up. It was a matter of step-by-step proceeding. We had, as I say, no difficulties on that because of the step-by-step difficulties and didn't bump anything. Some of us thought it was luck but I think it was just the cautious approach.

Q: How deep did the submarine submerge?

Dr. L.: Let's see. The depth of the water was probably about 140 feet.

Q: That's pretty shallow.

Dr. L.: Very shallow water. The submarine takes up 50 feet, so you

Lyon #1 - 37

had about 9 feet to play with and I think we usually split that and there was probably 30 feet under the submarine, which is pretty close to the bottom for a ship 300 feet long. Then we used the rest for clearing whatever we might run into. And we would pass under, I guess, ice maybe 30 feet thick or something of the sort at that time. Now, we were seeing on the screen other stuff that looked much thicker so we'd avoid that. Naturally, the sonar would tell you by the sound of the echo coming back and what it looked like on the screen was where we started to judge, that piece looks like a big hunk, avoid that, and go some place else where the sea looks pretty clear. So that's the way the sonar system worked out to guide us.

Q: I was wondering whether the submarine would respond that quickly?

Dr. L.: Oh, yes. We were going very slowly, between 2 and 3 knots. And that's another important point, particularly relative to the way a nuclear submarine works. These were all at very slow speed, so you have complete control for stopping or turning or whatnot, when you're going at such a slow speed. So there was plenty of time to become acquainted with what sonar looked like, make decisions, and make the proper moves.

Q: Were you with the skipper? I've often wondered as I read about you, as to where you were. Where did you stand? Were you seated by - Describe exactly the picture of you in relationship to the skipper.

Dr. L.: In this particular case, this was one of the problems we sort of ran into - the only way we could mount this equipment - the QLA scanning sonar system was in the conning tower, because it was a normal sonar system and was used all the time for going through minefields. The upper-looking echo-sounding system - the only place we could put it was in the forward torpedo room. That's the only place we had the space, so we had it in the forward torpedo room and that meant that I was doing all I could with it, operating it, which I had to do by talking to the skipper, who was in the conning tower. Art Roshon was in the conning tower watching that screen. So it was a matter of conversation back and forth about what was going on. The commanding officer did a lot of running back and forth to see what was happening in the forward torpedo room, seeing what was going on, interpretation, and the same thing was happening to Admiral McCann, who was running back and forth, too.

Q: Did you interpret it for them, or did they take both of these pictures and interpret them for themselves?

Dr. L.: No, at that time we did all the interpretation. I guess you can't say that we were any more expert than they were, but we knew what the equipment was and what it could do, so it was a matter of the operator knowing what he could do with his ship and what his background was, but primarily with Roshon watching his screen and saying what it is and more his background and long experience in types of targets that he had seen elsewhere on the sonar and saying what he was seeing on that screen and telling the commanding officer. And I was reading the echo-sounder system that was looking up and interpreting them, again basing my experience I had had with such systems with wakes and harbor defenses and other things. So, really, at this period, we are interpreting what we're seeing and reading that interpretation to the operator of the ship, and then he is making a judgment what he should do.

Q: How did you communicate with him? You said you were running back and forth.

Dr. L.: By a phone system. Then he'd get interested and come and look, too.

Q: It must have been nerve-wracking for him.

Dr. L.: Yes, I think so because he was responsible for the ship. That's one reason that Admiral McCann went on board for the first one, so that he could relieve the commanding officer of the responsibility for the situation the first time.

Q: Do you remember the name of the skipper?

Dr. L.: John Turner.

Q: And how far did you penetrate into the ice?

Dr. L.: Four or five miles, maybe. Then after that first one, we came out from that, which was just a sort of a probe to see what it was all about —

Q: How far did you go then, just 100 feet or yards?

Dr. L.: The first time, I think it was four miles. Then McCann went back to the Nereus, and the other submarines went off doing all kinds of jobs, surveying to see what the bathemetry was like of the ocean, taking the Nereus, catching biological samples, dragging the bottom, and all the things oceanographers do to understand the environment.

The Boarfish then did some more under-ice runs, and I think the longest was 12 miles, from the open-water in, 12 miles, and out again. That, I think, was the longest we did at that time, but with no incidents or any difficulty. But again in an area that we had good information, and a lot of that good information came again from Harald Sverdrup, because he had been on the expedition of the Maud, which was in the 1919-1926 period, which was a Roald Amundsen expedition in the Chukchi, East Siberian, and Laptev seas, all those seas north of Russia. What they had hoped to do was to repeat the drift of the Fram, the drift of the Fram across the Arctic Ocean in 1892-1896.

Q: When they left it in the ice to see what the currents would do to it?

Dr. L.: It drifted right across the Arctic Ocean. Actually, they hoped to make the north pole - prior to 1906, 1909, was it, when Perry made the north pole?

Q: Yes.

Dr. L.: Amundsen had outfitted the Maud, another ice-strengthened type of ship, and Sverdrup was a scientist on board that ship. She drifted around for a period of some seven years. She never went across the Arctic Ocean, but got into the circulating system of the Arctic Ocean north of Siberia, but did a tremendous job of getting oceanographic data over that entire area, to test the water, and some of the best work that was ever done on the physics and chemistry of sea ice. A tremendous amount of information was gathered.

And so, prior to the Boarfish, Gene LaFond and I — and later I was always in continual contact for everything I could get out of Sverdrup as far as that area is concerned — the type of sonar conditions to be expected, the entire story of the environment, what happened to the sea ice, how it grew, what it was like, anything I could get as far as information was concerned. But the Maud gave us a bathymetry which was very important. What the bottom was like of that whole Chukchi Sea, we had all of his information.

Q: Without that you wouldn't have known —

Dr. L.: Without that I would not have known what to expect. We'd have had no feel for what we were getting into, because Sverdrup gave us ideas of the currents, what the ice cover was like, how thick it was, what's it doing, how's it melting — some picture of the environment we were getting into, plus the vicinity. So you're in a very tight situation, space-wise, so you need to know the bottom as well as the top. There's a real debt to Harald Sverdrup for all of this, so far as the information is concerned. Plus he was sort of a believer and pusher in submarines because of his experiences on the Nautilus.

Q: How many dives did you make?

Dr. L.: In my recollection, maybe four or five, because you see we were only up there on the order of two weeks, possibly, in the ice cover and then came back with the Boarfish.

Q: What did you think you had learned?

Dr. L.: Well, really, what one had learned out of that - it was just the first time, you've got to do it first - so that told us, okay, we go from an open sea with the sonar equipment and avoid the ice, in the summertime, and see what we're traveling under, clear the bottom and avoid what's ahead of us, and go in and come out. That isn't sufficient to live in the ice cover or work in it. We recognized that. So that the next step was to be able to get away from that requirement that you must come back to the open ocean. So the next cruise that we set up, still with Admiral McCann in SubPac with the Carp's crew the following summer. This now, the objective was to try to go into the ice cover and stay in it. That means coming to the surface and recharging batteries inside the ice cover. So that was the objective set for the Carp's cruise the following summer.

Q: And again you were able to work with Admiral McCann?

Dr. L.: Right. He was still there at SubPac and was very happy with what happened with Boarfish and was a force in assigning submarines to continue. You understand there was no military requirement pushing this. This was just people interested in doing these things, because there was no thought at the time of military operations in arctic areas.

Q: Probably not too many people were even interested?

Dr. L.: Oh, there was so little experience by anyone, there was no reason for much experience, and some of the experiences people had were not the best either, because there had been work in the North Atlantic and people didn't want any part of that. For example they who had been on the Atule, had gone under and bumped the periscope which they were not very happy about. They could not see the use of submarines, they who were on the group of submarines that had gone up the prior summer, 1946. Many of the officers on those I met, after that, many years later, were left with a very poor experience of that run. They just did not want any part of anything near the ice because of their experience. But they had not been properly equipped.

Q: I think you explained that, that they didn't have the finances and research along —

Dr. L.: So they get the wrong feel or the wrong background, which is important. You generate two attitudes. The naval officer has the experience without the assistance in that new situation, he can come away with the attitude — I don't want any part of that, it's foolish to do anything with it. But if he has the other experience of being there when they are successful in attacking a new situation then he sees what can be done.

Q: And I guess the excitement of something new?

Dr. L.: This is an important part. Actually it appeared later, in another decade or two, by just these people by name, who had the different experiences, as a continuation of the focus, and that's important in many programs. The officer confident and the scientist confident make the first approach properly together. That first approach has so many problems and very much colors what comes later. The partnership between the naval officer and the scientist in this whole arctic game has been the key to the success in the end, and still is the main feature that we stress day in and day out in our arctic program now. We have a very tight relationship or coupling between the scientist and the officer at all times.

Q: Is your personality the guiding force in that?

Dr. L.: It has been my belief ever since I started with the Navy, maybe because I started that way back in 1941 during the war period, and was brought into the Navy, and that was stressed, and it always seemed the logical thing to do. The closer the feeling between the naval officer and the scientist, both with the aspect in which he's looking — it's really the consumer versus the person getting things for the consumer to use. The naval officer is the consumer. He uses what we're trying to produce, and if he doesn't use it right or isn't happy with it, you aren't satisfying your consumer from the marketing point of view, and the best way to do this would be working right with him — have both your market in hand, and you're making things for him to use directly and recognizing his problems and explaining at the same time. And at the same moment you get his viewpoint of what he needs — one of the most important things. Over the years I've noticed that we interpret what he needs because often in a new situation a submarine operator cannot really visualize what he needs. He sees something of where he's trying to go with his problem, but his background does not give him a feel for what the ocean is or what the ocean can do, and so we are, in a sense, refining his problem for him relative to what he's trying to do in the ocean.

Q: Especially in the north?

Dr. L.: Particularly in the north. I guess it should be done even more in an open sea operation.

Returning to the Carp, it was easy, then, to get McCann to assign another submarine, and so this job was set up for the Carp with the same equipment set up as on the Boarfish but, now, to go into the ice cover and learn how to surface the submarine inside the ice cover. That means searching out, with the sonar system, for open water overhead, because in the summertime we could observe as we went under it with the Boarfish that there were many big spaces of open water, no ice overhead. So if we got a technique for finding that open water and getting the submarine underneath it, we should be able to surface the submarine inside the ice - like in a lake between the ice. And so that was the task set forth for the Carp, and this was then for the commanding officer to work out, his turn and move to locate the submarine under the lake between the floes, and make the submarine ascend to the surface under control, and not strike the ice. The commanding officer was Commander J. H. Palmer of the Carp, and he and the whole group on board took a very strong interest, lively interest, in the problem and worked out the techniques, which was a stationary ascent for the submarine, which is not standard practice, because normally they come up under speed on a slant. To quickly come to the surface was to get good control of the stability of the submarine, come around underneath the open water, check the sonar system, and be sure that it's open overhead, and make the ascent. And so this was done for a period of some two weeks.

Q: How much experience did he try to do before he ever went under the ice?

Dr. L.: Oh, they practiced the technique all the way up from San Francisco to Vancouver and from Vancouver north. Every time they came up, they came up that way.

Q: Where did you board?

Dr. L.: I went aboard in Vancouver, British Columbia, and then from Vancouver went up to the Chukchi again. We had a partner with us, another submarine, the Blower. She was just sort of a communications escort. They go in pairs. But we did exercises just to see how we could talk to each other under the water across underneath the ice. The Blower was not equipped to go under the ice, so she stayed outside the ice cover.

Q: Did you add any more equipment to the Carp?

Dr. L.: No. Just as the Boarfish, other than we did take some temperature recorders to try and get some more information about the temperature and the salinity of the water that we were working in, because we found we were in very unusual water situations, in very mixed up water, clouds of warm and cold water. Very strange region. Something we'd never really experienced. We noticed that on the Boarfish and so took along a little more equipment to get more of the sotry of what kind of water we were in, with regard to its temperature from top to bottom and with regard to its changes of temperature as you proceeded horizontally, due to the melting of the ice. When ice melts, you get all kinds of clouds of water of different salinity and temperatures in the sea water, and so you get a very cloudy type of water situation, speaking as to temperature that one doesn't experience anywhere else.

Q: What does that affect?

Dr. L.: That affects entirely the sonar transmission. Again, the way a sonar beam goes through the water, it's very sensitive to temperature change.

Actually the Carp went very straightforward because of the long effort they put into their training for their ascents. And again we had experienced people on the sonar systems for both the QLA scanning system and for the echo-sounding system, so their interpretation of sonar was nothing new. It was just to see whether we could handle a boat underneath the ice cover and make these ascents. So that operation was straightforward according to the book and according to the plans. It was completed and we came out of it. There were no changes in the plans and the operation and data obtained were just as expected. It was cranked in, cranked out, and put in the book, and we knew then that we now could navigate under

— that is pilot, I should say — we could pilot ourselves underneath the ice cover with the sonar, and we could find the open spaces, or lakes, the word we use is "Polynya," the Russian for open water space, in the ice cover, get under it, make a stationary ascent, surface in the water, and submerge again.

Q: How far underneath did you go this time?

Dr. L.: We must have been in 50-60 miles, I guess, into the marginal area, into this open part of the ice cover. But again it was all north of the Bering Strait, in the Chukchi Sea, where we knew the areas we could penetrate, so we were not concerned with trying to explore a new area. We were concentrating on operating the submarine in the ice.

Q: What does Chukchi mean?

Dr. L.: It comes from the people who lived in that area, the Chukchi Peninsula.

Q: It's an odd word!

Dr. L.: It is, yes. The sea that's just north of the Bering Strait is the Chukchi Sea. It's a very shallow-flat-bottomed area.

Q: It's a long — well, you were going to tell me later, so I won't bring that up now, because it does go a long distance as shallow.

Dr. L.: Oh, yes, it's shallow and a tremendous area.

Q: And "polynya" means?

Dr. L.: An open water space in the ice cover.

Q: So that was again uneventful?

Dr. L.: Right, and it —

Q: I shouldn't say "uneventful," but it went as per plan, as you said.

Dr. L.: It went as planned. It kind of closed off this first go at under-ice work, because now we could go underneath the ice, wander around underneath, knew what we were doing, could surface in the open water, recharge the batteries, proceed to the next lake, the next polyNya, surface again, as long as we were in areas that we knew. We knew what the bottom was, knew what ice cover to expect, and that we could be assured that there were open-water spaces to surface, because we needed to surface in order to recharge the batteries.

Q: I was wondering, as I read some of the material, whether it would be possible, suppose a ship had surfaced, for an airplane to direct a submarine to an opening in the ice?

Dr. L.: Well, we thought about this and, in fact, with the Carp we did use an aircraft with us to give us the total picture of what we were working under. However, the communications between our aircraft and the submarine were pretty difficult and not very useful because you have to be surfaced in order to receive messages and when you're surfaced you've already solved it!

Q: It wasn't ever possible to make the transmission under the ice

Dr. L.: No. We do, later on, speak about receiving transmissions, which we do on very long wave lengths. We do receive transmissions under ice with modern submarines, but at that time we did not. So we surfaced and did talk to the plane to get what the whole area looked like, that was the only reason for it.

Q: But you had no problem with navigation or orientation or anything?

Dr. L.: No. The aircraft did help on the first trial with the Carp, to be assured that we weren't wandering off into very difficult areas. We used it in that sense. So, the Carp kind of ended that first trial period, but than at that time, the close of 1948, some decisions had to be made, personally and what do we do next type of thing, and what we recognized then was that we had a tremendous problem by the tail which we didn't know anything about. We knew how to pilot the submarine around as long as we were in situations that we knew about, we knew the bottom, and we knew pretty well what the ice cover was, and in the summer only when there was plenty of open water among the ice floes, and you wouldn't wander in too far. What we didn't know anything about was sound transmission, that is how bad or how good or what the distortion would do to the way the sound beam would wander around in this icy environment, which we didn't have too well described as far as temperature was concerned. We couldn't go anywhere else, but just in the Chukchi, because we didn't have any charts, we didn't have any bathymetry. If you look at a chart of that period, you find that the Arctic Ocean is not known, nothing to guide us other than the drift of the Fram with a few soundings. We didn't dare go east of Point Barrow, if you can think of the chart, we were straight north of the BEring Strait, this big wide Chukchi Sea, and the coast of Alaska, and Point Barrow kind of sticks out near the Arctic Ocean. And at that time there was no information east of Point Barrow, and we recognized that ice conditions changed, and we didn't know anything about it, and didn't know what we'd run into without something, so we always did all these first trials where we knew, in the Chukchi Sea. So we recognized that we must get information on the rest of the Arctic Ocean if we were going to run submarines. We must get information on what happens to the sonar's transmissions in ice. We must learn something about ice, so we can understand this material we're dealing with. And then also try to work in other seasons than just in the middle of summer.

Q: No one at that time even knew much about the chemistry of ice, did they?

Dr. L.: The only work on ice was the work that was done by Malmgren and a couple of others, primarily by this physicist that was with Sverdrup on the Maud expedition, and after all ice was the thing that we were contending with. This is sea ice, which is very different from fresh-water ice. We had to know all its properties, its chemistry, and particularly acoustically, which no one had done -- what sort of a reflector it was, how did it scatter sound, how did it change with the temperature and pressure when it is under water in the sea, and so forth.

Q: Was that an exciting challenge for you?

Dr. L.: Well, as you found from reading that report I sent you, Report 88, was written in 1948 right after the Carp, and the challenge then was it looked as though we could take a submarine and, if we did it right, go anywhere we wanted to. It looked as though the whole thing opened up for exploring the whole Arctic Ocean. Now it seems so commonplace, it has no meaning. But at that time, in 1948, we knew nothing about the Arctic Ocean. The only information we had was the drift of the Fram, aircraft flights over it, which don't tell anything but that it's got a lot of ice, and the data that had been released by the Russians when the landed in 1936 near the North Pole in an aircraft and drifted out on the ice floes. That was the extent of the information.

Q: Who invented that? They landed in an airplane?

Dr. L.: They were landed by aircraft —

Q: Oh, landed by aircraft.

Dr. L.: Near the North Pole in 1936 or 1937, just prior to the war — a party, and drifted on the floe from the Pole out to the Atlantic Ocean, and were picked up by a Russian icebreaker. So we had the data they collected on the weather, the temperature of the water, and the drift pattern. But that information and the drift of the Fram and the drift of the SEDOV, which was during the war period and hadn't been released. There was very little information. The chart of the Arctic Ocean at that time just shows a big bowl, just a big basin and nobody knows anything about it.

Q: I was wondering to your personality whether that was a challenge or so overwhelming that -

Dr. L.: No, it was definitely a challenge. The challenge that I was interested in was the development of the submarine as a vehicle to go and do things with. Of course, there was the exploration of the Arctic Ocean which was a challenge, too, but the main thing I was interested in was really as an engineer, how to use these things.

Q: You sound almost more like an engineer than a physicist!

Dr. L.: Really, at times, I guess, you're mixed up with engineering, and at other times you're mixed up with the basic information to help the engineering department, especially when you're doing work in the sea.

Q: But I was interested in you as a person, and sometimes scientists in the esoteric world without being concerned as to a practical use, and I gather that your research has always been with the practical and -

Dr. L.: I've always had pretty much a feel, I think, [maybe I didn't] prior to being involved with the Navy, but I always accepted this. If I must deal with the Navy, I must have one foot in the practical use of whatever is being done, as well as you possibly can gain knowledge and information, you need that, too. But you also need to show what you're doing with it. The market is always there. If you don't, you don't continue to get support given to things. That may be just the fact that some of us have a little bit more of the feeling that we've got to have a little practical business about us to keep going. To keep going where you want to go you've also got to show a good reason why you're doing it, some time, to get the support of the public as a whole - or the support of the market, whatever you wish to call it. And almost all work has an aspect of it, if you just present it in that form, some usefulness at all times.

So 1948 was a kind of a crossroads, as far as I was concerned, on a personal basis too, because I saw that what I wanted to do as far as this under Arctic submarine was concerned - and some of this challenge also came, I must admit, by that sort of opposition, not really opposition, but you know you still receive a challenge from others who disbelieve or give you an opposition. It is a part of that, I think, of anyone's nature because at that particular time, for example, of finding the official documentation of the Navy, the statement, "Okay, the Carp has demonstrated that you can go running around under ice cover, but also in the next sentence it says that an Arctic submarine is complete fantasy." So this is the official documentation from the Chief of Naval Operations. And that gives you kind of a challenge - okay, I'm going to show you "you're wrong type of thing." So there is that side of it, and all the way along there are these personalities whom you find who felt some of that challenge - "okay, we don't believe the official, but we'll show that there is another side, too." So there's that side of the challenge as well as just something new. Part of this something new is that you are alone and it gives you another kind of a feeling. When you are alone, you have a little more feeling of doing work as you see to do it than if you're involved in problems of research or development where a great number of people are involved. You have more freedom to proceed. So there's that side of it, too, which appealed to me I know, and it appealed to the group that I still have, the fact that we're sort of left alone to get on because we've always been flying a little bit contrary to the directives or the cardinal rules that have been set down as to what the Navy should be doing. So there is that side of the picture.

Well, coming back again to the question of 1948 —

Q: I think it's interesting to stop to get your personal reaction about that time, too. That's you, rather than just the story of what happened.

Dr. L.: Well, the way the picture stood in 1948 was — okay, we've got this thing, we can go pushing around in the Arctic in a submarine. At that time I had to make up my mind for the commitment that I had to UCLA physics department, because when I left UCLA I was committed to return as a staff member, because I'd left there as a staff member, and they gave me up until 1948 to make up my mind. After the war in 1946 the offer came, am I going to return to the university or not, because, they said, we've decided what the staff is going to be then.

I went back, actually, during 1948, and was a member of the staff because I'd accumulated so much leave during the war period that I'd go up there and teach two days and work down here three days. So I was teaching at UCLA all during half the year of 1948 and half the year of 1949.

Q: What was your subject?

Dr. L.: A lower division course in electricity and magnetism in the Physics Department, and in the upper division spectroscopy courses. But this gave me at least something to decide on. I could go back and do some teaching and see whether I wanted to do that. At the same time I was facing the submarine problem, and at the same time I had to decide how I would be operating inside of the Naval Electronics Laboratory in administrative command, because I was running a division of 150 people with a very much broader program than just Arctic submarines. So, this was the question, and what came out of it was I decided that I didn't want to go back to university teaching, I was not cut out to do that, especially at that time of life when I had this other thing to do which was far more challenging or interesting or something — to go running off in an Arctic submarine. And the other decision was I had to change my place in the organization of the Navy Electronics Laboratory, and they reorganized that year, in 1949, so I resigned from head of the division. It was taken over by Ralph Christenson, who later became director of the Laboratory. I took a group of about 12 or 15 people who had been involved in the Arctic submarine game, and we went off and were our own little division, or branch, or something. Anyhow, an organization where NEL could do special research. At that time, if we had used the word "Arctic science" or "Arctic submarines" or (arctic) anything, we'd have been out of the business right away because it was not recognized that there was any need anywehre in the Navy to have such an organization. So I think we called it special research or something of that sort.

Q: Which covered a multitude of sins!

Dr. L.: Miscellaneous!

Q: But you actually were working on Arctic problems?

Dr. L.: Right, and this is an important point. It was during the 1948-49 period that this all came about and we had to make up our minds what to do here. Then, in the summer of 1949, Rawson Bennett was still at NEL as commanding officer and we did take another expedition up north which you won't find in the literature, but then began a very different series of expeditions.

Q: Did it please you to have a unit with one specialty?

Dr. L.: Right. This was all my doing. I'm making a decision in my career now, and I recognized this. I had to make a decision at that point, and I keep telling my younger people, you've got to make up your mind in the same way. If you decide that you're going to make your career in an administrative goal or a director-type of goal, you're going to go for directing research and make it an ultimate, or you're going to go as an expert in a particular field as chief scientist in this particular field. Don't try to do both.

And so that was what I realized I faced then. I would either stay in the administrative-directing side of laboratory science, because I was a division head and just about one down from the top - I was either going to be an administrator and director of science, or I was going to go into one particular field. And I chose to go into one particular field and I'm still happy I made the choice because that's just the way - I mean a person has to decide which way you're built, which way is the happy way for you to go. You have to recognize that you're liable to make much more money in one direction than the other direction, and all kinds of things are very different.

Q: Weren't you fortunate, though, to be able to make the choice between the academic life or the type of life you led within the research field?

Dr. L.: Oh, right. I can't guess how many people actually had that happen, but I think I had it come almost everything at once, which I think other people sort of have these decisions and they don't quite recognize them because they're very gradual.

Q: They don't even know that they're making a decision!

Dr. L.: They don't even know that they're making a decision, obviously, don't see that there's a crossroads. But at that time it was pretty obvious to me and I remember thinking about it a long time - I am at a crossroads, I've got to make up my mind. I can't run this division and do this other thing. It was very obvious because I wasn't doing things that I should be doing as a division head for all those people, and I wanted to do the other, so it was pretty clear which way I wanted to go, which way I was going to have to be going, and that was the decision I made.

Then, from that point on, I was concerned with organizing and running expeditions for one particular purpose, and that was for getting the maximum of information on the Arctic Ocean area, with the ultimate objective in mind of running submarines in there, even though we didn't have submarines we still had to gather information. So we find that from 1949 through 1955 we obtained most of the information by icebreakers or other ships, not by submarines.

Q: I think I stopped you when you said you went on another trip that wasn't in the books, which was —

Dr. L.: Which was in the summer of 1949. It was the first of a series of expeditions to simply learn about the Arctic Ocean area. And in 1949 when this began a group of joint work with the Canadians we brought in and got together, and we had very closely cooperative programs with the Canadians from that point on. And this was based on the same people that I met much earlier. In 1949 we took the submarine which was NEL's submarine, the Baya, up north. We also took the Marysville, which was NEL's surface ship for oceanographic work, and the HMCS Cedarwood, the Canadian oceanographic vessel from Nanaimo, and we put together a joint program with Jack Tully and Bill Cameron and their people out of British Columbia, and Gene LaFond who was in the group at NEL, and my own people in this submarine business all along in these ships. This, of course, was all organized while I was head of the Undersea Research Division, because NEL still hadn't reorganized, so I could take all this stuff, and put it into an expedition up north. That was the last time that the Navy Electronics Laboratory mounted a big operation of their own joined with Canada.

It was a very intensive type of thing, with sonar transmissions and studies of water conditions and the whole oceanographic sea physics type of study with these ships. But it was kept again in the Bering Strait and the Chukchi Sea, which we now were trying to measure the sonar conditions in these areas we had been playing around in the other two years of 1947 and 1948. That year, we also went to the Bering Strait and kept a little group right on Cape Prince of Wales on the Bering Strait, where we tried to measure how much water was flowing back and forth through the Strait. That was a first try. I mention it because two years later we established a permament station there which still operates. It's a one-family station, there's only one family making measurements, which is part of my group with the Arctic Submarine Laboratory. 1949 was a complete expedition, just for lots of data, and it's all been written up in many papers that have come out on the study of the Chukchi Sea.

Q: Did you go under the ice?

Dr. L.: No, everything was concentrated on what would be called straight scientific information. We were putting hydrophones down and sound sources and measuring what the sound was traveling between. Nothing in the sense of operating, just straight measurements of what was going on. And we didn't have any of the fleet operators. These were laboratory ships. It was different than in 1947 and 1948, which were with the regular military fleet operators. This was more like a science group going in there and doing pure science, so to speak, and working up the information.

Q: Did you find that as interesting as going with the operations people?

DR. L.: Oh, yes. It's really just the difference in the way you do things. The way you organize is different, you have different kind of people you're trying to work with, and have a lot more to work with in the sense of ships and whatnot that the Navy is involved in, and I guess you concentrate entirely on the accuracy of getting your information. It's a difference. You change your personality and your approach, so it's different. You set up the experiments of what you're going to do differently, than when you're working with the fleet operators.

Q: How long were you up there?

Dr. L.: That was not the entire summer, from early July to late September 1949. Then comes, after that, a whole series in 1950 and 1951, 1942, up to 1954 - that is almost a continuous story, although it was a new expedition organized each year it kept the continuity. From 1950 on, we concentrated on learning what the Arctic Ocean was like east of Point Barrow, so this was going into an area on which we had nothing, and this was done using icebreakers as prime vehicles. Each one of these expeditions now was organized jointly with Canada, but was done through the service squadron here in

San Diego, Service Squadron 1, which was the controlling command of these icebreakers at that time. So the icebreakers organized under Squadron 1 would be assigned to go up there each summer, and then we would use them for our scientific parties. We welded together again a very close cooperation between the scientists and the fleet operators, but this time the fleet operator was the Service Squadron. Now, we had also reorganized the Navy Electronics Laboratory, and I was head of the special research division, but it got these field trips organized and these expeditions organized where I reported to the Service Squadron commander. We did the entire organization under the Service Squadron commander, so it was a fleet-organized operation, not a laboratory operation, very different from 1949. The 1949 situation was under the command of the laboratory because we were using laboratory ships, but for the next years we organized these expeditions under the Service Squadron command. And so I simply reported to them and took whatever we required for the various laboratories, but the Service Squadron was the military commander, and I'd report to him as the chief scientist for him, and then draw in what we could from everybody we could get hold of, including Canadian laboratories, Canadian surveyors, the Hydrographic Office of the U. S. Navy, and the Hydrographic Service of the Canadian Navy — wherever we could find somebody who was interested in going up there and working, we'd draw them in and form them into these task assignments.

Q: How many would go? Varying numbers?

Dr. L.: It varied. The Office of Naval Research played an important part here because they were supporting places like the University of Washington, Oceanographic Department. Clifford Barnes of the Oceanographic Department there was one of the prime individuals of this period - prior to the war he had been working up in the north and was very much interested in Arctic oceanography. So, he was a prime mover, and we had a number of oceanographers, students, and so forth, from the University of Washington. We got one or two from Scripps Institute of Oceanography, and then a few Canadians, Bill Cameron's and Tully's group from Nanaimo, one or two from the Canadian Hydrographic Service, and maybe one to four from the Hydrographic Office of the U. S. Navy, and then a few of our own people.

Q: Did you always go?

Dr. L.: I always went, yes, because my contribution was to organize these things each year, and then we'd have to set up what are we going to do this year, how much survey did we get done in the Beaufort Sea and the Canadian archipelago, what is the next step, and then each year be sure that I went to the Squadron to get the icebreakers lined up, go through the Chief of Naval Operations to get the things all assigned, go to each one of these institutions and be sure that the people were available, and be sure that the Office of Naval Research got the money for the right people.

Q: That was a tremendous logistic job.

Dr. L.: Getting all these people together —

Q: You still were doing administration!

Dr. L.: Right. Everything was focused on this one objective, nothing else. There was a lot of freedom because nobody paid any attention to us. And, again, the key people were in various places. For example, this is where McWethy came into the picture. Robert McWethy was the executive officer on the Burton Island in 1950. He was a submariner who got interested in ice-breaking and icebreakers. I'm not quite sure how now. So I got acquainted with him because the Burton Island was the first icebreaker that I had assigned by the Service Squadron, so I met him there and we just naturally got together, being submarine types interested in Arctic submarines. Then, he went from there to the office of the Chief of Naval Operations, to the submarine desk, that's Op-Nav 31. He went there and the commanding officer of the Burton Island after 1950 went to the Office of the Chief of Naval Operations to the icebreaker desk. So with those two people there, and Service Squadron 1 right here in San Diego, it was easy to bring these things together. The icebreaker desk in CNO kind of acted as the focal point.

Q: Who was the skipper of Burton Island?

Dr. L.: At that time Commander John Swartz.

Q: How many trips did you make?

Dr. L.: Oh, let's see - we would have a trip in the summer, and we'd have one in the winter. We always had the summer cruise, and then in the winter we'd have one of the icebreakers in the Bering Sea to study the ice cover. So there would be two cruises a year.

One year we had three - we had a summer cruise, a winter cruise, and a spring cruise. That was a bigger year, all year round.. But they were kept going so that we kept gathering information and moving further and further into the Beaufort Sea and around in the Canadian archipelago. This whole program was pretty well spelled-out by a meeting that was kind of a key to the whole thing - I should have mentioned it - back at the end of 1949, after we came back from that joint expedition of the Cedarwood, the Baya, and the Marysville. I recall that on the Cedarwood I came back from Bayh and we met with Dr. George Fields from Canada, who was a key individual for the next few years. He was chief scientist for the Defense Research Board of Canada. Jack Tully was there, who was from Nanaimo, and Fred Sanders, who was head of the Pacific Naval Laboratory - the Canadian Naval Laboratory in Esquimalt. And that's where the plan was laid out. What we didn't know was this Beaufort Sea and Canadian archipelago, and the point was made then that, some day, we shall have to worry about submarines in that area, particularly Canada in the Canadian archipelago, because of that intricate set of passages they have up there, the entrance to the whole of Canada and the U.S., and it just seemed obvious that some day a submarine would try to operate in the area.

So it was then that we laid down the fact that we did not have any information about those areas, and the submarine was the primary objective that we should get the information for. And so the series of expeditions which followed in 1951, 1952, 1953, and 1954 were sort of laid out at that time and agreed as best we could with the power we had, which wasn't too much, at least on my side of the house. I talked it over with George Fields, who was in a very high position, to work out these cooperative programs. We had a lot more freedom in those days than we do now, as far as handling arrangements. The bureaucracy and the organization of government has increased so that you can't put things together like you could at that time.

Well, that's the main planning meeting that did take place, and then we really sort of carried it out from that point on. In 1950 we had the Burton Island up there. In 1951 the Burton Island again. In 1951 we established a field station on Cape Prince of Wales to continually monitor the exchange of oceans across the Bering Strait as best we can. In 1952 we had the Burton Island and the Redfish. That came about because of what I mentioned before we were taping. Between 1948 and 1952, why we did not have submarine activity with these cruises, other than the Baya, was because the personality of the force commander in the Pacific - he had no interest in the Arctic. But in 1952 Rear Admiral Momsen moved from Op-31, and he had a real interest in the Arctic. He had an interest in just doing new things. The Arctic was a new thing, and that's how his interest came about. So he wrote himself a letter on leaving Op-31, the submarine desk in CNO, to the force commander in the Pacific to go and do something about the Arctic, and then when he got out to the force commander, Pacific, he received his own letter and assigned the Redfish to carry it out. So we had the Redfish assigned to this joint Canadian-U.S. Beaufort Sea expedition of 1952. We had also that year Burton Island then under the command of Commander Maher, whom we mentioned, and the Canadian small vessel, the Cancolim, directed, all under the command of the Service Squadron. Fortunately, the man who was the Service Squadron commander was a submariner each time. That happened to be a billet that was always filled by a submariner, so the thing was put together very nicely. At that time Captain Grenfell was the flotilla commander, and so I remember that we organized the whole expedition between the submarine and the icebreaker under discussions with Grenfell. He was the flotilla commander, the Service Squadron commander was a submariner, and Admiral Momsen was SubPac, and Captain Daspit was Momsen's Chief of Staff. These personalities all sort of fit together in this story as we go along.

That expedition put together a tremendous amount of information. As I remember, it included all of the scientific groups from the University of Washington, Scripps Institute, and the Canadian agencies. The Hydrographic Office had a big part, and the U. S. Coast and Geodetic Survey had a big part - it provided special equipment for positioning accurately the icebreaker and positioning accurately the submarine by electronic positioning, which was specialized equipment for getting the exact position of a ship relative to the shore. The Redfish was assigned a new task of holding her position in the ice cover northeast of Point Barrow. This was the first time we had taken a submarine east of Point Barrow, because we had gathered information during 1950 and 1951 on the bathymetry so we felt that we had some information and were not still afraid to go east of Point Barrow. So this was our first experience of actually taking a submarine there. We had again the same sonar set-ups that we had had on the Carp. We were equipped to pilot ourselves round underneath the ice cover, and also to surface in the open polynyas in the cover. So Redfish was assigned the job of holding a position northeast of Point Barrow and, working with the Burton Island, we made a lot of sound-transmission studies which had to do with the detection of submarines. Now we're starting to think about warfare problems of submarines in ice cover and what the problems might be. So we ran exercises of submarines versus icebreakers in the military sense on this particular expedition, and carried out a number of experiments with these submarine-simulated attacks on the icebreakers, the icebreaker attempted to detect the submarine. I think, as far as the submarine was concerned, the most interesting thing was that the Redfish maintained her station in the ice cover without benefit of aircraft or icebreaker or other information for a week, holding her position by the electronic position-indicating equipment to a position within a tenth mile at all times.

Then at the end of the week, after the sound-transmission studies had been completed, with ice completely around her, on all sides, and without any knowledge of where open water might be, we had to dive and get out on our own. So we had the real crucial experiment to conduct, "how does a submarine act without the benefit of any outside assistance."

J: Let me clarify. Where were you when the week was over?

Dr. L.: This was about northeast of Point Barrow, right out in the ice cover. We were holding our position. We were holding a position for radio communication and listening on sonars at the listening stations on the surface, and we had no information from the help of aircraft or anywhere else where was open water, what way do we go, and that sort of thing. We had to depend on our knowledge of what the ocean was like, what the vicinity was, and our own capability to get out.

Q: How far were you under the ice cover?

Dr. L.: We didn't have the slightest idea, because we had gone to this station and we knew what it was when we had gone there. It was now a week or more later and the ice cover had likely completely moved by miles. so it was really the test.

Q: Had you reached your point when you submerged and then surfaced?

Dr. L.: No, we reached our point partially - some submerging but mostly by surface with the icebreaker, together. We had gone as a pair. Then we were there for a week to ten days and the icebreaker had gone off 100 miles away doing other things plus making sound transmissions to us. So now we had to get out of there, and meet the icebreaker again on our own. So we were required to submerge. We were completely surrounded by ice as far as we could see and we hadn't the slightest idea where the ice cover was, and now we were depending strictly on our piloting and being able to surface in the open water lakes wherever we could find them to get out, or to proceed, and that's what we did do and were able to do, knowing our information of the ice cover, which was a matter of keeping track of the ice cover overhead, keeping track of the water temperature we were going through, and knowing which way to look for open water. We were using our knowledge of the ocean, and our sonar systems to get ourselves out of that situation. It was a demonstration of what we believed we could do, and we had to do in this case.

The next two days were taken in making an under-ice cruise, surfacing, re-charging the batteries, and proceeding under the ice cover so that we got ourselves into the open water, just east of Point Barrow, and then we proceeded on the surface the next 50 or 60 miles to the rendezvous with the Burton Island.

Q: Was that a tense time when you were submerging and not knowing where you were going to be able to come up again?

Dr. L.: The only tense thing that happened in that affair was just as were submerging, after being surfaced for this long period of time, we got a report from the after torpedo room that we were flooding, which shakes anybody when you're on a submarine. In this particular case, the gaskets on the after room hatch were not holding. We'd had this happen twice. The main induction also had it happen. Apparently the rubber in the cold temperature had lost its resiliency and was not properly sealing, so the flooding came in just because the gasket wasn't holding. Fortunately, nobody had left any dirt of anything on the seat so that what we finally ended up when the pressure got high enough was just a metal-to-metal seal and it held well enough.

Q: It corrected itself?

Dr. L.: It really corrected itself once we got down deep enough. I think that was the only excitement for possibly ten minutes or so until we realized that we weren't going to have a complete casualty. They took in quite a bit of water. I remember, there was considerable water in the after room. We couldn't surface again because as we came down the ice was right against us, it just closed over - well, we could have surfaced if we had had to in an emergency, but it would have been damaging to do it. That was the only point of excitement, I think, the rest of it was pretty straightforward. It was a long run with a battery diesel boat because we had no idea how far we should go, so, of course, every precaution was taken to conserve our battery power and conserve oxygen. And we did run for - I don't recall now, but it was a good number of hours before we did surface again for re-charging.

Q: Were you going South ?

Dr. L.: Yes, we were going towards where the open water should be, depending, of course, on our knowledge. Now we had knowledge of where the ice boundary should lie, where to expect the open water, most open-water lakes, because of the way the currents flow at Point Barrow, the warm water comes up along the coast of Alaska and swings out north of Point Barrow and in these kind of areas one can expect more melt-out between the flows and so we were guided according to that. We could watch what temperatures we were getting as we went along as to whether we were approaching the proper areas or not. So it was a matter of keeping track of the temperature, the type of ice cover, and knowing the direction and what the bathymetry was, and where the ice margins should be. We got ourselves out of that situation.

Q: Were you still reading the pictures and instructing the commanding officer?

Dr. L.: Yes, at this time we were still the interpreters of all the information, and informing the commanding officer what our best estimates and guesses were. He would make the decision what to do with the submarine on the basis of that information. The ship was not operating this equipment. The special equipment was being operated by civilian specialists.

Q: And it was still located distances apart?

Dr. L.: There was still not much choice of that, again because all this equipment was experimental and was only put on for special situations and were working on a regular military boat, so we still had that communications problem but did the best we could.

Q: Was there any other equipment on the Redfish than there had been on the Carp?

Dr. L.: Not relative to ice cover, no. The only other special equipment we had was some communications equipment and the electronic position equipment for knowing our location exactly, nothing else special.

Q: Did you feel an additional challenge after the Redfish? You'd been able to do something increasingly difficult with each expedition?

Dr. L.: The Redfish was a demonstration of what we could do, and we took Redfish then — well, we did all these exercises which really opened up a whole new thing. It didn't really open anything new, it just underlined what we believed — that a submarine had complete mastery of the Arctic Ocean, wherever there was ice cover the submarine had mastery of everybody, I don't care whether they were aircraft or surface ships, because the submarine could wander around under the ice and she knew what she was doing, but nobody on top knew what the submarine was doing. The surface ship just was a complete loss as to what was underneath her. Her sonar systems couldn't detect anybody under there. Redfish could wander right under the icebreaker and look up with a periscope and count the propeller turns, look at her hull, or do anything, and the icebreaker didn't have the slightest idea that she was down there.

Q: Was that because of the density or the temperature of the water?

Dr. L.: That's because there's not only the mixed water, but just because of the ice cover. The icebreaker is completely involved in struggling with the ice, breaking the ice, making so much noise, and her sonar systems cannot be extended while she's going through ice cover. A submarine can go out under the ice and come in at any angle. Any vehicle on the surface is committed by the ice to do the things that the ice wants, really. The icebreaker does not have too much choice of where she wants to go. It's the ice that determines where the icebreaker can go, whereas the submarine is completely free to go wherever she wants.

Q: So if you had a war game there wouldn't be much doubt about the winner, would there?

Dr. L.: That was pretty obvious, and when you have this complete sort of sonar-radar camouflage, the submarine is completely lost or covered, or however you want to say it, by this ice cover. She has freedom of action. This is the kind of belief that came out of the tests, which also showed that we needed different kinds of weapons, different ideas. Things that you did in the open sea just did not apply to military operations in this sea ice canopy.

Q: Were you making recommendations all the time to CNO or some senior person interested, or was anyone interested in what you found?

DR. L.: Well, let's see - out of that one we would write reports. We always reported from that point on under the Service Squadron. It was a typical patrol report or task report, which came out under the command of the squadron. It was a military report. There's a drawer full of documents. They're all there, as far as that's concerned. These were all reported, but they only caused interest in certain people who were interested.

Q: What he did with them, that is the —

Dr. L.: Sure, they went through. Everybody got to read them if they wanted to read them.

Q: You made the comment that 1953 was a bad year for Redfish. What did that mean?

Dr. L.: 1953 was then a continuation of the same expedition of 1952, that is a study of the Beaufort Sea with the joint Canadian-U. S. program with Service Squadron 1. Now, having completed the work that we did with <u>Redfish</u> in 1952, and especially with this demonstration of mastery or whatever you wish to call it, could-be mastery of a submarine operating against surface ships or other warships in the ice cover, and a demonstration by <u>Redfish</u> where we took her all the way across the Beaufort Sea up to the entrance to the McClure Strait - we felt that we had done as much as we could do with a fleet submarine and her standard sonar equipment without making any special modifications to that submarine, because I was concerned with what happens if we go into the ice cover for quite a distance and we find that we cannot find an opening big enough for the submarine to surface. Then, what do we do in order to recharge the battery. The submarine should be therefore modified in some way so that she could push her way up through the ice cover above her in the summertime. In the summertime, you understand, the ice cover is not cemented and tight, and so you can push your way up between the ice if you don't find a nice big open clear spot.

Q: You know that now, but you didn't know that then, did you?

Dr. L.: At that time we already recognized from running around underneath that we could get into areas where, from what we had seen both from the icebreaker and from underneath, the ice was broken but packed together into a contiguous mass. We did not know these packed areas ahead of time from the oceanography. Therefore, we had always done our operating up through 1952 in places where we knew that due to warm waters circulating underneath we'd have some nice big lakes somewhere available. We had not simply gone off into unknown areas just assuming that we could get to the surface some place. We had not done that.

Well, in 1953 I did not ask for a submarine, but Momsen was still out in SubPac and he said - the Redfish was there before, why shouldn't the Redfish go back and see what you can do with her. He was interested in using it although it was recognized that we didn't have any really new critical experiments that we could do with here, because she still would be this straight equipped submarine that she had been before with just the addition of a special echo-sounder looking up to take care of underneath the ice cover. And the test that did occur in 1953 with Redfish was packed broken ice with no polgnyas. In the long term it was a good thing that we did take her because we learned some things about ice and submarines that gave us what kind of extreme situations one might get into in the type of ice cover that we should plan to be able to handle, which we might not have recognized if we hadn't continued. Although at the time it looked like the operation with the Redfish was a complete fiasco, because when we got into the summer of 1953 it was one of those summers where the ice cover stays right against the entire beach from Point Barrow east to Amundsen Gulf the entire summer. There's no open water at any time.

And at the time of 1953, and with the submarine being not equipped to handle anything in the way of broken ice cover, it meant that the submarine was at the complete mercy of surface ice conditions and having to operate on the surface, because we could not find any open lakes through which she could surface to re-charge her batteries. She had to operate on the surface, and it was something like the situation down in Antarctica where we were not prepared to operate in broken-up ice with no open water.

Q: This taught you that in the summertime there isn't always the open place that you had thought there would be?

Dr. L.: We knew that, but it was the first experience I had had where there was no open water near the beach at any time. The experience that I had had in the area was in 1950, '51, and '52. In each case there was always a large stretch of open water between the Alaskan coast and the ice. In 1953, we had the other case where the whole ice cover of the Arctic seemed to shift over to our side and was against the beach the entire summer. So, we came in there this time the Northwind, the Burton Island, and the Redfish. The Burton Island went through early and did survey work in Prince of Wales Strait in the Archipelago, with a whole group of people on board from Canada and the U. S., and this was the first summer in which we were also beginning to do some work for the DEW line (distance early warning system), which came in later. At that time the Air Force primarily became interested in the north as to where it should put in its radar. So we had a combination of what we were doing for submarines, plus trying to do some early work for that radar line which just started in 1953.

So one person we had on board was Colonel Joe Fletcher, who had gotten involved in airplanes and submarines. He's the Fletcher who was on Fletcher's ice island, the big ice island discovered by radar from aircraft back during the war, and then was a drifting ice station in 1950, maybe. Yes, I think that was when the Air Force established a camp on it, a drifting ice station. And actually in 1952 Al Crary, the chief scientist on the ice station, set off some explosive charges (large acoustic sound sources) well out in the middle of the Arctic Ocean. We listened for them and received the sound pulse on board the <u>Redfish</u> far south in the Beaufort Sea. Hence, we could receive sound across the whole of the Arctic Ocean, which was the first time anything like that was done.

Anyway, Fletcher was on <u>Burton Island</u>, Commander Pat Maher was still the C.O. on <u>Burton Island</u>. Also the Canadians were on <u>Burton Island</u>. They were doing a survey in Prince of Wales Strait and on the north coast of Alaska and Canadian Archipelago for the DEW line. We had <u>Northwind</u> and <u>Redfish</u> together struggling around in the ice mess off the north coast of Alaska. <u>Redfish</u> never really did any diving that time. She made a couple of short dives near Point Barrow, but the rest of the time she was just fighting ice on the surface. Again, we had to use tows and all kinds of things to move the submarine and the icebreaker around in that complete ice cover. There were no open waters. So, this was a real lesson in what a submarine must be able to handle, if she's going to be a fighting ship in that area. She must be able to meet such kind of ice conditions, which means that the hull configuration had to be different than just a normal open-sea submarine. It also brought home a lot of information on the oceanography of the sea ice of the area, being the first experience really where I had seen this complete cover of ice right against the beach almost the entire summer, and all the problems that arise even from moving the icebreakers through such an area.

Q: How far did it extend?

DR. L.: It, of course, extended clear across the Arctic Ocean, but the ice was in and out against the beach, and there just wasn't any open water along that north coast of Alaska at the time we were there, which other summers had had a big wide open-water area.

Q: You say that came because of currents?

Dr. L.: That comes because of prevailing wind patterns. The ice cover in the Arctic Ocean is sort of like a big mass, and sometimes the prevailing winds can be such that it all comes over against the American side or the Canadian side or maybe it's more or less all against the Russian side. We don't know the whole picture, but winds can influence greatly where the ice cover is, and then if you get a lot of prevailing wind that is blowing towards the shore from the Arctic Ocean, you're just going to have ice cover right against the beaches. The north coast of Alaska is a large, long continental shelf, shallow water, and ice cover. It's just a bad situation as far as the submarine is concerned. You get ice building up there under pressure, huge mounds of ice, where heavy, thick pressure ridges form. These were the problems, and which any discussion of cargo ships, oil tankers, or oil finds up there must solve if it is intended to have any shipping off of that coast. The ice is just forced down by the wind system against the beach and it's piled up.

So 1953 was a real education in what the Arctic Ocean can do, the other side of bad ice conditions and what can happen along the north coast year round particularly not expected in the summer, closing in against the beach and just not leaving any room for operating in open water, whether submarines, surface ships, or icebreakers. Everybody had difficulty. The Burton Island broke some blades off her propeller, and just because of the heavy ice all kinds of things happened that year, although a considerable amount of information was gathered as far as oceanography is concerned. The Burton Island worked all the way up and down the Prince of Wales Strait, which is the little passage between Banks Island and Victoria Island in the Archipelago, as well as in Amundsen Gulf, and the Redfish and Northwind learned a lot about ice conditions between the submarine and the icebreaker.

Q: Did you have the same towing and scraping situation as you did –?

Dr. L.: Oh, yes, we went through that again. It was not new to me but it was certainly new to everybody else on board the Redfish – same Northwind but a different submarine but the same squealing and pushing and howling and bumping that one gets when being towed through ice. We didn't do too much of it but we did do some.

Q: Were you able to calm shattered nerves by telling them that you'd had that happen in the Antarctic?

Dr. L.: I told them that it was to be expected, but I don't know that that helped, you just sort of experience it, anyway. It's irritating, that's what it is. It's not so much fear as it's just irritating. It just sort of frays your nerves, more than makes you fearful.

I'm not talking about the winter cruises because those were strictly icebreakers, but in between on these summer cruises we did go up into the Bering Sea with one or two icebreakers to see what the ice conditions were like in the Bering Sea. During winter we were pushed halfway down the Bering Sea by the ice, and so we were operating icebreakers mainly to see what icebreakers can do, further study sonar conditions, oceanography, and understanding the ice cover at all times of year. That paper you have on explosives, icebreakers and ice, a lot of that was done in winter cruises.

The summer of 1954 was a contrast to 1953. 1953 the ice had been very tight against the Alaskan coast. The summer of 1954 it was wide open, just the opposite. We could have gone through there with the whole U. S. Pacific Fleet without seeing any ice. In 1954 we mounted again —

Q: You say going through there, how far could they have gone?

Dr. L.: They could have gone all the way from Point Barrow clear around into the Canadian Archipelago without seeing ice.

Q: Clear into the Archipelago?

DR. L.: No, not into the Atlantic. You get into all those tight little passages between the Canadian Islands before you run into ice, although they could have gone - we're getting ahead of the story here a little bit. But in 1954 we had again the Burton Island, the Northwind, and we were joined this time by the new Canadian icebreaker of the Canadian Navy, the Labrador. I should have probably mentioned that on the 1953 cruise we also had as one of our people on board Captain Robertson, RCN, of the Canadian Navy, who was to be the commanding officer of the Labrador, and so he was on one of the U. S. icebreakers so he could see how they operated, because he was prospective commander and builder of the Canadian icebreaker. I had known him before that, but then I got acquainted with him again, and he became another one of these personalities in this whole problem. He was a real prime mover of Arctic work in Canada as far as the Royal Canadian Navy was concerned.

Well, in 1954 he was commanding officer of the Labrador coming from the Atlantic. From the Pacific, the Service Squadron here in San Diego, we had the Northwind and Burton Island again. Now we were concentrating on oceanography and bathymetry in the Canadian Archipelago itself, because we'd covered the whole Beaufort Sea as far as we could go into the ice cover with the icebreakers. So now we were concentrating on McClure Strait, which no ships had been through, and Melville Sound, the whole passage from the Pacific side of the Beaufort Sea straight through to Baffin Bay in the Atlantic. The Labrador, coming from the Atlantic side, was to meet the two icebreakers in the middle of Melville Sound. We were surveying that area. See, all of this at that time was sort of unknown. We were straying out in new country. All of the areas I've been talking about were areas that had not been surveyed. There had been ships in and out but by surveying I mean you must know exactly where you ship is, so that you have information and intelligence to make a chart with exact latitude, longitude, and depth of water. At that time, the position of the islands was not know, so part of the work in 1954 was to put a geodetic party on shore at Banks Island and take a whole set of star sights. When you have 24 hours of daylight, you can take star sights if you are a geodetic expert, and thus position that island. The Canadian Air Force had taken full photographic maps, but that did not give the position, i.e., the lat-long of the land. We had the photographic outline and so forth, but it meant that we had to get a party ashore to establish the actual geodetic position.

Q: Were you able to get the depths?

Dr. L.: The depths were taken by icebreaker wherever we could get them, and the position of the icebreaker was taken by the same equipment we'd had all the time, which the U. S. Coast and Geodetic people (who were with us and had set up two camps on the shore) were positioning the ship by electronic pulses between the ship and these two stations. So we would be surveying with the ship at sea, and at the same time a party was on the beach getting the position of the land. This is the kind of thing that was going on. So in the summer of 1954 we had the <u>Burton Island</u> surveying again the passage Prince of Wales Strait on the east side of Banks Island, the <u>Northwind</u> up the west side of Banks Island and into McClure Strait. This was the first ship to go into there. Fortunately, that year was a very open year. We went through McClure Strait clear into Mercy Bay, repeating

McClure's cruise of 100 years before. We did in a few hours what took him maybe three weeks. There on the wall is an etching I got in London a couple of years ago of McClure going through McClure Strait. It is rugged country. So we did get our one survey of McClure Strait, which is a deep southern passage and that's why we were primarily interested in it. It's very spectacular country. The interesting thing to me was that while piloting Northwind through the McClure Strait I was reading McClure's diary and the diary of a surgeon on board McClure's ship. I'd read hair-raising tales of fighting the ice hour by hour through the passage, whereas we had bright sunshine. I was out on the bridge in my shirt sleeves in about 50° F. sun twenty-four hours round the clock. Beautiful open water with a power-driven ship and not having to worry about sails or anything, reading the story of that ship going through right against the rocks on the beach. Sometimes they were so close that they were dodging ice hanging off the cliffs. Incredible story!

So we completed the survey through McClure Strait and then all the ships joined the Burton Island which came up Prince of Wales Strait and the Labrador came from the east, and the three ships met in Melville Sound. That summer a lot of surveying got done, which was then later used by Seadragon in her submarine transit in 1960 summer.

Well, 1954 ended a Period. It had been a very, very productive period because there were continuous operations winter and summer all under the Service Squadron, and we gathered a tremendous amount of information and really had surveyed the entire area from the Chukchi, where we first went, all across the Beaufort Sea,

Amundsen Gulf, all these passages, established the positions of the islands, and felt very familiar with it both oceanographically and its bathymetry. They'd collected animals and bottom samples and geology. In the literature of oceanography and geology you'll find papers by all of the people from the various universities, where it's all spelled out. So it was a very productive time.

But in 1954, there's a break because that is the last year. Then, the early warning system (1955) was being built. So from that point on, all icebreakers and all ships were assigned to the building of that DEW line. This brought an end to being able to use ships for what we had been doing. Now the entire concentration of both the U. S. and Canada or anybody involved Arctic-wise was to get that early defense system in.

So for me personally 1955 — I went back now, not as an organizer of cruises, but as an adviser to the task force commander of the amphibious forces for installing the DEW line. So I went back and worked with the three icebreakers, as a sort of icebreaker pilot, or helper, or whatever you want to call it. To assist in getting that great horde of ships along the North Alaskan coast we had three icebreakers - the Burton Island, the Northwind, and the Staten Island - a number of small helper icebreakers with the Coast Guard - at least three or four, and some sixty ships to get round from Point Barrow clear across that whole north Alaskan coast, to carry all these supplies and people and everything else that was to go into the DEW line. That was a tremendous operation, and what happened was that 1955 was as bad an ice year as 1953. In 1954 we could have driven the whole thing back and forth with no problem. 1955 turned out to be one of these years where the ice was against the beach all the time, and here we were taking these big cargo ships, AKAs of 12,000 tons, APAs, all kinds of LSTs, and CBs, all these cargo craft loaded with equipment and people and oil, tankers, all along these various locations where the stations were to be built.

That's a whole story in itself, but it was just a matter of plain hard labor and work by everybody concerned with the enormous task force, and the icebreakers doing all the heavy work of guiding the ships back and forth through the continuous ice cover.

Q: How long were you up there?

Dr. L.: From 1 July until October.

Q: Was it possible, under the circumstances, to do any research at all?

Dr. L.: No.

Q: You were just completely involved in the -

Dr. L.: I was just on the Northwind, which was the group commander for the icebreakers and all we did was worry with ice and with getting those ships back and forth, and trying to guess what was happening to the ice conditions and advising that particular ship over there dongt put your anchor down, keep drifitng with the ice, because you're liable to get holed by the ice, and that type of thing continually. Just using the experience that I had been in the ice and what could happen, advising what should be done and what shouldn't be done, moving the icebreakers and the ships through the ice 24 hours a day.

Q: Were you constantly in communication with the ships and -

Dr. L.: I was with the commander of the Northwind because I'd been working with him the year before. I had been on Northwind the entire year the year before, so this was just a matter of being with him all the time, and he was in charge of all the other icebreakers, and all the icebreakers were the escorts trying to get these ships through, so it was just the day-to-day business of advising or putting in my two cents' worth on what I thought we ought to be doing about those three freighters over there that are mixed up in the ice cover and how to get them out and when they should move to the next place - just guessing what the ice conditions were going to be and how to move from point to point.

We did have the help of air reconnaissance information. Aircraft would be flying back and forth over the whole area as far as the ice cover was concerned, but this had to do more with simply intimate knowledge of each point along that entire coast and what you might meet and what was happening right around the ships, and what would happen due to change in tide, due to change in wind, due to what the immediate environment was doing, the weather conditions, whether the ships were in danger where they were or whether they should be moved maybe a mile this way or two miles that way.

Q: Were you on the bridge all the time?

Dr. L.: Most of the time, because on an icebreakers the cabins - the captain's cabin is on the port side and they have another cabin on the starboard side for the force commander, which I occupied. So you're in contact all the time, and being on that ship all the information kept coming in and the advice going out as to what to do with each icebreaker and each group that they were struggling with. There was a complete chain back and forth. The task force commander stayed at Barrow in the communications ship and so his problem was, as task force commander, he'd talk in large units as to what they were trying to do, and our problem on the icebreaker was the immediate situation - what was right around us within a local mile, what was the best thing to do.

Q: Almost within your vision?

Dr. L.: That's right, or within the vision of your helicopter.

Q: I'm sure you were immensely valuable with your knowledge of previous experience!

Dr. L.: Well, that was the reason why the icebreaker's skipper asked for me to go along because I'd been with him the year before and he knew I'd been through the 1953 period and actually, of course, operating along that whole coast for, by then, four years every year each year.

Q: He knew what he was doing when he asked for you!

Dr. L.: It was just sort of a natural thing to do because it was all done through the Service Squadron right here in San Diego, so it was all sort of a family affair. So 1955 was just kind of a lost year in the sense of going ahead with the submarine programs, but it was very instructive as far as ships and the problems of logistics and surface craft and all those things that arose in an exercise of that magnitude, which was really a huge operation. At the same time, my group was involved even on the eastern side because Robertson had the Labrador over there, and he had the same kind of problems on the eastern end with the Atlantic force, so two or three of my group were with him with the special ship positioning equipment using the electronic position indicator, and did survey work in Foxe Basin and Hudson Strait and areas around there in connection with the DEW line. So in 1955 and 1956 we were pretty much involved in the DEW line operation and didn't, in that period, get on with the submarine business in the field.

I should probably return to 1950, because it was in 1950 that we realized that we needed a laboratory where the work that was specific to these problems, that arose with submarines in the Arctic, could be done. You couldn't do everything in the field, you couldn't do everything by just taking a submarine and trying things. You had to have laboratory work. So in 1950 when we made that first approach to what do we do about a laboratory there wasn't any such thing anywhere as far as the Arctic was concerned. I had to approach the question from my then new position in the organization at NEL. We had at that time a scientific council which made all decisions on what projects to pursue, what facilities to build, what major plans should be drawn, etc. I remember I made discussion before them on what the Arctic submarine problems were, and the things to do in the laboratory. I didn't get any reaction out of the council. These were the major scientists at NEL and there was just no reaction, so the only way to handle the lack of approval was just go ahead and do it until they tell you to stop. That's exactly what we did do, starting in 1951. We just had to build a laboratory, and that's when the Arctic Submarine Laboratory started or was formulated.

Q: Is that the picture that's in one of the pamphlets?

Dr. L.: In 1948 actually it, in a sense, began because the lab I had had all during the war had a lot of high-pressure tanks and devices for testing cables and sonar that we took to sea on submarines. I ran out of space in the little building that I had occupied and been in since I first went there. It was just a little building at the Naval Electronics Lab, so we had hunted around for a place to put these pressure tanks, and found one of the old gun batteries that belonged to the Army which was called Battery Whistler. Its mortars actually fired in 1942 for the last time, and it was, of course, obsolete and surplus, so we moved in and turned it into a laboratory. I had it in 1950, so we had the space. It was just a matter of adapting it to the Arctic problem. We had a pool there for testing sound gear, so it was just a question of turning that pool into an Arctic pool. So it started in 1951, and we didn't get that thing operating until 1960, actually completed. But that's a whole story in itself.

Starting in 1951, we said - okay, we've got to have a laboratory.

Nobody paid any attention, so we said – okay, we'll just go ahead and do it until somebody says no. The means by which we funded it could not be done today. We didn't have a funded project, because there was no recognition that the Arctic was a problem. But in the 1950s things were a little different than they are nowadays, and normally in a laboratory then we had the power to shift funds. What would happen – a lot of problems would be funded in a laboratory, and you'd come to the end of the fiscal year and not all the problems were using all the funds. So I had to arrange with the commanding officers all during this period to use any excess funds. He was in favor of what we were doing. It was just the organization of a committee as a whole (what these councils were), and which are very different from people. You can often get a person interested in something, but you don't necessarily get a committee of people interested unless they themselves have some reasons. A committee has a very different personality than a person.

I could get the commanding officer interested during this time; it was still Rawson Bennett at that time, also the following commanding officer. Each one became very much interested in the Arctic submarine program, even though there was not a directive from the top down. And so we were able to milk off a little bit of money each year from what wasn't used at the end of the fiscal year. So that was the way it got build, by this increment method.

Q: It took nine years?

Dr. L.: It took nine years. We stopped in 1956, and that's a story in itself. It started in 1951. We got started, and then each year we got a little bit more in the way of equipment. No one knew how to build it, no one had ever built such a thing, so we were on our own.

Q: No one had ever built an Arctic Ocean Laboratory before?

Dr. L.: No, no. In Russia they'd gone through this.

Q: They had gone through it?

Dr. L.: Yes. We knew that they had ice model basins, and that kind of thing, because they were very active in Arctic work, of course. Right after the war they started very active Arctic work again and are continuing still today. So they had laboratories, this we knew. We didn't know what they were, but we knew from visitors that they'd got Arctic laboratories. So we were on our own in developing our own laboratory.

Q: Did you design it?

Dr. L.: Yes. Then we used the pieces - we designed it and re-designed it, I guess three times. That's a whole book in itself, but quite technical. We left off at 1955-56 with DEW line, but in the interim, of course, we'd been slowly building the laboratory. 1956 was kind of a special year because everything began to change then. Not only the DEW line sort of shut off the field work, but the whole direction system and organization of the Navy started to change during that period, that's during the Eisenhower administration.

It's hard to put your finger on just what may have done what, but that is the time when restrictions started to grow between what one department could do with another department in the Navy, and there had to be more organization on directives, and we did not have the freedom of choice in the lower echelons to do what we felt should be done.

Q: More rigid channeling?

Dr. L.: More rigid channeling started to appear, and this had its influence on us because then we began to come up against this problem of not having the Joint Chiefs of Staff establish a strategy that said that the Arctic Ocean was a military high priority. I mean, all this starts to trickle down to what we're doing.

Q: I want to have you clarify that. You said there was *not* —

Dr. L.: There was *not*. At no time, other than such a time as a DEW line, which is not military operations in the Arctic, it's a defense against something coming through the Arctic, but it does not require you to be in the Arctic Ocean for military operations, and that's really what we were involved in. Nor anywhere was there a belief that a submarine would be involved in ice cover in military operations. We were strictly still in that situation.

Interview No. 2 with Dr. Waldo K. Lyon

Place: His home in San Diego

Date: 31 January 1971

Subject: Biography

By: Etta-Belle Kitchin

Q: I think in chronology we were in the year 1955, and you made a comment that there had been on aspect of the Redfish operation that you wanted to refer to before we went on.

Dr. L.: I think I should return to Redfish for a moment. In 1953 after her return when we had had so much difficulty in 1953, and actually had some damage to the Redfish in towing and in striking a great deal of ice. It meant the ship would require considerable repair, and hull repair particularly, to put her back as a first-class fighting ship. We suggested and got concurrence from the Bureau of Ships to have the Redfish assigned to Arctic research. This was in keeping with the plan for the Redfish even before we took her north, because at the time that Momsen had her assigned in late 1951 or early 1952 it had been planned to retire Redfish from service. That's why Redfish had been chosen for the Arctic cruise, and then expected to be taken out of service after the cruise.

However, there was a change of command in ComSubPac between the end of the 1953 cruise. The command in the Pacific at that time had no interest in the Arctic and needed submarines in the forces, and therefore demanded, or requested, that the submarine Redfish be put back in first-class fighting shape, even though we had then talked to people in the Bureau of Ships, the design section, to go through a complete design for modifying the Redfish to an Arctic type hull which we could use for going under the ice and actually breaking up through the ice cover into what we, at that time, thought a hull should be changed to do.

As a result, the Redfish was returned to the Pacific Submarine Force in first-class shape after considerable overhaul and rebuilding in the yards, and she served for many years actually, and just recently about two years ago was retired. This was an instance, I think, of how Arctic work has succeeded by having people in various places interested - they had to be in key spots - and the work carried on that basis when any one of these key spots changed to a different point of view the continuity was lost, because again, all of this was, for all the years, the work really went by understanding between individuals in sort of key spots and not by a documented paper direction from the top of the command, because the Arctic wasn't a high-priority problem. It wasn't recognized as a military problem.

Q: I think that's interesting and you have mentioned it, and I know that it will be brought out frequently that the Navy at no time, perhaps even today, has made an operation order which says, here is where the Arctic operations fits into the scheme of Navy military operations.

Dr. L.: Right.

Q: So, in my view, you were the one item of continuity interested

Lyon # 2 - 96

in this development, which is why you and what you've done are so important, because you kept the continuity in spite of the reassignment of various people who were as individuals interested in the development of the Arctic.

Dr. L.: Well, I think that's probably true, and I've always - and a group of engineers and scientists with me - stayed in one place, and this has been our purpose for all the years. So we've been the focal point, and then there have been these individuals all through the Navy with the interest, and they move about to various spots. So you see the pattern happens, depending on what position they're in - how the work proceeds. However, we've always been the focal point because we've stayed on this one problem for twenty-five years.

Q: Well, that's why I feel by talking with you I'm going to get the chronology of the entire problem of exploration from the Navy's viewpoint. So, then, in the years 1955 to say 1957 you found the key people particularly important, did you not?

Dr. L.: Maybe we should say that we hit one of those patterns with people in positions which reached the minimum advantage to us. No key spot was filled by an Arctic friend. Also, in that period there were changes progressing in the management processes in the organization of the Navy, and the Defense Department over-all, that made documentation and rules more important than had been previously, or I should say that individuals didn't have quite the freedom to react and do things in various key spots that they had all during the war period and for a period thereafter through the Korean affair.

This is, keep in mind, the close-out of Korea, so that after Korea there was again an adjustment being made to be more formal in the way everything was managed and arranged, and as a result managers looked more to their paper directives and, again, the key people in the Bureau of Ships that we had always used in naval operations were just not there at that moment, which meant that the Bureau people relied more on what their paper directives said. And, as a result, direction came from Bureau of Ships managers that all Arctic work at the Naval Electronics Laboratory stop, because there was not the financial backing or the military directive for doing Arctic work, and so relative to all other kinds of work it must stop.

Q: How did you react to that?

Dr. L.: Well, then that action came to the Naval Electronics Laboratory command to carry out. However, the technical director at NEL was Franz Curie, and the military commander was Captain Phelps. Both individuals believed very strongly in continuation of Arctic research. So, in effect, they simply lost the instruction from Washington in the mail system for about six months and no action was taken, although we did meet with Curie a number of times just to discuss and relate our plan, exactly what we would do with the funding remaining if we had to finally simply act on this desist business. In late 1956, or about the summer of 1956, as I recall, the plan stood that if we must carry out the instruction we would continue maybe two to three people involved at Cape Prince of Wales field station, and all other personnel in the group of some twenty-five would either be reduced in force and sent away or we would find some other kind of work for them in the Naval Electronics Laboratory. However, again, that instruction we just sort of didn't think about it, let it drift around and not take any action. So we are indebted to the technical director and the commander for not carrying out their instruction at that time, or we would have simply lost all continuity in personnel and we would have been probably dissipated and you could never have gotten them back again.

Q: How did you feel personally when you realized that this was the instruction from higher authority?

Dr. L.: Well, it was really nothing new because we had this continually year in, year out, although it was always hanging and we knew that I was working on a personal relationships with so many different individuals in key places and we never did have any paper backing for what we were doing. So that we just sort of expected this problem. We were always living kind of on a brinkmanship type of situation.

Q: But there was a paper that directly stopped it!

Dr. L.: It was perhaps - oh, it wasn't the first time, but this was a very real case of an instruction to actually stop. In most all other cases we never had a direct instruction to stop. It was always we never had any instruction to do it. So this was sort of different, and I think what is pertinent is that, at the time, the laboratory command itself had the power to decide its own futures and to do its own control of what it was doing far more than it does today. In today's atmosphere of the way laboratories are operated, and the way they receive their funding and directives, I think this would be almost impossible, but at that time, in the mid 1950s, they still had flexibility, the commander had the right to shift his funding within his own organization to what the command or the top scientific group, together with the command, felt should be done. So they could go counter to some directives they received from above, and the agreement of the laboratory command with the command from, say, the Bureau of Ships. The command of the laboratory had to justify what they did, but they didn't have to justify it item by item by item. The Chief of the Bureau of Ships could give to them pieces of money to do various projects, but the command of the laboratory had the authority to shift that around a little bit to do things the way they saw them, and then each year they would have a confrontation, so to speak, where the command said this is why we did this, and the Bureau of Ships people would say - well, why did you do that, this is the way we want it, and they'd come to some mutual agreement. But there still was a flexibility at that time, which was essential to us in what we were doing.

Q: You didn't lose any of your people then?

Dr. L.: We did not lose any of our people, and we did keep the work going, but by the end of that year, the end of 1956, we were in serious difficulty. McWethy, in OpNav 31, and I met with Dennis Wilkinson, commanding officer of the _Nautilus_, and had discussions. There were some other individuals involved as well.

Q: Where did you meet and under what circumstances?

Dr. L.: In Washington. At the time, I was East for something else, probably with regard to the Arctic program. Though I think I was East primarily with regard to doing x-ray work on castings for the nuclear power plant, because we at the laboratory here at NEL had a betatron with which we were able to do x-ray work on very thick stainless steel castings, necessary for the nuclear power plants which were being built on the West Coast. Being involved with that, I just happened to be East, and Bob McWethy was in the CNO's office and, of course, had had a continuing interest in this whole Arctic submarine program, and he had gotten together with Wilkinson, and Wilkinson was looking at the problem of the Arctic and wanted to use *Nautilus* in the Arctic. So it was just sort of a meeting of the interests. And it was at that time that mention was being made of Senator Jackson ---

Q: Excuse me, but what transpired at the meeting between the three of you? Any particular goals or direction?

DR. L.: Other than somehow to get the Navy interested, i.e. the CNO command and the command of sub forces in sending the *Nautilus* into the Arctic area. It just seemed like a natural to try a nuclear-powered submarine under the ice. It would be definitely a show of what a submarine of that type could do, and at that time, of course, it was the only one. So it was Wilkinson who had a real interest of wanting to use his driving personality and his very strong force in getting the *Nautilus* into the Arctic.

Q: I assume that you supported it with all of your —

Dr. L.: Oh, right. I was brought in because it would be for me to provide the instrumentation and the capability for the submarine to go under the ice, because the nuclear-powered Nautilus did not have the necessary equipment. She was prepared to run in open sea only. McWethy was in the right spot in the CNO's submarine warfare branch, which would be involved in such an assignment. So it was really sort of three-pronged - the commander of the ship, the individual in CNO, and then for me bringing the instrumentation necessary for the submarine to meet the task.

Q: This was an unofficial meeting?

Dr. L.: Oh, this was an unofficial meeting. We were just really discussing that it could be done and ought to be done, what do we do now. So the thought then came that one method was to interest Senator Jackson, who, being from the state of Washington, had been active in Alaska in observing the ice cover, and had an interest in the Arctic and, of course, a very strong interest in the Navy. He was the one who then asked the Chief of Naval Operations, Admiral Arleigh Burke, at one of the exchanges of information in the Senate committee meeting, "What is the U. S. Navy doing in the Arctic?" - interesting question. Then, started a chain reaction. The Chief of Naval Operations went back to his department and asked to review what Navy is doing. That comes back down the line, and, again, the Op-31 desk, which is the submarine branch, which is where McWethy is, has to answer the question.

Q: I can picture the scurrying in the CNO's office and ---

Dr. L.: It was typical of these kind of procedures. So when that question was asked, McWethy had to prepare the answers, and hence called me back to Washington. It was early January, then, and I remember being with him for a number of days to answer what are we doing and surely we do have a plan or program ---

Q: Did he call you back to help him prepare the papers or present the papers?

Dr. L.: Prepare the papers, because the paper is just prepared and is given to the CNO ---

Q: Just sent through regular channels?

Dr. L.: The CNO was the presenter, of course. We didn't try to do any presenting, but providing information, it was done in this manner.

Q: How long a paper was it that he presented? Did it go into a lot of detail?

Dr. L.: I don't recall. I think Bob McWethy prepared what would be a CNO Op-Nav instruction, which really revised one that we had written in 1951 when Admiral Momsen was in Op-31. The only piece of paper that ever existed in Navy through all the years other than the typical cold weather bill, which doesn't address itself to submarines, was an instruction written while Admiral Momsen was in Op-31 in 1951. He wrote an instruction that said the Navy should be doing something on submarines and the use of submarines in the Arctic. That's the only piece of paper to back up anything done. That doesn't state priorities or anything of that sort. It's just an instruction that we should be learning everything we can about the use of submarines in Arctic waters and sea ice. I had a hand in the writing, and it was written to cover what we were doing.

Q: You played a part in writing that?

Dr. L.: Oh, yes, at that time. So it did cover what we were doing, and it was the only reference we had for the work going on. THis was really updated then, in early 1957, or late 1956, when the question was asked of the CNO to say what we were doing. That would be obviously the main document to show what the Navy was doing, and intended to do, in the Arctic.

Q: Do you know whether he presented it personally, or did he just send it through channels?

Dr. L.: I've forgotten. I don't remember just what happened and the details of it. What followed then was the interest - from this little affair, it did get generated for sending Nautilus and it just sort of seemed natural. After all, here was Nautilus a new ship with all kinds of capabilities not freely recognized what she could do, and this was an opportunity to demonstrate the real unusual capabilities of being a true submarine. And it caught the fancy of a number of people, both in the submarine forces and the ship, of course, and Dennis Wilkinson himself. So, in early spring of 1957, we started preparing for taking Nautilus that summer.

Q: May I ask you a couple of questions before we go on. Did Sputnik have any relationship to the impetus?

Dr. L.: No, this is prior to Sputnik. Sputnik did have, certainly, an impetus on the 1958 program, but not at this point because this was the spring of 1957 and this was when there was activity in attempting to send up satellites by both Army and Navy, but this was prior to any actual demonstration. So this was truly submarine business of itself. It didn't have any pressures from that point of view.

Q: What did Admiral Rickover think of sending the Nautilus under the ice?

Dr. L.: I was not privy to any discussions with him. He certainly was aware and I judge that he was favorable.

Q: I read somewhere that he opposed it because it was his first nuclear submarine, and I wondered if you knew any information on that subject?

Dr. L.: I was in on some of the discussion for 1958, but not any discussion with him regarding the 1957. And 1957 was really one of the first trials. It was very straightforward really from the submarine's point of view. There was another key individual involved, as far as we were concerned, in preparing it. That was in the Bureau of Ships. At that time the Bureau of Ships was responsible for all of the preparations, the equipment, and what submarines took part and the equipment and work at yards and so on to be ready to do their particular operations, and the key individual then was Lieutenant Commander Carvel Blair, and he at that time in his position in the Bureau had the authority to move funds and do things to get the job done, which again I make the point strictly because the power is not now available any longer in the way the Navy is reorganized. But at that time, the submarine desk in the Bureau of Ships had the authority to use funds and the responsibility to get jobs done, and this was essential to get <u>Nautilus</u> prepared both in 1957 and 1958. I think it would be very difficult in the present organization of the Navy to do what was done at that time.

Q: Was there any secrecy concerning this 1957 operation?

Dr. L.: The 1957 operation, other than normal secrecy, the normal confidential level and typical submarine operation. Nothing special in secrecy to it. The <u>Nautilus</u> was around here in the Pacific early that year, in the spring of 1957, and that was when Wilkinson was relieved of command by William Anderson. Some time in May, maybe, of 1957, <u>Nautilus</u> stopped in here at San Diego and we put on board the equipment that had been in the laboratory ever since the <u>Redfish</u>. (1953)

Q: Can you describe to me the equipment you did put on the <u>Nautilus</u>?

Dr. L.: The equipment on the <u>Nautilus</u> was the echo-sounder system that looked upwards, measured the ice under which the submarine was traveling. By 1957 we no longer had available the QLA scanning sonar system. It had long gone from Navy use because the Navy during that long period since the SEcond World War didn't go through any minefields, and so very few submarines, if any, still had scanning sonar systems of the QLA type left on board. There certainly were no systems available anywhere in the stockpiles of the Navy. So all we had available was the standard equipment, which I don't recall the name now, on the submarine, which was for the detection of submarines, very low frequency and not the type of sonar that one would want for avoiding ice at one's depth such as we required when we were running Redfish or Carp or the others up in the Chukchi. So we just did not have that kind of a sonar system on the submarines any longer. The Nautilus didn't have it. However, we did have these upward-looking echo sounders systems that we had had on Redfish, so we put those on board.

Q: That had been developed at NEL?

Dr. L.: Right. It had been developed at NEL. There was only one set and that was experimental equipment that we carried on each submarine every time we went.

Q: Oh, you were taking it off and re-installing it on succeeding tests?

Dr. L.: Yes, we put it on Carp and we put it on Redfish, and after Redfish we took it off and there it was in the laboratory.

Q: Oh, it was only one set you had?

Dr. L.: Only one set. You see, we never went through the procedure of developing an under-ice system because there had never been any demand for a number of submarines having this type of system because there was no steady requirement for it - for submarines in the Arctic. So you don't go through that whole manufacturing procedure of prototypes into a regular standard contract developed system to put on submarines.

Q: Tell me where this device was installed on the submarine.

Dr. L.: This was put on the Nautilus, and was a series of sound projectors on the deck from bow to stern, so that one had an upward-looking sound beam over the length of the ship, and again inside the ship it was in the forward torpedo room where the data were read out when we wanted to see what was above the ship. The same as we had on the other submarines. It's the one place on board where there is space to put in something of an external nature without disturbing all the equipment which is normally in the control room area, particularly when this is done for just a short trip, and for one experiment, and then take it off again, so the forward torpedo room was used, and this is what was done on Nautilus.

Q: And there was another picture in the control room?

DR. L.: No, there was no picture in the control room on the data that was being taken looking upward. The control room of the Nautilus had its standard sonar equipment which is good for the detection of other submarines.

Q: I'm trying to relate this to the other time when you said on Carp there was one picture forward —

Dr. L.: The Carp had the QLA scanning sonar.

Q: Oh, I see, and you didn't have this?

Dr. L.: We didn't have QLA on the Nautilus, so we had no picture in control of what they were seeing other than the standard low-frequency detection system which gives some picture of the ice cover, but not a discreet detailed picture of exactly what was ahead of the submarine with regard to the ice. So, in a sense, Nautilus had less - in fact did have - less sonar systems for under-ice work than we had on either the Carp or the Redfish.

Q: No one had salvaged that off --

Dr. L.: There had been no need for this equipment expressly at that time, because it was built for penetration of minefields, a standard military function. And so when the later submarines of the 1950s, that is, the standard fleet submarine of the 1950s, and also Nautilus, there was no requirement for sonar systems which would take it through minefields. They did not have that type of sonar on board.

Q: And you couldn't locate any of the old submarines that had the equipment and salvage it?

Dr. L.: We couldn't really find anything quickly, and it would have been very costly to locate it and refurbish it to go on board because it meant modification of the hull and mounting it - it would have been a very costly process just for going and doing the two-week experiment.

Q: Did you have any hesitation about going without it?

Dr. L.: Not really because this was a different story now. All the previous work on submarines had been in the Pacific which had required one to operate in very shallow waters. You can't get into the Arctic Ocean from the Pacific except by going through the Bering Sea, Bering Strait, Chukchi, and that's where the very shallow water is, and you must then have the scanning type sonar equipment. But in 1957 we were going up in the Atlantic, and the Atlantic is all deep water so one can just stay deep enough; don't have to worry about the bottom restricting to avoid ice. One can stay deep enough to go underneath it, and do not need the mine-avoiding type of sonar system - ice-avoiding type of sonar system. In fact, all of the cruises: Nautilus in 1957, Nautilus in 1958, Skate in 1958, Skate in 1959 up until the Sargo cruise, we were blind as far as operating in depth was concerned. We did not have equipment to tell us that ice was in the path in front of us. We simply operated deep enough to avoid any ice that might extend down to us. We were restricted in all of those cruises during those years to working in the deep Atlantic. It was not until the Sargo cruise in 1960 that we made the attack again on the shallow water of the Pacific.

Q: So, now I stopped you where you had brought the Nautilus back to San Diego to install the —

Dr. L.: The Nautilus got the equipment and she went through Panama and on to the Atlantic. Then it was in the summer of 1957 that the assignment was carried out for a very brief thrust into the Arctic Ocean with Nautilus. And I recall I was on board with one man to help me and one person from the hydrographic office. We were up in the Arctic Ocean in the month of August for about a two-week period. So this was the first trial with a nuclear submarine under the ice cover, the first under-ice penetration since the Redfish. This experiment was another kind of first because, for me, it was the first experience with a nuclear-powered submarine which is entirely different from operating with an ~~oil~~ diesel battery ~~diesel~~ submarine. It's a really true submarine. Even after reading what it can do and what it would do, one didn't realize what that meant until one actually took part. BY that, I mean, we'd stay submerged at whatever depth chosen for as long as required - days at a time - which is an entirely different experience from being required to surface every few hours to charge the batteries. Plus the speed at which one is capable of moving at all times, say, up to 20 knots, which just had been inconceivable with a battery diesel operated boat. So this change meant that the equipment that we had used for the various relatively slow-moving diesel battery submarines did not completely fill the requirements of this fast-moving, continually submerged type of submarine.

Q: Didn't it reflect the information quickly enough or far enough ahead or what was matter?

Dr. L.: It didn't resolve the profile to the ice cover as well when moving at such high speed. In other words, it - the width of the sound beam which I was using looking upwards was too broad. It was quite sufficient when I was moving slowly ahead, a fairly broad beam looking up, but when I was moving fast I needed a very narrow beam in order to resolve all the roughness and character to the ice cover that was overhead.

So this was the first thing that was shown by this trial in 1957. Other things we learned were that particularly in trying to surface in a lake in the ice cover the sail wasn't strong enough. At that time, the <u>Nautilus</u> had an aluminum constructed sail, and it got damaged a good deal, just from touching a small piece of ice, and the periscope projected above the sail even when it was completely housed, so it got bumped. The deck plates just didn't stand up. The other thing that occurred was that after we made a number of probes under the ice we made the attempt to reach the north pole, but when very close to 87° North, we lost power, (400-cycle power) which energizes the gyrocompass, so we lost the gyrocompass, which is very essential item as far as knowing where one is going, for getting headings, etc. Even though the power was lost only momentarily, we could not be sure that we had recovered and held our direction correctly. So, on this basis, Captain Anderson had very little choice but to turn around and try to head out of the Arctic Ocean and not continue to the North Pole because we could have become lost with this loss of direction. And so at 87° North, the <u>Nautilus</u> did turn around and we didn't make the attempt to reach the pole on that particular cruise. This experience gave impetus to getting an inertial navigation system as a backup on <u>Nautilus</u> and aboard the submarines.

Q: I want to ask you a question that's actually connected with that move. Did you have any qualms about going on this nuclear-powered ~~instrument~~ submarine?

Dr. L.: Oh, no, not in the least. This was a very interesting opportunity, I should say, to get into the really new submarine, a true submarine, because it's just an entirely new world to ship from a battery submarine to a nuclear-powered submarine, an entirely different world, because the diesel-powered submarine is really a surface ship that sometimes submerges, whereas the nuclear-powered submarine is a submarine which sometimes surfaces. It's a submarine. You do everything underwater and you don't come to the surface unless you just have to because the water gets too shallow or you've got to go into port, but any other reasons to come to the surface you really wonder why one should and you've got to have a good reason. So it's an entirely different viewpoint. This was really an outstanding opportunity as far as I was concerned to get into a true submarine.

Q: Did you have a feeling of excitement about being able to go aboard?

Dr. L.: Oh, I'm sure. There certainly was a feeling of being right in the front of things because, after all, the Nautilus was just out, the first, and here was a firsthand opportunity to see what her capabilities were.

Q: Did you have a sense of the crew's reaction?

Dr. L.: The crew and the officers and men on Nautilus and on the nuclear-powered submarines of that period were outstanding individuals and had, of course, been chosen by a fairly elaborate process of picking the best of the best. Every one of the individuals, both officers and men, were outstanding individuals. There was a feeling of excitement in the <u>Nautilus</u> just being with those kind of people. They were exciting people who were on board that ship. There's no question of the difference between being on that type of ship and being in any other ship in the submarine force, and even the submarine force as a whole was a special chosen group of people, so here you had the choice of the choice.

Q: Could you describe your day activity?

Dr. L.: On that particular cruise the day's activity was being practically up all the time and operating the equipment. There were only two of us so we had to split our time.

Q: Did that mean a twelve-hour - or how did you do that?

Dr. L.: As I recall, we split it maybe four hours - four hours on and four hours off and catch a few hours' sleep. I've always been an individual - when I'm at sea I don't sleep very much, on the average maybe three or four hours a day. I find that quite sufficient, so I'd just catnap two hours at a time. It's always been that way, as far as I'm concerned. When at sea one doesn't have sufficient physical activity to require more than that, and there's enough going on all the time and enough to be done that I'll split the day in, maybe, two-hour naps, one in the early morning and one in the late evening, or something of that sort.

Q: That was enough to keep you going?

Dr. L.: Oh, plenty, yes.

Q: You were up in the forward torpedo room?

Dr. L.: Yes, we were in the forward torpedo room in <u>Nautilus</u>, and so we were relaying information aft, but in this particular case, the information on what the ice cover was or what the ice is overhead doesn't really govern the movements of the ship very much, because the ship is operating well below any type of ice projections that could possibly hinder a ship. So the only time that communications from the forward room to the control are important is if the ship is trying to surface, then it becomes very important, and that type of conversation showed that we did need, of course, the portrayal of what was involved right in control. You just could not give this information over a talking system to have the ship safely surface between the ice. And that was part of the reason why in one case we did bump a chunk of ice, not a very big chunk, right on top of the sail and put a dent in it and the periscope. But it was well that was done, because then between 1957 and 1958 all of these ships were corrected, and the sail was strenghened, and it was recognized that radars and periscopes should retract below the top of the sail, and the sail should be steel, high-tensile steel. These changes were made between 1957 and 1958.

Q: How big were the screens you were looking at?

Dr. L.: In this case there were a number of recorders, that is, paper about ten inches wide on which the profile of the ice overhead is being drawn out.

Q: You have pictures in your papers which show that conjectural.

Dr. L.: Right. It portrays a picture on chart just similar to what you get from the bottom echo-sounder.

Q: You were in ample deep water so you had no problem with that?

Dr. L.: No. The water had been well sounded, so we had some bathymetry, not too much. But, again, we were indebted, completely indebted, to Sverdrup and the earlier Nautilus. The only data we had after we got north of Spitzbergen was the information taken on the temperature of the water, and the ice cover, and the bathymetry by the 1931 Nautilus research by Wilkins, and this data of Sverdrup's, and I had with me all his original papers and charts, because this was the only information we could get, and that information paid off, dramatically, when we lost the gyro-compass. Our problem then was we were heading south from 87° North; we had turned around, but we were not at all sure that our compass was correct because it had lost its continuity of power. We had to depend on any kind of other information to try to back up what the compass was saying. What we did use was the appearance of the ice cover, and the depths below us, and the temperature of the water to guide us as to whether we were steering correctly to get out of the Arctic Ocean through the slot between Greenland and Svalsbard, really a very wide slot, but we needed a wide slot considering the loss of direction. If you come south from the pole you could very easily be off by a few degrees, and you'd have ended up then, when you get south near land, quite a ways from the slot.

Q: Weren't they referred to as something roulette?

Dr. L.: Oh, yes, that's Captain Anderson's remark. I can't recall it, but what he meant was that if you lose direction up there you can practically spin the wheel and end up anywhere, because if you're going south from the pole it depends on what longitude you're coming south on as to just where you're going to end, and whether you get out between the islands and the continent. We were coming south and the only thing we could check against was whether the bathymetry and the soundings below us seemed correct, whether the temperature of the water seemed correct, and whether the ice cover looked appropriate. And this was all governed by water temperatures, and ice cover governed by the outflow of ice, which is along the east coast of Greenland. There is an outflowing surface current, the east Greenland current, which is a very cold current, and flows along the east side of Greenland out of the Arctic Ocean, and, to the east of that, is a branch of the Atlantic water, which is warm, which circulates north around Svalsbard then south and sets up an interface with the cold Greenland current. We used that interface to judge whether we were in the right spot. If we were too far to the west, towards Greenland, it meant that the water was going to be very cold, and to avoid Greenland we should be getting into somewhat warmer waters more to the east. So we did make a turn as we were coming out, because it did appear that we were in too far to the west, and the turn was made to the southwest, which was correct, and brought us out without any trouble.

Q: That data on this was derived - ?

Dr. L.: We were relying on Sverdrup's information that he had taken on the Nautilus. He had taken these temperatures and we were measuring temperatures at all times that we were going.

Q: And you were the person that had this information?

Dr. L.: Yes.

Q: And if you hadn't given them this information the ship wouldn't have got in the right place?

Dr. L.: Not necessarily. We might have used something else, but it certainly gave us the support that we needed to make the judgment. We were using everything we could.

Q: But you were the one making adjustments, were you not?

Dr. L.: That's correct. Whatever the ocean was telling us, to make decisions, both as to bathymetry and as to the ice cover which showed the type of ice cover we had, its thickness and its characteristics. It also indicated we were not in the right area.

Q: Captain Anderson relied entirely on your statements?

Dr. L.: He relied entirely on that and also on what the navigator could feel and what his compass was doing. So everything was sort of chained together, but we had to use all bits of information that we could get hold of to make the right decisions. It all fit in. No, my task was understanding and interpreting the ocean, and the navigator's task was trying to get the best interpretation he could out of his equipment and the compass.

Q: How were you getting these temperatures? You didn't reach out

Lyon # 2 - 118

Dr. L.: What we would do - the submarine carries a continually reading temperature device. That's standard equipment, for water temperatures.

Q: Where is it?

Dr. L.: It's an instrument in the control room.

Q: Oh, I see, it's reflected into the control room?

Dr. L.: It just draws a continuing graph of the temperature. We were also measuring, drawing samples of water in the engineroom from the sea-water circulating system, and we'd measure the temperature and salinity of the sea water. So we were drawing samples from the sea, and also recording temperatures on board. So you do know the temperature fairly accurately at all times.

Q: So the thing you were doing were measuring the temperature of the water, the salinity of the water, the ice cover, the surface of the ocean's floor and the ice bottom.

Dr. L.: All, that's it. That's the extent of the data at that time.

Q: But I can understand that you were thoroughly busy because of the continually changing situation.

Dr. L.: Right. The two of us were busy all the time running the data and, of course, watching what the submarine was doing, advising, and getting acquainted with an entirely new submarine.

Lyon # 2 - 119

Q: This 1957 operation was divided into two parts, wasn't it, in that when you tried to surface the first time the periscope was damaged? Did you not come out from under the ice cover in order to make the repair and then return?

Dr. L.: Let's see. The ship did make a very outstanding repair in the field there because the periscope was bent over, and they repaired the periscope so it could be used. I can't recall whether that was done right in a break in the ice cover or out on the edge of the ice -- very likely out on the edge of the ice field. We had another submarine with us, a diesel battery boat --

Q: The *Trigger*?

Dr. L.: The *Trigger*, right - to go along. And we talked to each other. The *Trigger* went under the ice and made one of the longest excursions any diesel battery boat has ever made. There's nothing very odd in that, after all *Nautilus* went 1,500 miles under the ice, and *Trigger*, I think, did 75, which is an outstanding feat for a battery diesel boat, but under the shadow of *Nautilus* it's kind of obvious it didn't have much meaning.

Q: The repair job is given much story in several books. Do you have a recollection of it that isn't --

Dr. L.: No. I think it was well stated, and it was a real feel for the mechanical capability of the ship to make such a repair and get the 'scope working again. And it was needed because *Nautilus* was assigned her primary task of working with the Atlantic Fleet after this particular Arctic expedition. It again was the first time that a nuclear powered submarine worked with fleet units, and she needed all her capability to demonstrate what a nuclear boat could do.

Q: And that was a fantastic example of the physical prowess of those men, being able to stay in that temperature —

Dr. L.: No, it wasn't so cold as later on some of the winter cruises, but the ingenuity that they demonstrated in making repairs with what they had available was amazing.

Q: They had to build themselves a little tent and use the welding equipment —

Dr. L.: What they had, yes, to protect from the wind so that it would work because of the low temperature and wind chill.

Q: What was your reaction after this was over? Were you pleased or were you just — ?

Dr. L.: We learned a great deal and recognized what was required in changes of equipment. We recognized what an entirely new and real submarine could do toward opening the door to a whole new world, as far as the submarine was concerned, and immediately forgot about any other kind of a submarine, once you had that kind available.

Q: There was some conversation that everybody aboard the ship was disappointed because the Nautilus didn't get to the pole, and there were many comments on their determination to get to the pole, and I wondered if that was kind of a story, or actually did people aboard actually care about getting to the pole?

Dr. L.: I don't recall now, but I'm sure that among the crew and officers there was disappointment. Once you start on something of that sort, then to turn around and come back and not make it, is a real disappointment. For me, I was so involved in all these other things I don't recall having any impression whatsoever about whether we did or we didn't. There was too much else involved in the case that I don't recall any particular disappointment at all in that regard. Well, it's hard to say now after all that has taken place afterwards, whether at the time I might have been even a little bit relieved because we didn't have all the instrumentation we should have to do it, but I don't recall.

Q: I picture you as being a little bit more dispassionate in your approach to the situation and having a driving ambition to perhaps do something dramatic that maybe you didn't actually prove anything.

Dr. L.: Not at that time. The pole never really had any particular goal, as far as I was concerned. Crossing the Arctic Ocean had, that was the real goal. To me, to cross the Arctic Ocean from the Pacific to the Atlantic was always a goal, if there was any particular goal. And I think some of this came about from discussions with Sverdrup and his background, because this historically had been always sort of the ultimate of demonstration of what could be done if you could make the crossing and use the Arctic Ocean as an ocean, not just go to one point up in the middle of it, such as the pole.

Q: I can understand that, because man's desire to find the northwest passage has gone back in history, too.

Dr. L.: And I know when Sverdrup left San Diego in 1947 or 1948

— 1948 was the last time I had any discussion with him — that the promise was then — okay, the next time I would see him would be that I had crossed the Arctic Ocean by submarine. Now, speaking of 1957, it was while we were up north in the <u>Nautilus</u> that Sverdrup passed away in Norway. In 1948 he went back to Norway to head the Arctic Institute in Norway, and he ran that Institute for all their Antarctic cruises and Arctic work from 1949 until 1957 when he died. He died while we were up there actually.

Q: He certainly made a marvelous contribution to —

Dr. L.: Oh, yes, he made an outstanding contribution. He was sort of the father of oceanography as far as I'm concerned.

Then, coming back, the <u>Nautilus</u> put in to Scotland, and we took all her equipment off while she was in Scotland because then she joined the fleet exercise which was from England, a large NATO exercise between England and the Mediterranean. Rex Rowry, who was helping me, and I spent a week wandering around Scotland and England, and then came back to San Diego.

Q: Flying, I presume?

DR. L.: We flew back, right, with the equipment.

Q: When you say you flew back with the equipment, I can't picture the equipment being anything that you could take on an airplane.

Dr. L.: No, I guess the permanent equipment didn't come back then.

I think the equipment went on board the submarine tender. That's right. We put the equipment on the submarine tender, which was in Rothsay, Scotland, where the Nautilus tied up. We left the equipment on the tender, a big ship, and we flew back and when the tender got back to the U.S., probably two months later, we picked up the equipment. That's the way it was.

Q: Now we're almost at the beginning of 1958, aren't we?

Dr. L.: In the fall of 1957 things began to happen. There was no release on that cruise. That was all kept under confidential order - no public release for the 1957 summer cruise until late in the fall of 1957, but it was released about the same time Sputnik took place, so no one ever noticed it in the press. You'll find the press release that did come out at that time, but there was no attention paid to it whatsoever because of Sputnik.

Q: Was Sputnik in October?

Dr. L.: I think it was October of 1957. You remember the reaction, nationwide. Everything was wrong. Our schools were wrong, the education system was wrong.

Q: The Navy was wrong!

Dr. L.: The Navy was wrong, everybody was wrong just because Sputnik had occurred in Russia. It was kind of a special situation. Well, that was much of the pressure, I think that gave to authority for the 1958 across the Arctic Ocean cruise.

Q: In effect, it worked out to your advantage, didn't it?

Dr. L.: Yes. It was the obvious thing to do but it might not have had the push that Sputnik put behind it. The story from that point on is pretty well documented in the books.

Q: The president's press secretary and aides.

Dr. L.: Certainly, the press secretary, Mr. Haggerty, and Captain Aurand were the two key individuals in the White House. Captain Aurand is now Rear Admiral Aurand now in the Pacific with ASW forces, but he was the active individual in the White House setting up the Sunshine Operation. For me, from 1957 through the rest of 1958 was an incredible year. It's difficult to recall all the activity and the day-by-day action that took place, and, of course, under the various unusual, almost storybook conditions, with the secrecy involved.

Q: Can you remember when you got the word that you would go to - from one ocean to the other?

Dr. L.: There were all these preliminary discussions and things got down to real hard cases in January of 1958, but I can't be sure.

Q: Did someone ask you your opinion if it could be done?

Dr. L.: Well, we had all along from my position in the electronics lab and from the position I had for the submarine forces and because I was always reporting or writing or answering directives to the submarine division of Op-Nav in CNO, all during these years I reported directly to the submarine division in CNO, it came about because all of these submarine cruises were always fleet-operated.

so I always worked under their direction rather than under my own command in the laboratory. So I had been involved in preparing and writing letters with suggestions or a proposal for the next experiment or the next program, and this is one that we had cranked into the system, I guess in 1957, that what should be done with Nautilus is to make the crossing.

Q: This was before you'd been aboard her?

Dr. L.: It came about during that summer when we first started to work in 1957, and it was obvious after the work with her that summer how it should be done, and I know that fall we turned in a letter proposal that this should be the next operation. But then that got whatever you want to call it, superimposed or set aside by a directive from the White House to proceed on this Operation Sunshine under very different secrecy rules than we were proposing to the staff in the office of Chief of Naval Operations, because what was desired was impact on the world scene. There was absolutely no knowledge of it till it hit.

Q: You mean that there were other accomplishments than the Sputnik?

Dr. L.: Right. It was a demonstration for national prestige and that was a real part of the action.

Q: Do you remember where you were and how you heard that there was to be this operation?

Dr. L.: I don't remember who called me. It must have probably been the people in the submarine branch, CNO, because they were the ones who always did.

Q: But you were here?

Dr. L.: They called me to come to Washington. All discussions were carried out in the Pentagon, in the Chief of Naval Operations' office or in the submarine warfare division office. Then, I remember, I met with Anderson and, at that time, it was Rear Admiral Daspit in Op-31. He had been chief of staff for Admiral Momsen back in the Redfish days. He was Op-Nav 31. I think that's where the discussions took place. That was after Anderson had his discussions with Aurand at the White House and the thing was beginning to formulate.

Q: Was your opinion asked, or was it just a matter of a group discussion which really decided that, yes, it could be done?

Dr. L.: At that time it was a discussion of various ideas as to how, when, and whether we could do it relative to the crossing, which direction, and the main question was whether we could get through the Bering Sea and Strait and the Chukchi Sea with Nautilus, being fully aware that she did not have the equipment that we had had with earlier submarines, and the chances that had to be taken were well recognized. But this was spelled out and it was a matter of preparing Nautilus to do the job. She had to have all kinds of things done.

Q: Did you have any qualms again about whether it could be done with this lack of equipment?

Dr. L.: No, not under the qualifying requirements that were necessary, which meant that the time of the year had to be chosen to get through the Bering Sea and Bering Strait when the ice would permit us, so that we could run surfaced or submerged and get through the shallow water before we would strike ice and be in the problem of having to pilot ourselves through shallow water in heavy ice. So there was a bit of give and give back and forth. They wanted the crossing as early as possible for - I don't remember what the reasons were, some timing relative to the World Fair in Brussels at that time which was going on. But there was some desire for special timing relative to what was happening on the world scene and I don't recall the details.

Then, that relative to whatever the ice would permit us to do. So there was give and take. I know the desire was to do it as early as possible, so we were pressed into some taking a risky guess out of this, but making a guess as to how early the ice would be back and we could make it.

Q: Were you willing to go in June?

Dr. L.: Right, on that basis, that we were going to make the best of whatever we could do, and we did go earlier and for the first time a little too early and we had to return and try again.

Q: Before we get to that, I'd like to know what changes or modifications were made on the Nautilus from August of the prior year?

Dr. L.: Many changes were made to the ship. The big one was to obtain inertial navigating equipment. In that I had only the part of advising. The real pusher in all this was the commanding officer of the ship itself through Carvel Blair in the Bureau of Ships. He

Lyon # 2 - 128

He was a key individual at this time for securing things that were necessary for the Nautilus. She had to have her sail modified and he had that done.

Q: Was it replaced with steel?

Dr. L.: It was replaced with steel. Steel sail made and made sure that all periscopes and radars retracted.

Q: That was a major job!

Dr. L.: Major job. We had to have that, so I say that's why the Bureau of Ships had the power and authority at that time with people who could act and do things. This was all done in New London, as I remember, and it was a very active year for getting all these changes made. And then the inertial navigation system -- there just wasn't any such thing at that time for the ship, and so there was a bit of scurrying around. Captain Anderson on the ship, and wherever he could get the help, did an outstanding effort at finding an inertial system from the ex-Navajo missile that had been scrapped. And so North American Corporation, who had that inertial system, was brought in to modify it, and get it to work on board ship when, after all, it had only been designed to work on a missile that was only going to last about eight minutes at the most, and here it had to last for 80 days.

Q: Was it a system that they took manually and modified?

Dr. L.: And fixed it so it would run for long periods of time, and sent their people with it to make it run. So that gave Nautilus and gave Skate, which also went up in 1958, an inertial navigation system, which was a backup to the gyros. It really became the primary navigation system and the ship's gyros became the backup.

I think it's explained in the books, but there needed to be a cover story for the Nautilus —

Q: Before you get to that — is that all that was done now?

Dr. L.: No. The other one that was necessary, which involved us, was to change the the upward profiling system. The one we had was just not going to do the job. So we came back to the lab and the fine group of fellows I have there frantically and feverishly and rapidly devised or rebuilt and engineered and put together a new profiling system from scratch, which was an experimental system and looked it, but got put on board by the summer of 1959.

Q: How did that work?

Dr. L.: That worked very well and gave us very good records.

Q: I mean, what did it look like?

Dr. L.: It looks similar, except the big change was that we had a very narrow profiling beam so we could see detail of the ice profile.

Q: Was this something put in the nose or on the top or — ?

Dr. L.: This time we put the equipment — mounted the equipment — right in the control room, so that we had in the control room all the data coming in on the ice cover.

Q: Do you had nothing in the forward compartment?

Dr. L.: Nothing. Everything was in control, so that as far as equipment for observing, that was the only change - a new type of equipment, high resolution for high speed and mounted in the control room.

Q: Because you said you modified it for high speed and that would have been the weakness before.

Dr. L.: That had been the weakness. We also put on equipment that recorded the submarine's depth accurately at all times, so we knew what depth we had in order to measure the draft of the sea ice, because you get the draft of the sea ice from knowing your ship's depth versus what the beam looking upwards measures at the lower side of the ice. It had these two numbers. So this equipment was put together and put on board.

Q: And what kind of a picture did you have to look at to read the findings of the installation?

Dr. L.: The same presentation that we had before. It came out on a paper tape and was drawing out the profile.

Q: That required who to read it? You?

Dr. L.: Right. One of us had to be there to operate the gear, even to know what it was, and to read the information.

Q: Who went with you this time?

Dr. L.: Two different people. On the first trial we made in June across the Arctic Ocean, Rex Rowray was with me who had been on the

1957 cruise. But then on the final crossing Archie Walker, another one of my people, was with me.

Q: I think we are getting a little ahead because you had started to talk about the -

Dr. L.: It's necessary to bring in the cover story, and this was really carrying out what we had turned in as our program and it was a little bit elaborated from what I originally asked, which was one submarine, another diesel similar to the 1957 cruise. Instead, they put together Skate and Nautilus and a diesel submarine to go north and have a very intensive study of the Arctic OCean with two nuclear submarines. This was carried as a normal confidential operation, just like the 1957 operation or like the operation of the Redfish et cetera. It was going to be a ComSubLant operation and we had all the meetings and carried it out, and this gave us the cover for making modifications to the Nautilus. Everything was being prepared for this dual submarine study of the Arctic Ocean in the summer of 1958. So it was perfectly logical for everybody to be busy getting both ships ready, both Skate and Nautilus, and laying out a program. So everything was done in a sense, but in the background, the ten people who knew about Operation Sunshine knew that Nautilus was really being prepared and everything was getting ready for her transit across the Arctic Ocean. So it meant for us that we had to get two sets of equipment ready and be prepared to both give equipment to Nautilus and to Skate and be ready for both. So what we did was just that - get together two pieces of equipment and get equipment for both ships, but we only were able to build high-resolution, high-speed sonar, echo-sounding system for one. There just wasn't time or manpower available to build two and there really wasn't much point. We might as well go and try it with one and see how it would work out before we built another. So we only built the one equipment for Nautilus and I want in Nautilus, of course.

Q: Was it built here, actually constructed here?

Dr. L.: Oh, yes, we constructed the whole thing right in our shop.

Q: That must have been a tricky operation!

Dr. L.: It's normal for an electronics lab. Nothing unusual. We were just under a little bit of pressure to get it done in time.

Q: There was nothing outside the submarine? What is outside that reflects on the echo-sounder?

Dr. L.: There are sound projectors which were mounted on the deck or in the deck for projecting the sound and cables had to be run through the hull. That's the only thing that's on the outside.

Q: And you were in charge of installing that, as well?

Dr. L.: Right. This was all done at the Electric Boat Company in Groton.

Q: You took the material that was made here and shipped it back east?

Dr. L.: Three of my people went with it and all the installations were made there.

Q: Were you there while they were doing it?

DR. L.: In and out, but the engineers with me did all the work. They did the design work and did the installations, checked it out, and so forth, and I'd be in and out with that, because there was also involved all the other bits and pieces of getting Nautilus ready. So I'd be there for a period of time. They were there all the time. We had to do all the drawing up of the plans and the diagrams, and be sure that all the equipment and what data was to be taken, and personnel, and so forth for each cruise. So this meant running around back and forth. Plus it was complicated in the spring of 1958 because of the secrecy on this Nautilus cruise. And often I ended up as being messenger boy for the operation, because there was no way of handling the secrecy except by an individual really relaying by memory or word of mouth what was going on in one place to someone else when it had to do with the Nautilus' special operation. And really I was the one person who could go back and forth, because Captain Anderson was on board. He could not leave the ship. Some things had to be done on the West Coast, and there was no way to get this information back and forth, either by phone or letter, because the secrecy was such that it was simply not transmitted by phone or mail, because the secrecy required only individuals who knew of it, and those individuals were known by me.

Q: As I recall, even the CO of NEL didn't know about it.

Dr. L.: That is correct. No on in San Diego was privy to the information, except I. So, my commanding officer, nor technical director, nor no one else knew anything about it.

Q: Did they get mad when they found out about it later?

Dr. L.: No. The other individuals knowing were the CHief of the Bureau of Ships, and he was the only individual, and Admiral Rickover in Ships. They were the only two individuals in the entire Bureau organization aware. The only people knowing in CNO were the CNO himself, Arleigh Burke, and O3, Vice Admiral Combs, Readiness and Operations, and Admiral Daspit immediately below him from the Warfare Division, and then his people who did all the work with whom I was in continual contact - Commander Duke Bayne and Captain Walker.

Q: And the President!

Dr. L.: The President and Aurand, and the Captain of the ship, Bill Anderson.

Q: Have you told me why you decided to go from west to east?

DR. L.: West to east was - I don't know who made the decision -- but it was the way to go because you had to go through this shallow area first, and once you're in the deep ocean, then the rest is straightforward.

Q: Whereas you could have made all the rest of the trip, and then the whole thing would have failed?

Dr. L.: Then you'd be caught by the shallow water, and would have failed, then you'd have to turn around and go out, and you couldn't have said anything. Because it was agreed that if the ship made it and everything went right, then it was going to be one of impact. If it was a failure, nothing would be released.

Q: And you found out right away whether you could do it instead of waiting for days.

Dr. L.: That's right. No, it was much easier this way because the ice was retreating over the shallow water and so you could get up and follow thr retreat far enough to hit deep water and then the rest was straightforward. If we had had the systems that we had on Redfish and the Carp, the sonar scanning systems, we could have done it at any time. But just because we did not have those old-time sonar scanners available on Nautilus we were not able to cross the Bering Sea and Chukchi Sea . Our main attempt was to try to find such a system but under the way the thing was being set up I could not probe very deeply, otherwise somebody would guess what I was up to and it would have broken the cover of the whole thing, because the cover story said we were going to take Skate and Nautilus into the deep Arctic Ocean from the Atlantic side and there just wasn't any need for having the scanning sonar system. So if I was wandering round in all the many places one could find - possibly find - such a sonar or on one of the other boats and demand that we must have it on Nautilus, it would immediately have been an indicator of what was up. So we just had to be careful and we just couldn't push to try to get one of those systems.

Q: Weren't you slightly nervous, going without?

Lyon #2 - 136

Dr. L.: Not really - well, certainly we were at the time of year where we knew it was touch and go in some sense, but with what was at stake, why, you do it. But we recognized our shortcomings, that's about the way to say it, and the shortcomings showed up when the decision was made that we wouldn't try to press our luck, and that's why Anderson chose to return to Hawaii, which was correct, and then wait for a while until the ice had retreated further.

Q: And that's when you told me of the overflight you made and all the secrecy of your going aboard.

Dr. L.: Oh, that was a long, involved story.

Q: You almost didn't get back to go aboard the ship!

Dr. L.: We need journals to follow that. I'm depending too much on memory now.

Q: As I remember, you went on a Bush Line small, two-engine plane to go over the route, along with Captain Anderson?

Dr. L.: There was a lot of frankybusiness! Keeping the secrecy appropriate for the mission. Of course, Nautilus came around to the West Coast under the cover story that she was going for the indoctrination of the Pacific Fleet into nuclear power, since none of the Pacific Fleet had had any contact with nuclear-powered submarines until Nautilus did come around in early 1958. I think it's reported in there - one other thing happened on that cruise that is important to arctic submarines. We had a small fire on board, insulation, approaching Panama Canal and that brought everyone up short from noting that fire on board could be a very severe problem if under ice and you couldn't immediately surface. But between the time that Nautilus came through in early spring of 1958 until she went north in June, this was corrected by putting on board very quickly an air-breathing system so that every individual on board would have a mask that he could connect into the air system and get air independent of the air inside the ship, in case of smoke.

Q: Everyone on board?

Dr. L.: Everyone on board, and this was essential and has proven so in years past, but it was, I think, a real feat to get that all done between the time that she came through Panama Canal and the time that the ship went north.

Q: Where was it done?

Dr. L.: In San Francisco, as I recall. The ship came round, I think, to San Francisco Navy Yard.

Q: Oh, you didn't travel on the Nautilus from the East Coast?

Dr. L.: No, I didn;t have anything to do with Nautilus during this period, except running back and forth from the East Coast to the West Coast with all these instructions.

Q: And getting the new equipment installed?

Dr. L.: Getting all the equipment installed and then checked out as it came around, because we had installed it before she left the

East Coast, while she was in the yard on the East Coast, and then while she was around on the West Coast we had opportunites to check it out. But I didn't participate in them - some of my people would go on the basis of checking the equipment out, because that seemed logical to do and for them to do. Many fleet units participated in cruises of the <u>Nautilus</u> in the Pacific at that time, which was for demonstration to the fleet, and finally brought us into Seattle in June.

Q: You were going to tell me about your flight over the ---

Dr. L.: June then was the time to try to get some reconnaissance of what the ice cover looked like at that time of the year, but again there was no really easy way to bring in Navy flights, or any other kind of available flights, without telling the people why they were needed. So that was when we used the suggestion of just chartering a small plane and flying out from Kotzebue, Alaska, out over the Chukchi and getting a look at what the ice cover was at that time of year, and then trying to make a judgment as to whether to go ahead or not.

Q: What did you see when you were up there, besides a lot of ice?

Dr. L.: I picked up Bill Anderson - he joined me from Seattle, Washington - and we flew up to Kotzebue and picked up the plane there and flew out over the Chukchi, had a good flight. The ice was there, but it looked as though we might possibly sneak by it and get sufficiently far to avoid any big pieces and might make it, but recognizing it was a touch-and-go situation and, of course, much could happen between the time we were there and the time Nautilus would get up there. So it was a matter of trying to judge where it was then and what where it could possibly move to by the time the Nautilus actually got there.

Q: You were still willing to make the try?

Dr. L.: We were pretty much committed to try to make it as early as possible, anyway. So this just gave Anderson somewhat of a picture of what it might look like.

Q: Did you have any trouble on that flight?

Dr. L.: Not really. We had to put down once on the beach to pick up more fuel in order to reach Point Barrow. That's pretty routine.

Q: Hadn't you been refused landing at one place?

Dr. L.: Well, I think the pilot, as I recall, asked for landing at Lisburne, which was one of the big radar stations, and he was refused landing unless there was a very emergency situation, because you had to have clearances to go into a place like that.

Q: And he thought you were both civilians?

Dr. L.: We, technically, were both civilians. Of course, I was known all over the area because of our field station at Cape Prince of Wales where we were always doing things like this, either flying out on the ice looking at something or having people in or out, or running LCVPs on the beaches and doing all kinds of things. So, as far as I being there, there was nothing unusual, or flying around. However, the fact that a civilian from a Navy lab — I didn't have any particular clearance, or hadn't asked for clearance, of course, to go in a place like that, so the pilot wouldn't have had any reason to assume that I had a clearance to go in there, and Anderson was flying under an assumed name as a civilian from the Electronics Laboratory, so he didn't have any clearance. So the pilot was correct in saying he had two civilians with no clearance. So, then we put down on a beach a little further north, Point Lay, maybe — I'm not sure. But this was fairly typical at that time in those areas where you land on the beach, which is dragged into a strip for landing for these small villages, and they have fuel and gas drums. So we landed and pumped some fuel into the plane from available drums.

Q: Was there someone to take care, to do it, or did the pilot have to do it himself?

Dr. L.: The pilot did it with the help of some of the Eskimos who came down. They're always around, you know, from the village. It seems to me he pumped it in, but I can't recall.

Q: It sounds like it was near the place that Will Rogers and —

Dr. L.: That would be too close to Barrow. I just don't recall, but it seems to me it must have been still quite a distance from Barrow. Anyway, we went in to Point Barrow that night. We flew all one day around the ice cover, then went in to Point Barrow, and returned to Seattle the next day. The ship sailed sometime thereafter. I know that Rex Rowry and I had to sort of hide out in Tacoma for a few days.

Q: That's what I was going to ask you about. Did you have any trouble keeping your identities - ?

Dr. L.: Oh, we did. We couldn't stay in Seattle because we had to be sure that we weren't seen by ship's company, and be sure we weren't seen by any of the people I knew at the University of Washington. I had to stay away from Seattle, the oceangraphic department there. Of course, Clifford Barnes and all these people we'd worked with for so many years knew I wouldn't be in Seattle unless I was doing something in the Arctic. They'd wonder what I was there for, so I just stayed out of Seattle. Plus we couldn't be seen by any of the crew. The crew did not know that they were going into the Arctic Ocean. At that time only the commanding officer, the executive officer, and the navigator were aware that <u>Nautilus</u> was in Seattle to cross the Arctic Ocean. So if any of the crew had recognized me from the 1957 cruise, and whenever I showed up they knew they were going to the Arctic, and Rex Rowry had also been in 1957. So we both were around, and if they saw us they knew something was up, so we stayed in Tacoma till the day the ship sailed, and drove over from Tacoma and were met - I guess we had a rental car. So we dumped off the rental car and got in a taxi, and were met at some corner in Seattle by the navigator in his car, and then taken in his car to Pier 90, where the ship was tied up, and went aboard while one of the other officers who knew was watching the gangway, and all crew members were down in the crew's mess being briefed on their duties - not on the Arctic cruise, but on the cruise they were supposed to be taking into the Central Pacific. So then we were taken below while the crew was in the crew's mess. We went into the engineer's cabin.

Q: Did you feel like you were playing cops and robbers?

Dr. L.: Well, all during the spring of 1958 there was certainly a continual feeling of pressure -- don't do anything and think of every move you're making to be sure that you're not in any way compromising the possibility of the leak of information.

Q: Your family as well as everything else?

Dr. L.: Yes, the family, of course, had no knowledge of what was going on. The laboratory had no knowledge. Everything had to be prepared and spoken of in terms of the dual operation of Skate and Nautilus.

Q: That must have been a very wearing experience in addition to the job you were having to get done!

Dr. L.: I think so. I'm not too sure now, but as I recall, that I think was the difficult part about it, meeting and exchanging information and being sure that you were not making some move or doing something that could possibly jeopardize security.

Q: As I recall, you even brought Captain Anderson sealed orders in person, did you not?

Dr. L.: Oh, right. Again, there was no way of doing anything by phone, unless you had prearranged words to mean something. There was no way of writing anything unless you could cover it by something that was to do with the dual operation. There was no means of sending a message. This was the security. Even though you put "top secret", this was more than "top secret" and you had no means of communicating, except by word of mouth, speaking to each other. That's why I spent a good share of my time running about catching people.

The Nautilus was around on the West Coast in, I guess, late May and the orders for the Arctic cruise, of course, had special secrecy and had to be delivered. One way to do it was that I went to Washington, was given the orders, signed out by CNO, and had to get them to the submarine, and I could not go directly to the submarine. That, again, would be an indicator, so I carried the orders and Anderson came from San Francisco to Los Angeles, and we were supposed to meet in the airport at Los Angeles and I would pass them to him. There was something, I don't remember what now - change of flights, mine was ahead or his was late, or what, but we never did meet there and I ended up in San Diego because there was no way to talk to each other. I could not tell what happened to him, so I just carried the orders to San Diego. I got in and I heard from him that night that he had been delayed and he came to San Diego and I met him at the airport in San Diego. So on a park bench out behind the airport, we traded orders - two ordinary looking civilians.

Q: Did you ever feel a little silly doing all this? Or was it just a strain?

Dr. L.: Sometimes it just seemed like - at that time I guess there weren't so many TV shows like Mission Impossible or something like that - you had that feeling. Sometimes it seemed unreal, but it was very real and one was very much aware of the impact improper release would create. In fact, one episode did happen that brought this home even more.

Sometime, I think it was in April, there was a meeting here in San Diego conducted by the Office of Naval Research, a symposium on research in the ocean or some such - I don't remember the title. I had to give a paper on what we had been doing in the Arctic Ocean in research. This had been scheduled long in advance. I gave a paper, and there were a number of people here. In fact, Captain Robertson, former C.O. of Labrador (Canadian icebreaker), was here, and Bill Camerson was here from Canada, all these people that I'd been involved with in Arctic work over the past years. They were in the house, and we were discussing all these problems of the Arctic, so that was going on, and there was conjecture at the symposium on what submarines could do or couldn't do, and I remember that the press picked up someone - I'm not sure who, but my impression is it was Rear Admiral Heyward, who at that time had the air command in the Pacific, and he made some remarks about what submarines after the 1957 cruise of Nautilus in the Arctic Ocean, and the capabilities of submarines in the Arctic, that certain things should be done and what not. In the Press it looked very close as though something had been said.

Q: And he actually was speaking only ---

Dr. L.: It was all conjecture and had nothing to do - no one had any knowledge here, except me, of the operation. And I recall very private phone calls coming in at that time saying - what's going on out there, and who's releasing information. I assured everyone that nothing had been released. It was just plain guessing and conjecture on the part of the people at the symposium. But it did bring home again the importance of holding the high security of this particular operation and made one a little more touchy about the whole situation.

Q: Going to the extent they had, if it had been leaked, it would have been disaster almost, wouldn't it?

Dr. L.: It would have completely negated the impact that finally was achieved. Of course, an even greater risk but also, I think, greater achievement of showing what can be done with personnel in submarine forces was demonstrated later when the first attempt was rebuffed by the ice and we came back to Pearl and by then the entire crew knew what was up, and everyone was briefed that they must hold this extremely tight and that there was no leak, I think this was an outstanding show of what can be done when people realize and know why something must be kept - that there was no breach of security between the two cruises.

Q: Of course, in the first place there were only ten people who know!

Dr. L.: Right, but once we went to sea, then everybody knew.

Q: But on this one, that would have been how many? A couple of hundred?

Dr. L.: No, I guess it was probably 125.

Q: 125 and they were ashore.

Dr. L.: That's right. They were ashore because the ship went back to Pearl and many of the crew went on liberty clear to their homes on the East Coast.

Q: On the East Coast?

Dr. L.: Yes, the ship arranged for flights back and forth across the country for crew members to go to the East Coast, have liberty or leave, and return to the ship.

Q: There was how long a period there? About a week?

Dr. L.: No, it was longer than that. It must have been a period of two, three, or four weeks.

Q: Oh, it was from about June 8th to August !

Dr. L.: No. From late in June to mid-July, and during that time we made corrections to equipment and all kinds of things that could have easily - somebody slipped up, because they had to take care of the types of clothes they had, nothing to indicate that they were going north.

Q: It's almost unbelievable that that many people could keep that secret.

Dr. L.: To me, I think it's outstanding. Whether any of them did possibly let slip somewhere but whoever they let slip to also kept the faith. But so far as anyone has ever been able to tell, it certainly showed that when Nautilus did cross it made a real impact - nobody had suspected, although a few people suspected but there was no public release in any sense.

Q: Now, do you want to go back to when you were smuggled aboard the Nautilus?

Dr. L.: No, let's see -

Q: That was June 8th, was it?

Dr. L.: Sometime in June, I don't know the dates. Nautilus left Seattle, because onece she was out of port then everything was wide open for the crew and everyone.

Q: Can you tell me how it was told to them and what the reaction was?

Dr. L.: Oh, it was told to them strictly by again calling everybody - those who were not on watch - into the crew's mess, and doing it in two sessions, I guess, reading the orders, and the executive officer or the commanding officer, I don't know which, reading the orders and discussing what the cruise was about. Of course, this created excitement and lots of tales and stories, but after all you had a superior type of crew and they just took it as part of their Nautilus would be proud to do and I'm sure all of them expected to do it sooner or later. So I don't think there was any special, you know -

Q: They didn't fall back with their mouths open!

Dr. L.: No, not actually.

Q: Were you there at the time?

Dr. L.: Oh, sure, I was part of the discussion as to what we might find and what our chances were, and all that kind of thing.

Q: Were there lots of questions from the crew?

Dr. L.: I don't recall. I imagine there was some discussion as to how it was to be done and new equipment, but I think they had that discussion and, of course, after we were - we could not make it because of heavy ice in the Chukchi -

Q: Describe it, can you, on a day-by-day situation? Can you put it in that context of your trip north?

Dr. L.: I don't think so, any more. I'd have to read the journal, because it was very straightforward until actually reaching way up above, about north of where we had done our aerial survey, and we were submerged and running and then, again, of course, we only knew what we're going under. We do not know what we could see in front of us. We were blind as far as seeing eyes ahead, other than to know that we were approaching ice but we cannot judge by the equipment we have on board how thick it is, whether it is projecting down into our path or not. And on the particular date - I couldn't give you the day now -

Q: It would just seem to me that would have been an almost unacceptable hazard, to not know what was ahead of you and ice projections down -

Dr. L.: No. We were having to depend upon retraction or retreating of the ice sufficiently far and leaving no extremely heavy pieces so that there was real consideration of some luck here, too, or a probability of running into very heavy pieces to make an opening that we could both surface and do some submerged running to reach the deep water. That was simply the hoice that had to be made.

Q: Could you tell from the ice overhead whether there was a likelihood of a projectile being in front of you?

Dr. L.: Not too well, no.

Q: It was just strictly luck?

Dr. L.: Pretty much. Running on the chances that the heavy ice would be retreating. Now, we did at that time lack some information that we got later but we didn/t have then, and that is just how much heavy ice was in the strait or in the Chukchi Sea, because at that time we just didn't have any foreknowledge of what the total amount or percentage of heavy ridged ice was. We hadn't had the experience, we hadn't had any way of knowing, and it's nothing that could be observed from the air. And I was depending to some extent on the monitoring we'd been doing at Cape Prince of Wales field station, and at the moment I did not realize that some of the data that I had there was not too reliable and perhaps - I know - was misled to some extent by that information.

Q: Of what type? Could you expand on that?

Dr. L.: At the field station we had for a year or two kept echo-sounding systems very similar to what we had on the deck of the ship on the bottom of the strait measuring the ice that was passing back and forth through the strait, but because we had lots of other equipment in there we only sampled periodically - one hour out of any number of hours, we'd use that sample trying to guess then what was the total amount of ice going through there, just sampling once or twice per day. And out of our records, which I looked through, and which had just come in early that year - in fact that was the year that we were doing this - so I didn't have too much data, and I couldn't ask anybody to analyze it, and give me the real results because, again, that would indicate something. So I looked through the data, and made the best guess I could out of it, and from that I think I got - I know I got - a somewhat false impression of perhaps what total ice was there: one from the fact that we did not sample all the time, and we apparently missed by our lack of total sampling some of the real heavy pieces that did go through there, such as the kind of a piece that Nautilus squeezed under. And I had not seen on any of our records pieces of 80 feet draft.

Q: Was this your first trip up in ice that thick?

Dr. L.: That's right. And from the sample of the records on Cape Prince of Wales Station I think we saw 40 and 50 feet as seemingly the order of magnitude of the draft that showed on those records. Apparently we just didn't happen to sample at the time when one of these great big fellows went through. So I was expecting maybe 55, 60 feet, or something of that sort, as the maximum, whereas Nautilus squeezed under a piece, when we turned around, on the order of 85 or 90 feet.

Q: That was when you decided to return?

Dr. L.: To withdraw, yes. That was the first time that I'd observed that heavy a draft in a ridge.

Q: But there's no way, as you go under the ice cover, and knowing how thick it is, as to whether you're likely to turn into that sudden —

Dr. L.: Well, in a sense, we did that because we saw that for the first time — a 90-foot piece — we didn't know how many more there were there, so that's why we turned around. But there's no way of knowing as you change from 20 feet, to 30 feet, to 40 feet, that you now might expect 90 feet.

Q: I see. There's nothing in the chemistry of the ice to know that this is the kind of ice that's —

Dr. L.: It's all jumbled, and so you have to go by the area where you are and what to expect, and I was depending on the data from Redfish, Carp, and all the rest, and the sampling that we'd been doing at Cape Prince of Wales for what to expect. Although knowing full well that from seeing what ice is backed up on the beach that you could have much heavier ice than that. That I was fully aware of, but I had — well, along the north coast of Alaska from all the icebreaker cruises, and from what we had seen off of beaches near the Cape Prince of Wales field station we were fully aware that there was ice of much greater draft than this 55 or 60 feet, because the ice piles up and reaches to the bottom and there it sits. You know it sits, and fully aware that that could melt free and be drifting around. But I had no indication at that time that this type of ice ever reached down into the area in which we were.

Q: Down as far south? Did you have a choice of routes when you went north?

Dr. L.: We didn't have too much choice. At that time we did not have the complete bathymetry of the area, except knowing it was pretty flat, which we had, but when it's so shallow you have to worry about 10 feet even or a mound of 15 feet on the bottom. And I did go through a lot of work trying to find the deepest - even taking another 6 feet would help in the Bering Sea and Chukchi area. The only way I could get that data was that I'd ask the hydrographic office to send me every single ship's log book they had that had ever gone through there, and their records. Recognizing that most of the time those ships don't have their position too well known, but just taking all of the records, which were hundreds, and just plotting out where they said they were and just looking at it and seeing if there seemed to be, ~~some ships~~ assuming big errors in their navigation, an indication that some area was a little bit deeper than another area, we would choose that, and that did prove somewhat useful - in fact, very useful. It did give us some choice in going through the Chukchi Sea. It gained us perhaps six to eight feet, or something like that, in depth, which perhaps was important. But I'm not sure now what difference it might have made because maybe if we'd been over in the shallow water we wouldn't have happened to hit the deep ridge.

Q: Was the data which came from Sverdrup helpful?

Dr. L.: Not applicable in this case. I would have liked to use the suggestion he made, which was to go to the west side of the Chukchi because he had an indication of a canyon, or a valley, in the western part of the Chukchi, but to the west of the U.S.-U.S.S.R. convention line of 1866, or whatever ~~it is~~ date, and because of th~~is~~ particular sensitivity in this operation and possibly wanting to run on the surface, we made no move to go to the west side of the convention line. So I didn't have the availability of that suggestion of Sverdrup's, which we did use to advantage on the SARGO cruise later, but we couldn't use it that summer of the 1958 cruise.

Q: Did you attempt to go at one place and come out and try another place with the Nautilus, or was it just a straight in and straight back?

Dr. L.: No, we made our choice on the basis of the data I had and made the run, but then, once we struck such heavy ice and having had no previous knowledge of that type of ice in that particular area from any previous work, it seemed that the only smart thing to do was - well, we had two choices - either to return to somewhere and then come back and try it later after a few weeks when the ice would have retreated much further, or we would have to operate on the surface, stay in the vicinity and just sort of move with the ice going north, perhaps stay in the vicinity there for two to three weeks while waiting for that ice to retreat. But we would have to stay on the surface in order to see what was going on.

Well, that requiring on the surface was difficult because of again the sensitivity and not wanting to be seen. If we were on the surface, then, an aircraft could have flown over or we were under the radar pattern from Cape Lisburne, from Cape Mountain, the

DEW line radar stations were in full operation at that time and could sweep the surface of the sea. And it could be that we might have been detected by tracking radar.

Q: The numbers were painted out, weren't they?

Dr. L.: Oh yes. The submarine would not be recognized because she was the one of her class only, and it was definitely known that if any of the military forces of the U. S. reported *Nautilus* the command would not recognize it. They would not get a report back, you see, saying "unknown submarine reported, is it *Nautilus*?" because *Nautilus*' operation plan was known not to any fleet communication net, so the response would have been "not U. S."

Well, I don't know about that, but it at least could have started an entire military circus into operation to determine what an unknown submarine is doing off Alaska, and that again would be an indicator immediately to people who had no knowledge, and it would be immediately released to a very large organization, and a very great number of people that something was up, because *Nautilus* was only known to a few, so she was not in the normal military circuits. So this was the principal reason why we returned south to wait. The most expeditious thing from the ice cover and getting through would have been to stay right there and go on with the ice, but then we took this risk of being detected, and not recognized, and that would have immediately broken the security situation. So, with that in mind, about the only choice Anderson had was to do what we did

The proper choice was to get out of there.

Q: Did he ask your advice?

Dr. L.: Well, we all talked about it. He had to make up his mind. It was one of those things one person's got to decide, and that was the proper thing to do. But also recognizing the risk about so many people knowing and they had a real security problem again. However, that was one that you sort of had control of, whereas this other one of being detected on the surface you had no way to control that one. So it seemed like the best thing to do, and it turned out to be the best thing to do, was to return and then come back sometime later and make the second try. The right decision was made and it turned out right.

Q: Can you describe the depth of the water, the dimensions of the submarine, and the free space you had above and below?

Dr. L.: No, I don't recall the numbers now but it must have been only 5 feet of clearance or something of that sort.

Q: From the bottom, or the top, both?

Dr. L.: On the bottom, I suspect we might have had 10 or 15 feet, but I don't think any moved any closer than that - probably about 5 feet of clearance -

Q: How long did those tight quarters exist?

Dr. L.: Only for a few minutes, as we passed under the ridge- We turned around, and surfaced, and looked at things. But when you come up to the surface, you can't see very far when the periscope is so close to the water.

Q: But this 90-foot - what do you call it, not a projectile?

Dr. L.: 9-foot pressure ridge.

Q: 90-foot ridge, that was from attempting to go -

Dr. L.: We were traveling north, you see, and up until that time we had been able to stay under ice, which was what we had expected. We went under this one particular heavy piece which would have had a draft some 30 to 40 feet more than anticipated - a real clincher as to what was - but we didn't have the full knowledge that we needed to make choices. We certainly expected to pass under 55, 60-foot ice in trying to get into the deep water.

Q: Did you hold your breath while you were going under there?

Dr. L.: Everybody did - didn't know what was going to happen - or whether it was going to get any deeper. Well, that's the same as when you have a fire or something else. I mean, you know you're in extremum and everybody's tight for that until you get through it.

Q: Did the commander say, "Why didn't you tell us we were going to see that kind of ice?"

Dr. L.: No, no, no, nothing of that sort. Everybody recognized we were covering new territory.

Q: And you surfaced after that?

Dr. L.: We surfaced after that and looked all around and sat around there thinking what do we do now, and that's when all of these questions were under discussion, as to whether we should sit and drift, or wait around, or return - we discussed all the pros and cons and after full discussion Anderson simply had to make a choice. Somebody's got the make the choice - the commanding officer makes the choice, as appropriate. And, having done that, then he had to send a message which had all been set up - particular messages could be sent -

Q: Which meant certain things?

Dr. L.: Yes - and this was sent and agreed to, and Nautilus proceeded to Hawaii.

Q: Did you run under that same 90-foot projection going back?

Dr. L.: No, we made our turn to avoid that.

Q: You knew where it was and so you avoided it. How many days was this, from the time you entered until you came out from the ice cover? Do you remember?

Dr. L.: No, I don't.

Q: Two or three?

Dr. L.: No, it was more than that.

Q: A week, maybe? Weeks?

Dr. L.: Not weeks, a week maybe. I'm not sure because we went under some ice off St. Lawrence Island, we had to make a decision which side of that island to go on. We did go round on the west side, in the deep water, but we had some heavy ice in that area. I don't remember the details now or how many days were involved. It could have been on the order of a week or ten days.

Q: Anderson, in his book, speaks of an attempt at a western route from which the Nautilus withdrew, and then an attempt to go by an eastern route and then withdrawing and then returning to Hawaii. What did he mean by that?

Dr. L.: No, I think that was on the west side of St. Lawrence Island there was deep water, but the ice hangs into that section and I think we did try to go around there and met heavier ice than we expected. We then made the choice to go on the east side of St. Lawrence. The east side is normally all clear because of the Yukon River which melts out all the ice and you can run the periscope there. The water isn't deep enough to run below periscope there. As I recall, we did go round the east side of St. Lawrence Island at periscope depth and went that way.

Q: And it was farther north than that you came into this east --

Dr. L.: Oh, the heavy ice was clear north of the Bering Strait, well up to the north of Cape Lisburne and near Kotzebue where we had gone out on our flight. It becomes quite shallow in that section and there's just no other way to go unless one can go to the far west and use the Sverdrup sea valley.

Q: You call it a sea valley named after him?

Dr. L.: Well, that's what we feel. He's the one that suggested it. I'm not sure that it's a completely accepted geographical name or not, but its valley is there and very useful for submarines just because of this ice cover it gives one far more depth of water to operate in.

Q: So, actually, the only way, at this time in history, to go north approaching from the Pacific was wait until the ice withdrew?

Dr. L.: With a ship without proper sonar systems. If I'd had the same Sonar system I had on our earlier ships I could have gone right through. This was the sad part about it. We did not have the capability that we had with the Redfish. We had nuclear power but we did not have the sonar systems.

Q: To a civilian observing it, it seems — although you had the finest of ships and yet lacked one piece of equipment which had been in the earlier —

Dr. L.: Yes, but, again, it was a very — if it's taken out of context — was a very special security classification. Then, it makes sense, so you have to look at it in terms of these special security restrictions which were completely unusual.

Q: Otherwise, you'd have been able to somehow get the other sonar?

Dr. L.: Otherwise, I could have got this equipment on board, but with the fact that the submarine was scheduled to operate in the Arctic, in the north Atlantic, there just was no reason to put that equipment on board. They'd spent all the money and effort in getting in getting the modification to the hull and all the other things that had to be done, but we just could not have justified it without saying that we were going to go through the Pacific.

Q: It just all has to be known and put in context for it to make sense!

Dr. L.: That's right. Otherwise, it doesn't make sense whatsoever. There were many other little things that occurred on that particular cruise that don't make sense unless one is aware of the security situation.

Q: Do you want to amplify that?

Dr. L.: What I'm thinking of now, but I remember them occurring - what you did with people, what you did with pieces of paper, what you did with communications or travelsorder for people - all kinds of odd things kept arising every day in the way you would not normally administer or direct an operation which had to be done in a special way because of the situation.

Q: Do you remember how the skipper approached the subject with the crew, of impressing them with the need for this security between the time they got back to Pearl Harbor, which was late June, and a month later when they were going to try again?

Dr. L.: Oh, there were very long discussions with the full crew and then individually everybody working and trying to think of things that had to be done. So everybody was busy on board, both as individuals and as a group, being sure they were going to do things and have their stories right and what they'd tell their families and everything else. This was very well and thoroughly discussed. For instance, people had put special markings on clothing, and they'd look at each piece of clothing they had to be sure they didn't take it off the ship and all kinds of things - anything that would be any indicator of what they were doing or intended to do was very carefully looked at, and must have been because there was not a breakdown in the security situation. Everything was kept on board and they kept reminding themselves, we are coming from a cruise into the central Pacific and returning to Pearl after a long time of endurance run, and appear to be coming from such an operation, rather than from the north.

Q: Did lots of things have to be put under lock and key?

Dr. L.: Oh, yes, all kinds of things were kept in lockers on board and that sort of thing.

Q: Where was the <u>Nautilus</u> in this roughly a month period?

Dr. L.: She stayed tied up in Pearl, and the story then was that certain corrections had to be done and other things before she started on the next leg to return to the Atlantic for the cover operation of <u>Skate</u> and <u>Nautilus</u> together. Then, you see, she left at about the right time, supposedly to go from the central Pacific back through the canal, through the Atlantic and to go north, and it seems to me that there was a change of orders then, that because of certain things going on in the central Pacific, not expressly stated, she would not return to the Atlantic and <u>Skate</u> must with the other diesel boat proceed on their own in the Atlantic.

Q: By the way, was the Nautilus number repainted before you got back into Pearl?

Dr. L.: Yes, they painted her just before we got in, so she came in in full condition as though she had been returning from this cruise in the central Pacific, and all the cover stories through the Navy circled themselves that these duration runs had to be further continued, which, at that time, were sort of part of the studies going on with submarines anyway, because it was a new type of boat. So that no one was too shook up about the type of story given.

Q: What did you learn, besides the fact that there were these deep projections that you had?

Dr. L.: On that particular --

Q: Yes.

Dr. L.: That was the only thing. We did not have the full story of the ice cover at that time of year.

Q: Were there any changes or modifications made to the Nautilus in the month period?

Dr. L.: No, not that I recall. I think everything was just - oh, there probably were, but I don't - I think it was just sort of an upkeep and bringing everything up to first class.

Q: What did you do in that period?

Dr. L.: I returned to San Diego, and Rex Rowray returned with me. We came back to San Diego, but there was a lot of tricky maneuvering to make sure that no one knew where I'd been and where I came from.

Q: Weren't you getting tired of that by this point?

Dr. L.: Oh, well, yes, because I remember getting off the <u>Nautilus</u> in Pearl Harbor, and there I had to be careful that nobody saw me, and knowing so many people in Pearl right at the submarine base. And I came up out of the hatch once and looked out, and there was somebody I recognized right off on the pier, and so I had to wait until he disappeared. The Navigator brought a car right up to the gangplank and I got off and into the car immediately to go to the airport. Anderson had arranged for my flight on one of the regular naval flights which was taking a lot of the crew members east and Anderson. I used the same false identification card that I had given him when he was flying up north. So that I went out under an entirely different name from my own. I didn't appear in the office to write in or check in, he checked me in, and I kept around the corner of the building or somewhere nearby, and when they got on board I just got on board the aircraft.

Q: That's so unlike your nature as I would observe it to be!

Dr. L.: This was going on all the time. So that I got in and out of Pearl Harbor without having my name show anywhere, because that would have been a complete give-away to the submarine forces.

We got into San Francisco then, and Anderson and I went on to Washington, and Rex Rowry - his name was not known - went to San Diego from San Francisco. Anderson and I went to Washington and were met by Duke Bayne there, and that's when everything was sort of laid out again for the next try.

Q: Was there any question ever that there would be the next try?

Dr. L.: Oh, there was no question about that. Then I went back to San Diego, Anderson went home, and then back out to Pearl again.

For the moment, go back before our cruise started. Of course, I always had to travel under travel orders, civilian travel orders. I had written what I told the command in San Diego, which was backed up by Admiral Daspit through some proper conversations with the lab. My cover story was that I was required in Alaska to assist the air command and the DEW line, which fit in the 1955-1956 period when I had been operating with them for so long. So I had orders to proceed to Point Barrow and Anchorage and that area, and report to the Alaskan Air Command and Alaskan Sea Frontier. Rex Rowry and I had those kind of orders.

Of course, Rex Rowry knew nothing about this until I got him into Seattle and told him - now, you go ahead to Tacoma and sit in the hotel. I'm taking your ticket. That was when I said - okay, this is what the real story is. So that was the first time he knew he was even going to the north. He thought he was going to Alaska to help do some photography and plotting and what not for the Alaskan Air Command.

Q: He didn't go on the second trip?

Dr. L.: He didn't go on the second trip, but he went on <u>Skate</u>. The second trip got even more hairy with regard to travel orders. When we returned, you see, from all of this, you always turn in your travel orders, where you've been and the whole detailed accountin

So, when we got back Rex Rowry and I had to sit down and make out entirely false sets of travel vouchers and turn in ticket stubs and so forth, which accounted for going to Anchorage, reporting to the Air Command for so many days -- I don't remember the whole business, where did we live, who did we get food from, our taxi fares, and all the rest of it. I showed I went Military Air to San Francisco, Military Air into Washington, which I really did from Honolulu, and then we went from Washington by commercial air. All of this was turned in as a legitimate set of travel vouchers. I've often wondered how a perjury case could be made on all this. Well, actually, a number of nights I was up at the lab, and I wrote travel orders for the assumed name of Bill Anderson, so that he was traveling on Naval Electronics Laboratory travel orders, with this identification card which I had obtained from Franz Curie, had been taken out of the NEL files of someone who had long left the laboratory. I split that card and slipped Anderson's portrait in, and he took the name. It was a card for an individual of physical dimentions similar to Anderson's; I slipped in his picture so that he appeared to have identification from NEL. Then I wrote out travel orders and forged the signature of the commanding officer of NEL, to give him standard travel orders from NEL, so he appeared to be a perfectly good NEL party -- with a false name. He was under that name all during the time --

Q: And what name were you traveling under?

Dr. L.: I was under my own name, because I was in Alaska and I was always traveling to Alaska, so there wasn't any problem there. But then when I got to Pearl, Honolulu, where I didn't expect to be, then I had to be somebody else. Then I took the same card and became that person when I went to Honolulu.

Q: That's very good!

Dr. L.: But then all the real trouble was getting all this stuff back into NEL and then having to turn in these vouchers for both Rowray and myself, which were completely false, turning those into the system and then going out again under another set of travel orders, only this time I had to send Rex Rowray to the East Coast to go on Skate. But that was was very straightforward because that one was completely in the clear. I needed him to go on Skate in order to have somebody with backup experience, because he had been in the 1957 cruise, so he could go on the 1958 cruise with the knowledge he had from 1957 on Nautilus to help out on Skate in 1958.

I then took ARchie Walker with me, another engineer from NEL to help me on the Nautilus. So again we set out with a set of orders that said we were going to return to Alaska Sea Command and the Air Force to help them with their DEW line defense problems along the north coast, and had all the typical tickets, and we had tickets to take us to Seattle and into Anchorage, which had been issued to us by the laboratory. In the interim, I had arranged through Pan American - I'd asked for space on Pan American from Los Angeles to Honolulu.

I didn't tell Walker anything other than he was going to go to Alaska and help me out with the same sort of problem Rex had been doing, and of course when he talked to Rowry, Rowry hadn't told him anything, so he didn't know. It was a highly secret job, that's all. So then when I got into Los Angeles I said, now you have your choice: you either go with me to the *Nautilus* and we go from here to Honolulu; or you have the choice, if you don't want to take part in it, you can return to San Diego, but you're under oath not to say anything about it. I could see he wanted to go. I was pretty sure he wanted to go, or I wouldn't have taken him. When we got to Los Angeles we canceled our continuation to Seattle and got our plane to Pearl. That way, nobody knew we were going to the ship. As far as the laboratory was concerned we had continued on to Alaska, and it was understood that they would never get any communications from us because we were out in the hinterland, and out of touch with communications, and also that it was a highly classified job, and we were just not going to communicate on the tasks that we were doing.

Q: There was an awful lot of maneuvering to do!

Dr. L.: So, we proceeded to Pearl, and the ship went from there, and the rest of the trip was very straightforward.

Q: Well, it was not completely straightforward, was it, because I want you to describe - of course, you had the problem of getting aboard the *Nautilus* again unseen?

Dr. L.: Oh, right. Of course, in this case, nobody knew Walker so I did have a contact. He could go back and forth to the ship and get things done and set out, and I stayed in the hotel down in the central part of Honolulu - of course, not anywhere near the sub base. So every time I got out on the street, I'd begin to wonder whether I was going to meet somebody. I think my prime worry was that my sister-in-law was in Honolulu at that time, as I recall. I'm pretty sure that Virginia's sister and her husband were in Honolulu at the same time. I thought they'd be probably down near the yacht harbor, and so we stayed away from that, because if we'd run into each other that would have been really confusing and very difficult to cover up with a plausible story.

Well, anyway, when it came time someone from the ship in a car picked us up in the early morning hours of the day we sailed, and took us again by car into Honolulu and to the pier, being sure no one was on the pier as we were getting aboard. Of course, this time we didn't have to worry about the ship's crew. One individual who knew about the cruise was ComSubPac, Admiral Grenfell, and he did come on board and we had a talk with him. He had to come and see me because the only way to do it was for him to come on board, and we had a discussion. The point of the discussion was, at that time, he was very much concerned about icing of snorkels on the regular diesel-class submarines during winter in the Western Pacific. This is part of the story which has to do with our pool which we should pick up, I guess, after we get through with the <u>Nautilus</u>. He did come on board just before we sailed to discuss this icing problem with the snorkel head valve on the submarines in the Western Pacific.

And then we sailed that day, proceeded up through the Bering Strait. Of course, by now, this was July and there was no ice until we got well north of where we had stopped before, and then became a problem again of searching around for a place to get the deep water, and we did search while on the surface for about a day. We went straight north of Bering Strait and found ice before we could reach the deep water, came to the surface, and started going northeast knowing where the Barrow Sea valley is. We were wandering right along the edge of the ice, and were able to reach the entrance to the Barrow Sea Valley before the ice completely stopped us. So that gave us deep water, and we could drop down to the Barrow Sea Valley, and go northeast of the valley, and then turn north off of Point Barrow in deep water, keeping in sufficiently deep water at all times.

Q: So you actually had no problems this time?

Dr. L.: No problems, no, because the ice was sufficiently retreated to get to the Barrow Sea Valley and get in, and we didn't need the scanning sonar system.

Q: Can you describe the instrument that is now in the control room? Can you describe your participation in the Arctic trip, and your reactions?

Dr. L.: Well, of course, all of it up to now again was just the advising what to expect from the ice cover and where to go and how to make the approach to the northeast and get into the Barrow Sea Valley, and that was some of the decisions that weren't binding advice given to Anderson as to where to go, and whether to take the chance of getting so close to Point Barrow, which is necessary to get to the entrance to the sea valley, and risk detection. Once in the valley it is a straight run, so from that point on I was just interested in gathering information about ice overhead and the bottom topography because we were going in completely new country. But the ship was just driving a straight course, and the ship was concerned with navigation and getting across the pole. Their entire focus was on navigation so that they knew where they were, and reaching the north pole, and crossing out to the Atlantic side. I spent my effort on getting the bottom bathymetry, the temperature of the sea water, and the top ice cover. So the two of us, Archie Walker and myself, were again a few hours on, a few hours off, and up all the time sort of thing for the 96 hours, I think we were practically up all the time.

Q: Do you say the bottom of the ice cover when you are cruising under it?

DR. L.: Yes, the bottom of the ice cover that was above us - the bottom profile. Getting that complete record, and also the bottom topography, since we were going to cross the Arctic Ocean and nobody had ever sailed through there. That bottom topography was all new information.

Q: Was this an exciting experience for you at this point?

DR. L.: I think so. I know so, because it was completely new. We had good information when we started out from the icebreaker work in the Beaufort Sea. We had information from drifting ice stations, Fletcher's ice stations, which had crossed part of the track, and some other ice stations. We had some Russian data, but that was to the west of the area we were crossing. We sort of extrapolate from that information as to what we might expect. We were going across the center of the Beaufort Sea, in which there had never been an soundings taken. So one is aware at all times, one is not sure, sort of guessing what the topography is in front, but one has to be alert as to some changes when approaching mountain ranges, and remain alert for the unexpected.

Q: Weren't you always under a situation of tension?

Dr. L.: We were always under some tension, but after it settles down, and we get into full deep water of the basin, then we begin to judge - okay, we're going over a broad basin, we're not going to expect any sudden cliff to rise in front of us and that sort of thing.

Q: You didn't know that that might happen?

Dr. L.: No, but you still have this from a knowledge of geology. It's just not something that's going to happen to reach from 2,000 fathoms up to the very surface. It's just not likely without some change in the topography to give you warning. In fact, Nautilus did go over a ridge, and we did slow at one point, because it looked as though we were reaching rising ground, so then we'd just go a little more cautiously than we we knew that we were in a big flat basin. And the ice overhead, of course, it just stayed the same. We had plenty of room for it, so there was no real worry there, and we had sufficient information to know that we were not going to have icebergs, which would easily reach to the depths at which we were traveling. But our knowledge of the ice cover in the Arctic Ocean from the drift stations, and knowledge where icebergs generated gave us assurance, as anything is assured in a science sense, that we would not meet any icebergs. So there was no worry in that sense. We could proceed at our 20-knot speed and depth and not have any particular concern except to be sure that we stayed on our track to the north pole.

Q: Did the inertial navigation system work as you expected it to?

Dr. L.: It did its job. They had special people, and they had their problems at times to keep the equipment going, but it did its job straight through, and got Nautilus to the pole, and the Skate to pole, and out again without any trouble.

Q: Was it an exciting experience when you found that you were at the pole?

Dr. L.: I guess, but by then you see it coming. It doesn't come suddenly. The whole thing is progressing according to plan, and I don't think there's any sudden shock of excitement. And when it was all through, as far as I was concerned - I think a couple of us were so tired there was no shock from it being done, because the 96 hours that the crossing took took two of us being on the job almost continually during that period with only very little sleep. I know that I was in a state of exhaustion almost when it was over. So there was no sense of excitement then.

Q: You're speaking now of when the whole trip was over?

Dr. L.: When the transit was done, and we were out, and we were in open water, and the ship was doing normal operations.

Q: Did you collapse?

Dr. L.: I didn't collapse but I certainly went *to sleep* and didn't wake up for a while.

Q: Were you two hours on and two hours off and on the all the time -

Dr. L.: I just don't have much recollection of much sleep or anything because the equipment we had required almost continuous adjustment and continuous care, because, remember, it was put together very quickly and, in a sense, we were still designing its use and working with it, experimenting with it the entire cruise, and to get the most out of it we just had to stay with it all the time.

Q: Were the crew members interested in it?

Dr. L.: Oh, yes.

Q: Did they come and watch it? Could they read it? I mean, could they tell what was going on?

Dr. L.: Yes, they could tell what was going on. Then, of course, again, being the first time there was, as you say, certainly some strain from that and being sure that all that equipment stays in and giving the information, and the only way of knowing when you're out is by such equipment, when you're in the clear again, out in open water. There is certainly a strain and that, I'm sure, we felt. I notice, looking at the photographs that were taken I look as though I'm about ready to collapse.

Q: It would seem to me that, here, you've had the responsibility for designing, developing, and making that equipment and following it and seeing that it worked and knowing that if anyone the whole crew would be on jeopardy, as well as the ship.

Dr. L.: Well, it's not quite that serious. Wouldn't be in jeopardy, it would just mean that you spent a lot of extra time going a lot further south to be assured that you were out in clear water that you don't need, but it's not a sense that it's black and white, that if it fails your life is in jeppardy.

Q: Well, but suppose there were unexpected projections down and unexpected ice cover? The only way you knew it wasn't happening was because of the equipment. Am I correct?

Dr. L.: Not quite, because the previous experience in 1957 because of the data et cetera, et cetera, we knew that, okay, we could go to such and such a point and there's bound to be open sea.

Q: Yes, but I meant you couldn't always be positive that there wouldn't be a projection at some point, could you?

Dr. L.: Oh, deeper than normal?

Q: Yes.

Dr. L.: Pretty much so. If the projection would be deeper it would be an iceberg and that would be extremely - we were sure it wouldn;t happen ,except, of course, we were using the profile data to get the first information to see whether we were correct in all this assumption. The only time that the upward-looking echo-sounding systems would have been absolutely critical to our safety was in case something happened on board that required an emergency, such as a flooding or a fire, or something that required us to immediately surface. Then, the entire life and everybody depended upon this system to find a place to surface. In that sense we're under a type of a dagger holding over our heads, because the equipment was the only key to getting the ship to the surface. But we're living with that all the time.

Q: Of course, I would think so. I'm certain, in retrospect, it wasn't as calm an experience as your words indicate.

Dr. L.: Maybe. However, for me, I don't think it was. As I recall the time, it was a lot of hard work, but keep in mind that I had also been through all of the diesel battery boats, which none of the others had, and experiences on the diesel battery boats where you knew very well that you must surface within the next few hours were far more of a pressure and in that shallow water that we operated in with the diesel boats. There was far more pressure on one all the time than in this particular operation, because here we had plenty of room, and a submarine that in normal situations didn't have to surface at all. It could live under the sea, and that gave one an entirely different sense of capability and freedom than the diesel battery boat had under the very tight ice situation that we had been in on <u>Redfish</u> and <u>Carp</u>. So, having that behind me, I don't recall ever having a feeling of anxiety or fear. Perhaps some of the others felt it because they didn't have that kind of experience. But the nuclear boats just sort of lost a lot of that apprehension that was felt a little more on the older boats.

Q: Could you have surfaced through ice with the Nautilus, or did you know that?

Dr. L.: Oh, yes. In an emergency situation, why, one does a lot more things than one would normally do. One just take higher risks of striking the ice cover. Of course, we had not done a great deal of surfacing with a nuclear submarine at that time. We hadn't had much experience. But if we'd had to, we would have done it, that's all.

Q: But you didn't surface with the Nautilus on this at all?

Dr. L.: No, because here again timing was the all-important factor, and spending time surfacing and looking at the ice cover and doing lots of other things was not the prime purpose. The prime purpose was to get across the Arctic Ocean, demonstrate, and get that one-flash impact from what we'd done.

Q: And let the world know that it had been accomplished!

Dr. L.: I was not in on that. That part of it was then carried out by Anderson being picked up at Iceland and the story broke at the White House.

Q: Did everyone, do you think, have a sense of accomplishment and pride?

Lyon # 2 - 177

Dr. L.: I think so. There was never at any time anything but that. Certainly, the Nautilus was given a tremendous reception at Portsmouth when she got in to England. The crew and officers when they were in London, or any part of England, could ask for anything, anybody did anything for them. Amazing the reception they received. Everybody on the streets even seemed to be interested. They just stopped a Nautilus sailor walking down the street and gave him a lift or started a conversation with a group of people immediately.

Q: That must have been exciting after all to be successful.

Dr. L.: I should think so.

Q: Did you return on the Nautilus?

Dr. L.: I came back on the Nautilus from Portsmouth. Archie WAlker left Nautilus there, because it was the first opportunity he'd had to return to his home. He was born in Scotland, and went to see his brother, I guess. I came back with Nautilus to New York.

Q: Did you have a ticker-tape parade?

DR. L.: Oh, yes, and that was quite an experience. That's only a once-in-a-lifetime thing to take part in a ticker-tape parade. I think everybody that was on board had quite an experience then, because, again, the reception of Nautilus in New York that week was amazing. You'd walk into a restaurant and you couldn't pay for your meal as long as you signed somebody's program or something.

All of the shows were available to the people on <u>Nautilus</u>. I remember we went to "My Fair Lady" and "Music Man."

Q: What indication, what insignia, did you have that you were part of the <u>Nautilus</u>?

Dr. L.: I didn't have any, but I was normally wandering around with someone from the <u>Nautilus</u>, either someone from the crew or some of the officers.

Q: When you were aboard the submarine what did you wear; a business suit?

Dr. L.: Oh, just khakis which I normally wear most of the time for being on board or working.

Q: Khaki shirt and khaki pants?

Dr. L.: No insignia, you don't have any insignia or indication of any sort.

Q: And all this time the <u>Skate</u> was —

Dr. L.: All this time the <u>Skate</u> was up north carrying out the original story! Gene LaFond and Rex Rowry were on board and people from the Oceanographic Office. So their entire effort was to carry out the original plan of operating in the area, getting ice cover, bathymetry, etc. They had a very different track from what the <u>Nautilus</u> had. So, together, we gained a tremendous amount of information. And <u>Skate</u> carried out what we had intended to do in surfacing a submarine in the ice, in the polynyas in the ice. She spent a great deal of effort going up and down in open-water lakes in the Arctic Ocean.

Q: That was in the summertime?

Dr. L.: That was in the summertime. She had an outstanding tour. She went to Norway, down into France, quite a wonderful time touring through Europe after her cruise and coming back. So <u>Nautilus</u> got the welcome in New York, and <u>Skate</u> had the tour of Europe that summer. It was sort of a high point, of course, for Arctic submarines that year and the following year. It was a golden age that just turned everything over from what we had been through before when no one paid any attention. All of a sudden we were paid almost too much attention, extremes.

Q: What do you mean?

Dr. L.: Well, the demand on time and people to do things, and ideas to use the ships, and everything from lecture tours to courses in schools - just suddenly growing, expanding in the extreme, people wanting information on what was happening and their use of the submarines and so forth.

Q: You told me earlier that the demand on your time, being on the lecture tour, was that at this period or later, or did it go on for a long period of time?

Dr. L.: That began immediately. While on <u>Nautilus</u> when we reached Europe a lot of mail had reached our ship. I didn't believe this was possible, but the mail that came aboard was just tremendous, and it was from all over the world. It kept everybody busy answering and reading all this mail, and then began the demand on people on board. And, in my case, I know I received all kinds of requests to speak about the cruise. If I had taken all of them I'd just have been speaking all the time. In fact, personnel of the <u>Nautilus</u> had to fill this demand because it was part of the Navy's publicity program. The ship's officers simply had to spell these jobs out, and go speak at the various affairs, everything from luncheons to dinners to programs of all sorts, to schools, to what not. The demand was tremendous, as well as all these letters —

Q: How did you possibly get your letters answered?

Dr. L.: Fortunately the letters - the big advantage that I was working for the submarine forces, and I was reporting to the ship, so the letters are addressed to the ship and not to me. So the ship could carry this burden. It was their show, anyway, so the Navy just had to handle them. On that trip back from England we spent all the time just working these letters over, and they'd be written in all kinds of languages, and we'd try to find somebody on board who could read them, then write out answers. We'd be asked for the buttons off the captain's coat!

Q: Not really!

Dr. L.: That's right. You'd get all kinds of collectors' items that wanted something from that ship.

Q: Did anybody want the engines?

Dr. L.: Not quite, but maybe they did. I don't know. There were the strangest demands and, of course, the cacheted letters that were written only a few, and there were all kinds of requests for any kind of materials from the ship. I had never realized that there would be this type of thing until I witnessed it.

Q: That was a fallout you hadn't thought about!

Dr. L.: No, I don't think anyone had really considered the fallout of that sort.

Q: What had they done? Heard of it and then written to catch the ship in England?

Dr. L.: They just wrote then immediately to the ship, of course - USS Nautilus at the New York fleet PO, or anywhere - and it would show up in great bags of mail.

Q: There must have been thousands, based on what you tell me?

Dr. L.: I have no idea how many messages and letters. All kinds of messages poured in.

Q: Did you hear from Mrs. Lyon at that point?

Dr. L.: No. At that point she got - I guess the press opened up on her. She was caught in the middle and really given a bad time for a while by the local press and all kinds of reporters asking for stories, and she knew nothing. And she said, "I know nothing," but they wouldn't believe her that she knew nothing. So finally she had to be just caustic about it and say she knows nothing and can say nothing. She just didn't know.

Q: Actually, in that respect, it was fortunate that she didn't.

Dr. L.: That's right. It was very fortunate.

Q: Let's see, then, you were finished with the Nautilus —

Dr. L.: In September of 1958.

Q: And your next assignment?

Dr. L.: A lot of that fall was spent ducking out of lectures! I tried to pick ones that would be just now and then of importance. I gave one to the local people here at Scripps Institute under the auspices of the University of California, billed as a public lecture, and I gave that once there and then, maybe, a couple of more trying to pick sort of semi-scientific; tried to be at least connected in some way with a scientific body. I felt that I should do that side. The ship itself could take care of the general public and general release, but I should only speak if it somehow had to do with the technology of the submarines —

Q: In your area of interest!

Dr. L.: In my area of interest, but I'm not speaking for the ship. It was the ship's affair, not mine, and a Navy affair, but I would speak if it had some relationship to oceanography, navigation of the arctic submarine, and the technology.

Q: If you'd been the kind of person who wanted publicity, you could have got mounds of it!

Dr. L.: Oh, yes, you could have run off but you'd spend all your effort doing that and we had many more problems to solve without doing that.

Q: The first trip of the Skate had been in the summertime?

Dr. L.: That's right. The summer of 1958 and that had all of the instruments and techniques that we used many times in the summer time, so there was nothing new in that whole set-up, except this was the first time a nuclear submarine did surface in open water in the Arctic Ocean. So Skate accomplished that.

Now, in the fall of 1958, we recognized that we had done all of our submarining in summertime, we were depending upon summer conditions in the arctic, and we should now try to extend this to wintertime. So the discussions in the fall of 1958 between the commanding officer of Skate, Commander Calvert, and I were over what to do about the wintertime situation, recognizing this was the thing to do, and I turned in then a program to CNO that this was the main next point to be attacked - how to operate a submarine in winter.

Q: Did he agree with that?

Dr. L.: He, of course, agreed with that and Calvert was very interested in making the try. A Skate-class submarine was the thing to do it with. It was the newer class, a compact submarine, and had the hardened sail, the strong sail required to make the break-through, or whatever method we were going to use, because this was all new now. We had to start thinking entirely differently as to what the problems were for the winter, and again we needed equipment to meet the situation, so we were updating the equipment that we had on Nautilus. There were certain shortcomings and it had been thrown together very rapidly, so during the fall of 1958, went back to the laboratory and took the equipment that we had on Nautilus and further designed it and particularly

combined it with the depth-sensing system that was carried on
<u>Skate</u>. So we would automatically have a system to measure the
draft of the ice, correcting for whatever the depth the ship was
operating in, and not something we had to do mentally. Until
then we would be reading the depth of the ship on one record and
reading the profile of the ice on another record, then mentally
had to subtract one from the other so that we could see what the
ice thickness was.

Q: I'm glad you did it mentally, without having to use a pencil
and paper!

Dr. L.: Doing it mentally gave us sort of estimates, but not
a real accurate, precise, quickly read ---

Q: Now, this new equipment would automatically give you this?

Dr. L.: It was just putting two figures together and getting the
engineering working properly. Again, a first try at it. That was
the main change between <u>Nautilus</u> in the summer of 1958, and getting
ready for the winter - to give an equipment that would compensate
for whatever depth the ship was operating in, and try to give us a
direct-reading record of the track we were on.

Q: Where you were between the top and the bottom?

Dr. L.: Yes. Just the draft of the ice accurately. Up until then
we'd always just been drawing a profile of it, but that didn't give
us on that same record the surface of the open sea so that we could
read directly the thickness. We had to go and look at another record
and transpose what it said as to the depth we were operating in, and

transpose it on to the record to get where the surface of the sea should be on the record, and then --

Q: And that would give you the thickness of the ice?

Dr. L.: Yes, but now, by putting the depth-sensing equipment directly connected to the sonar profiling system we could get a record that would already have written on it where the surface of the sea should be if there were no ice, and then the profile of ice beneath that. So it was all presented on one record.

Q: It didn't have anything to do with the bottom?

Dr. L.: Not the bottom, no. It had to do with wherever the ship was in depth below the sea surface. The ship could move up or down all the time, and it was easy enough to do this mentally as long as the ship stayed at one depth all the time. But if the ship was changing its depth, then one mentally had to correct all the time for whatever that ship was doing on the previous record.

Q: And in the event of emergency --

Dr. L.: In the event of emergency, it would be something one couldn't do rapidly, and it would be a real short-coming. This combined equipment was expected to be particularly important because on going in winter we did not know how much open water we would see, if any, then we had nothing to relate to because the open water was the sea surface against which we would calibrate our record or and depth sensing equipment. If you don't have any open water, then it's not easy to determine where the free sea surface is.

Q: A person who is unskilled with this sort of thing doesn't have any concept of the problems. I think you indicated that when you made your speeches to people who were uninformed. You might have said something that was terribly important and it would have gone right over their heads as an item that was so critical to you.

Dr. L.: That's right. Not being familiar, it's something that the average person just doesn't think about or have any everyday experience, or even have any travel experience with these problems.

Q: I think another thing is that as the public is accustomed now to things of science that are so remarkable, they to some extent take whatever is done in science as a matter of course.

Dr. L.: Right, and actually in this case and much of this arctic, the concepts are really very simple, except that they're just not everyday experience.

Q: When they're explained to you -

Dr. L.: Yes, that's right. We find this over and over again, that things that are obvious once we're there we didn't think about until we got there - the fact that it's just not commonplace experience.

Q: Commander Calvert speaks of your supervising the installation of a new inverted bathometer and floodlights and TV and strengthening the top of the sail.

Dr. L.: These were the things that were done. The strengthening of the sail followed from the experience of the Nautilus in 1957. So the Skate was built with a strong sail. The upward-looking echo sounder is just what I mentioned, this depth-correcting, direct-reading, under-ice profile system which we developed in the fall of 1958, and that was what was installed in Skate.

Q: The Bathometer - it was using that -

Dr. L.: The Bathometer and echo-sounder are synonymous. Actually, the word "fathometer" was originally a copyrighted name of the old Submarine Signal Company, which is now Raytheon, and legally, years ago, one did not speak of a fathometer unless one spoke of Submarine Signal Company's equipment only. And so the echo-sounder is more of a general name meaning all types of things that get data by echo-sounding, whereas the fathometer was the copyrighted name of Submarine Signal Company. That's many years ago and I suspect now the copyright is overage.

Q: It's referred to in the books many times just by the word fathometer, but I think your specific words describe it far better than the word "fathometer."

Dr. L.: Right. Echo-sounder is what it is. It sounds the depth or sounds the distance by echoes.

Q: And did you put floodlights on the Skate?

Dr. L.: Then, we thought it would be of value since we're going in the winter and winter darkness, we might gain some information by lights illuminating the ice and look through the periscope as well. The suggestion came, I think, there was an underwater television camera available through the Bureau of Ships and which we installed on board, just again to give us some more tools to see what we were doing. There's nothing like being able to look at something.

Q: And they were both topside?

Dr. L.: They were both topside. The lights on top and this TV camera which was - I can remember it being in fixed position, and just looking upward to have a look at what the ice looked like, or whatever else we could see. Additional equipment - I think those were the additional equipments. Otherwise, Skate was as she was configured for the summer cruise.

Q: And you were back in New London supervising?

Dr. L.: Right. This was all put on in New London. THe people involved at this time were Walter Schatzberg from my group and I, Walter Wittmann and maybe one other from the Oceanographic Office, and people to operate the inertial navigation system. Those were the specialists on board the ship to help. The cruise was in February, if I recall correctly, 1959.

Q: I show March 4th, which is essentially the same thing!

Dr. L.: I guess it was the end of February through March.

Q: The pressure was off for secrecy on this one, was it?

Dr. L.: I think this was wide open. Skate in the summer was in the open. Nautilus, of course, was not, but Skate I think was fully released to the press. In fact, it was released to the press so that we had a cover for the Nautilus, and I think the winter cruise was just a normal operation. Now, whether that was classified up until the time we got back, I don't remember, or whether it was released before then, I don't recall now.

Q: Anyway you didn't have to be incognito or anything like that?

Dr. L.: No, this was very straightforward, and everybody knew what we were doing, at least in Navy circles. Skate went by herself; she had no escort. It being winter, there was no one who could escort her, anyway. This was a very new experience now. There was nothing in our background -- any other experiences other than my work on ships in winter, which were icebreakers, no other submarine experience. This was a first again. To me, it was another new problem where we were trying to do submarining in the winter to see what the problems are. We were going there to see what the problems were.

Q: But you had one advantage in that you were going into the Atlantic?

Dr. L.: Yes, we were going into an area we knew very well, so we were not concerned with the area. What we were concerned with now is submarine versus the ice cover, and a new kind of ice cover, and what is it like in winter. We just had no experience.

Q: You had never been above the ice, actually, had you? From the submarine up to this point?

Dr. L.: In the winter?

Q: Yes.

Dr. L.: No. No activity any time on a submarine in winter. All of it had been in icebreakers, on the ice in the icebreakers, a lot of that activity in the Bering Sea, but no wintertime submarining.

So we went in and under the ice and I think the first thing that impressed immediately was that there was not any open water.

Q: Before you go on, I think it would be interesting, and you may have forgotten, the description that Commander Calvert makes of you. He describes you as learned, slight, soft-spoken, and unobtrusive, whose manners blended well with the atmosphere of the submarine. It was not long before his quiet self-assurance and keen mind gained the rapt and respectful attention. How do you feel about those descriptive terms?

Dr. L.: Well, that's nice! I'm not one the judge. I feel that I always have had good rapport with the people on board, the submarine forces, because every ship is a different personality. Long ago I learned that every ship has its own personality which is a mixture of all of its officers, particularly its commanding officer, and you learn how to work with that personality, because one comes with an expertise or whatever it is of your own knowledge and you need to work it in to whatever that personality is on the particular ship.

Q: Have you ever had any problems with any of the personalities of any of the officers and men on the various trips you've taken, all of which have been under some kind of tension?

Dr. L.: They've all been very different, but that's nice. I mean

All the people are different. I've had some very difficult experiences and difficult people to work with, but not on the submarines.

Q: Not once you were under way?

Dr. L.: Not on the submarines. These have been on shore establishments. Maybe it was well because my first contact with naval officers in my whole life was through the commanding officer at the Radio and Sound Laboratory when I came to San Diego, and he was always called one of the most difficult people to work with that ever came down the line.

Q: Was that Bennett?

Dr. L.: Oh, no, this was Wilbur J. Ruble, who had a reputation of being a real difficult person to work with, and he was very difficult at the Laboratory, particularly after the Division of War Research was established there, and a sort of conflict grew up between his command and the director of the Division of War Research. I entered the Navy under this difficulty, and learned how to live with it. And I think it always did me in good stead for the rest of my time, having learned how to work with him along the lines that I felt needed to be done.

Q: You were a very young man, too!

Dr. L.: Right, but once learning that, and learning a great deal from Leo Delsassor, who was in uniform, and I was out of uniform, the two of us working together to gain what we needed to under this particular commanding officer was a real experience; but it paid off because I learned that if you get acquainted with different personalities, and work with them and know how they look at things as men in uniform, and how we look at things as men in science, working together it is possible to get a great deal accomplished.

Q: But you also have the personality and you could do that.

Dr. L.: Right. If you don't have it you're not going to work in such a system as this. And if you do you're going to get ahead and get a great deal accomplished. But if you don't, why, you're going to be in continual trouble, and you just don't make use of the tools available, which are the military ships and military men.

Q: No matter how smart you are if you can't put it into effect —

Dr. L.: You're going to be ineffective in this whole setup, and that's a very important part of working with the fleet operators. That's part of the total system. You can't do your science and your beautiful engineering and development if you don't bring into your system the people who are going to use it, the operators and officers. If they're not brought in there and the whole supply system that keeps the thing put together, it doesn't matter how good your engineering is, it's just not going to pay off. That's part of the total engineering, but it's often forgotten. Today, it's one of the things that's again and again forgotten, and you get into more and more troubles with these more sophisticated weapons and vehicles because that side of it is forgotten. The whole training and the fact that a man, either enlisted or an officer, has to use it, and you've got to bring him into your system as part of it.

Q: I thought it was interesting and it's somewhat along the same lines, that Commander Calvert said - he didn't indicate that you actually held classes, but that you would talk to the men on board and almost teach them about ice and the Arctic. Do you have any comments on that?

Dr. L.: Well, we did quite a bit of that. Again, it was all new to us - new to them, new to me - this wintertime situation, and we did have considerable discussion like a seminar or lecture where we were talking - what do we know, what are we finding out, how is it fitting together, what doesn't fit - this kind of thing of our knowledge of the ice cover and what we were experiencing right there. Because we did some redesigning and rebuilding of the equipment underneath to meet the situations that were arising, and this was, I think, the 1959 cruise as well as the Sargo's cruise in 1960, the ultimate of a situation where the engineer-scientists and the operators were working together. And we were doing the experiments and the design and everything right there, right on the scene, and that was the only way to solve the problem.

Q: I was going to cover that more in detail when we get to some of the crises that arose ---

Dr. L.: Possibly. Now, no crises arose with the Skate. Oh, we bumped our head a few times, trying to break through ice that we were measuring wrong, and I had gone with the idea that at least I would see the crack of open water somewhere to do the calibration of the equipment, because on the way up we had to have a flat, open sea some time in order to calibrate this profiling equipment to get what is the sea surface. Well, if you never see an open, flat sea, you just don't calibrate. You can't calibrate in storm waves because the waves are moving back and forth plus or minus 10 feet and there's no way of knowing where the sea's surface is. So we expected to at least get under the ice cover, and sooner or later we'd see a crack where there'd be open water between the crack and the ice. But we never saw this, so we had to find out another way to calibrate our equipment, and the only way to do that was to actually go up and bump the ice with the sail, and then change the settings on the equipment for what the pressure gauge said the pressure of the water was, and where we thought we were in depth and calculate the position of free water surface. And the next time, try it again and see whether the equipment indicated correctly when we touched the ice with the sail. We did a number of tries just to get the equipment calibrated to where we estimated the open-sea surface to be. Once that was done, from then on we could measure with fair accuracy the thickness of the ice at whatever depth we were cruising, and the ship was able then to hit the ice with the sail and break through. (That photograph you see there is one of those cases when the submarine came right through.)

These were the first experiments where we actually made these stationary ascents, vertically upward at controlled speeds, struck the ice and broke through with the sail, and that has become our technique for all wintertime surfacings, all surfacings where there is no open water and one has to break through the thin ice to get to the surface.

Q: Did you never see any open water?

Dr. L.: Never, on that particular cruise. A couple of times we were surfaced and there were sort of weak little ponds off to the side, but any surfacings we did in the winter of 1959 were breaking through ice of maybe two or three inches, six inches, up to about thirty-six inches.

Q: And you were able to break through ice of that thickness?

Dr. L.: In each case, yes. So that cruise, over-all, was very successful because it gave us a technique and that removed then any restrictions on us, that we could move anywhere in the Arctic Ocean any time of the year so long as we could find these thin spots, and the information we gathered by running around over many, many miles we would judge how often we would be able to get thin spots. We'd find them every few miles so we were able to surface under such conditions, if need be. Of course, we had no reason to surface, other than to get up either to send out a message or to read the stars, or just look around.

Lyon # 3 - 196

Interview No. 3 with Dr. Waldo K. Lyon

Place: His home in San Diego

Date: 6 March 1971

Subject: Biography

By: Etta-Belle Kitchin

Q: You were saying that there actually wasn't any need to surface unless you wanted to send a message, but I was thinking that it might be comfortable to know where it was possible to surface in case you met an emergency.

Dr. L.: That question always stands that we must always be prepared for emergency surfacings, and communications are an important part, particularly if we start looking ahead to military operations where it is necessary to communicate, and we must have something through the surface in order to send a message, as well as there might be need for either aircraft surveillance or other tasks which a submarine might be required to do. Wintertime was a new study, working out something we had not considered prior to this cruise, although we had it in the back of our minds, or had been thinking of what would be the problem, and had given consideration during the period from 1956 up until this time. The physicists in my group had been concerned with the properties of sea ice, particularly the strength of it as a material, and had been doing work at the Cape Prince of Wales Field Station on seeing what was its strength and what would be required to break it. So I did have the information available from these experiments which had been done off Cape Prince of Wales, and was necessary for these tests that we did on <u>Skate</u>. Data that had been taken both in the Lab and at Cape Prince of Wales were with me when I was on <u>Skate</u>, because we needed the data to judge with what speed a submarine should rise to strike the ice to break. We had to have some feel for what the strength of the stuff is that we're hitting to judge what momentum to have on the submarine, and what speed it should have to strike and still not damage the submarine, but still get through and break through.

Q: Were you able then to evaluate what upward speed you had to have to break a certain thickness of ice? Is that what you're saying?

Dr. L.: Well, the first time we did this was a critical experiment because, having not done it, the question that I faced was what speed do I recommend to the commanding officer to rise to strike the ice that will not damage the ship, but will break through. And this was pretty much a guess. I mean, it's guessing with what data we had taken from the Laboratory data on the strength of the ice, how strong it is. We knew how thick it was by measurements from the ehco-sounders looking up, and we had had discussions with the engineers in the Bureau of Ships who knew the ship's architecture, the ship's construction, and gave me what they thought was the maximum pressure that the ship should exert by striking with its sail that would be within the strength of the ship. So between those numbers, why, then, it was just coming up with the best scientific guess one could make as to what the speeds should be. We had to make a number of assumptions, and then much of it was just, I must admit, intuitive, it just seemed right.

Something like the sense you have if you're driving your car and you have to strike something, and you have a feel for how strong your car is, and you can run into a plaster wall or fence or something that has material strength in it, you can get a judgment of how and of what speed you can run into that thing, and perhaps it would give you some superficial damage, but knock it down. It's the same kind of intuitive sense.

We could do some calculation, but there's a lot of numbers missing in the calculation, so you do calculations that give you some feeling that your intuition is about right. It's kind of a combination.

Q: Because the same depth of ice might have different characteristics of breakability?

DR. L.: No, the strength of ice is quite similar wherever one goes, and the thickness gives you the total strength that it has.

Q: I mean twelve inches of ice here, in one part of the Arctic, would be as easy or as difficult to break as twelve inches, say —

Dr. L.: Not necessarily. We wouldn't be concerned too much with that point at this time. Really, just what is the kind, what is its strength, or make a best guess at it, or, if it's real thick, what sort of strength does it have. What speed can I hit it with and be sure I don't damage my ship.

Q: At the first attempt to surface, there was some damage to the antenna, was there not? To the radio antenna?

Dr. L.: Oh, I think that's very likely, because the radio antenna is a small thing extended from the sail, and we recognized that we might do damage to protuberances sticking out, but our main concern was with the top of the sail itself.

Q: I seem to remember a picture of a lieutenant being lashed to this antenna to repair it.

Dr. L.: Yes, he tried to repair it.

Q: It wouldn't retract, I think.

Dr. L.: Yes, the lieutenant at that time made it so that it supposedly would retract. They didn't want it to get damaged, but in the cold many things happen that weren't anticipated by oil freezing and things getting tight and windows frosting up on the periscope, and things of this sort - all these little things which were learned from the wintertime experience, because this was the first time where a submarine comes from a temperature of water that's just at freezing to temperatures which are $25°$ or $30°$ below zero on the Fahrenheit scale, so a $60°$ change from the time you come out of the water and coming into the air. That means very quick freezing of seawater films. Periscopes and all kinds of things that have come up wet are susceptible. We learned all kinds of things that required handling in such a situation which we had not experienced before. In summertime the water and the air temperature were almost the same.

Q: I see, but in the wintertime they were far different?

Dr. L.: In the wintertime, yes, there's great temperature change.

Q: Did you observe the ceremony for Sir Hubert Wilkins?

Lyon # 3 - 200

Dr. L.: I didn't take part in it. I observed it from the ship. The ship's company took part in that ceremony, and I just watched it from aboard ship. I had talked with Sir Hubert Wilkins for the last time that fall at a meeting. In the fall of 1958 he was at a meeting at the Air Force Cambridge Labs, and I remember talking to him at that time and he died that December, and we went on the cruise that March during which his ashes were scattered in the Arctic.

Q: Was that a dangerous thing to accomplish?

Dr. L.: Oh, no. The submarine was surfaced when this was carried out. The ceremony was cold and windy. It was a proper and fitting tribute to Sir Hubert Wilkins.

Q: Did the *Skate* carry frogmen on this cruise?

Dr. L.: Yes, it did, I think. My memory gets all these ships mixed up, but I believe they did. It seems to me Dave Boyd, the engineer, took school and training and he and a couple of others; and they did have scuba divers on board. It seems to me they did. That was the first time, I guess, someone did it in winter. The trick was then to get out of the water and back into the ship quickly before you froze into a solid sheet of ice in the cold temperature.

Q: How long could they stay in this —

Dr. L.: Well, when they are in the water, the water isn't much different than any other time of the year. But it's the air temperature one has to watch. From the water and into the submarine is okay, but don't be caught outside in $30°$ below zero temperature too long. That's when one is all wet and freezes pretty quickly.

Lyon # 3 - 201

So it was a matter of getting out of the water, up the side of the hull, and down the after engineroom hatch into the warm ship again.

Q: These were ship's crew who had taken a special training?

Dr. L.: Dave Boyd was the engineer officer, and I think he had a couple of enlisted men - I can't remember - who were scuba divers and tried it out in the wintertime. This was not the first time, because we had had such diving operations off icebreakers before, but not with the submarine forces.

Q: Was there any situation involving the submarine itself - I recall there was a leak in the circulating pump. Do you recall any problems with that?

Dr. L.: On each cruise there were certain engineering problems which would arise. Particularly on the Skate class there were problems with the sea-water circulating pump that always seemed to arise. On Skate this occurred, and to make the proper repairs it was necessary to be on the surface for a considerable period of time, while the pump was broken down and resealed, rebuilt, and put back in operating condition. And so, this being in the wintertime, it was a new experience, maybe, to most of us. Certainly a new experience for the submariner in the wintertime of being surfaced in ice cover in which there's a great deal more action, and the fact that there's no open water - one isn't sitting in an open-water lake, as in summer. In winter the submarine was surfaced during these repairs on a frozen-over polynya, and the ice did move and the ice did scrape around the hull, and did make lots of noise, and this was disconcerting to eveyone on board, but by now was familiar to me because of the past experience of being towed around in the ice, and it's a very similar noise. So all that was required was watching the movement of the ice, seeing whether heavy ridges were moving in against the ship. The ship was not in danger so long as it remained in the thin ice, and that ice could move about and the motion would not damage the ship, but it if should start to close up, then big heavy ridges started to move great distances in towards the ship, then it could have been in danger. But it's possible to judge how much danger by how far away these ridges are and just simply continue to plot how much they're moving per hour. In this case there was lots of noise - thin ice moving around the hull, which is a screaming, screeching noise, particularly when it's so cold. It just screams, a piercing screaming type of thing on the hull. But, again, it just makes your nerves ragged, but it doesn't - if you go and look at it you find that there's no fear of being in danger, but when you're down inside and hear it it frays your nerves.

Q: Were you able to reassure the crew members as to the danger or otherwise?

Dr. L.: Right, and by going and looking, and of course, while surfaced, there's always an officer of the deck in the sail watching. So if one felt that the noise got too high or got worried about it, why all he had to do was go look and assure himself that really nothing had moved. It was just the ice screaming around on the hull. But these are experiences one gets by being there, and that's the only thing to do - to actually see it.

Q: But in each case your responsibility was to advise the commanding officer as to danger or lack of danger and what he could or could not do with his ship?

Dr. L.: And depending upon long experience, and having seen it before, and what to expect, and what pressures could be developed by the ice sheet, and explaining what these are, and what's needed. And over the years what we fulfilled is really the continuity of having the past experience, and we have each time on a cruise new people who have not the experience, so all we do is explain what previous experiences have been, and suggest what was done, and what should be done in this particular case.

Q: Of course, it was Commander Calvert's first trip?

Dr. L.: He'd been there in the summertime. Of course, it was the first trip of a submarine in wintertime, but I had had all the background of icebreakers in ice --

Q: He had taken the Skate up in the summer, of course.

Dr. L.: Yes, and he was an outstanding commander, and the two of us together on board provided a fortuitous opportunity to work out these new problems that were faced here between the top operator and I as a scientist from the past experiences. So, the combination is again what produced the top results in a situation.

Q: Were you again off and on two hours at a time and no sleep?

Dr. L.: Oh, that's right. On this one, we had a regular watch period between Walter Schatzberg and myself, four hours on, four that cruise, as I recall, I was doing the catnap process which I always use - just sleeping when I needed to.

Q: Did the floodlights and the TV give you any assistance?

Dr. L.: They were helpful because they gave us particularly some look for the first time, when we first touched the ice with the sail, we could actually see it with the TV camera, because the TV camera could look, but the periscope could not see anything because periscopes had to be retracted. The TV camera was down on the deck, so we could watch the sail touch the ice, and when you're doing it for the first time it was really helpful to see what was going on. You could see the cracks develop in the ice and could tell when we touched and see the airbubbles and whatever else was taking place. We also used it to see some of the fish that were around. That was just of interest, nothing new we were using, but it gave a feel of something of roughly what the environment looked likewhich we couldn't have had otherwise.

The lights did not help us as far as the periscope was concerned. Calvert learned that he could do a lot with his periscope, but the natural light coming through the ice of itself was quite sufficient. The moonlight, or what we would call the early dawn light of an Arctic day, even though it was 24 hours, was most useful in looking at the ice through the periscope and that became a part of the technique of surfacing, this visual watching with the periscope before one made the vertical ascent against the ice.

When the Skate cruise was completed, from this winter trip we had reached a point where now we could take a submarine into the Arctic Ocean through the Atlantic, summer or winter, and feel free to operate aywhere in the deep Arctic Ocean. We recognized now that we had that capability but we must stay away from areas where there were icebergs, because still we did not have a scanning sonar system that told us anything of the ice at our depth. We must stay away from shallow water, but we could operate in any season either in the dark or the light of the summer, and we could surface through the thin spots and find them.

So, now we faced the next step in developing Arctic submarines — to go into the shallow water.

Q: Which would have been on a Pacific approach?

Dr. L.: Right. That was recognized to be the next step, and to be able to handle icebergs, which meant Baffin Bay and certain parts around the islands off the U.S.S.R. where there are icebergs possible. But the big group of icebergs where they're thick is in Baffin Bay.

Q: No question that this trip certainly accomplished its mission?

Dr. L.: No, no question. We just set out to do it and did it, although maybe we didn't quite visualize what it was like before we got there, while we were there you get the visualization and corrections made to whatever little changes have to be done.

Q: I think Commander Calvert said you did surface eleven times and traveled 3,090 miles under the ice.

Dr. L.: Something like that. Each time, of course, on one of these cruises we'd go into different parts of the Arctic Ocean, so we'd get a whole new set of bathymetry and data on the ice cover and water conditions, so there'd be a new set of bottom profiles, bathymetry of an area, that hadn't been done before. Also, it was a real thrill, I think, because it was the first wintertime, an entirely different experience from all others which had always been summer. Just the darkness is different. You don't have the advantage of the sunlight to look at things, and when you're surfaced it's dark. The Skate cruise was late enough in March so that we did have quite a bit of light, in contrast to the cruise just completed, the Hammerhead, which was in complete darkness. It was early in November which was even closer to the December 22nd period. Everything was in darkness, and that does make a difference on attitudes and what people do when they never see the sunlight for a long period.

Q: Did you find personality problems on this trip because of so much darkness? On the Skate, I'm speaking of.

Dr. L.: On the Skate? Oh, I don't think so. Again, there was high interest. We never really have had any personality problems of any kind. They were very select people.

Q: We're going to pick up now at 1959 when the planning for the Sargo and its voyage commenced. Would you be kind enough to proceed to that topic?

Dr. L.: This would be in the fall of 1959, following the Skate earlier that spring. In the fall of 1959 we began planning for the shallow-water experiment in the Pacific, which was the crucial test for Arctic submarines — if they could go through the entrance to the Chukchi and Bering Seas in shallow water, particularly during the winter when it was ice-covered. THis depended on properly designed sonar equipment because when we get into such shallow water we must have sonar equipment that will tell where the ice ridges are, how deeply they project, so that we can avoid them, the depth of the water being about 150 feet in the whole of the Bering Sea, through the Bering Strait, and the Chukchi Sea. Ice ridges can easily project to 90 feet or more, so it means that the submarine must twist and turn to avoid ridges in order to get through, which is an entirely different situation from entering from the Atlantic Ocean, which was all the work involved with the <u>Nautilus</u> and the <u>Skate</u>, where there's great depth of water, and you could stay well below the ice cover, and never had to avoid ice ridges.

Q: All you had to do was go deep enough?

Dr. L.: Yes, you just went deep enough. And in the entrances to the Atlantic, of course, we did not have sonar equipment that would give us this avoidance - guidance to avoid ice ridges, so we did go <u>deep</u> enough to stay away at a 350-foot depth, a depth that kept us well below the ice. Entering from the Pacific, we must stay 25 or 30 feet off the bottom. The bottom is very flat, and we can run that close to it, but even so we can't slip under 90-foot ridges. There just isn't enough room. So we have to avoid.

During the year of 1959 Art Rashon and his group on high-revolution sonar equipment at the Naval Electronics Laboratory spent their time developing and building the particular sonar equipment needed for the next cruise, which would be the <u>Sargo</u>. So by the time fall came around in 1959 we had this piece of equipment built and about ready to install, and it was installed on the <u>Sargo</u> in late 1959, in preparation for a cruise in early 1960.

Q: How did it differ from the sonar that you had before?

Dr. L.: It was somewhat similar to the sonar dating way back to World War II, called QLA, the mine-avoidance sonar. A forward-looking, very-narrow-beam sonar system that scanned back and forth, with a very narrow horizontal beam so that you could see what was at your own depth. The sonar looked directly ahead and would sweep back and forth so that we could discriminate what was projecting down into our depth and watch such targets ahead of us that were at our depth and as we approached them tell how deeply they projected, and then avoid those at the depth of the operating vessel.

Q: How large an arc did it have?

DR. L.: It swept from $90°$ to port around about $90°$ to starboard.

Q: Oh, it had $180°$!

Dr. L.: It had $180°$ scan, or you could narrow this down to looking at one particular sector, if you wanted to, or narrow it down so that you only looked at $45°$, say, to starboard, so there was a $90°$ sweep in front, depending on what the situation was that one got into, and twist and turn to avoid pieces of ice ahead. All this was presented on a screen just like a radar system. It showed ice targets in front so we could make decisions as to which way to turn to avoid ice that was extending down.

Q: Where was the screen located in the Sargo?

Dr. L.: In the control room, to one side, right where the commanding officer could watch the screen and give the commands for turning the ship. So that this was a special piece of equipment put on borad, plus the all-important equipment, plus again sonar echo-sounders for profiling the ice cover. These two sets were the pretty essential parts, the one that profiled the ice that we passed under, and then this scanning sonar system that looked ahead. That and the echo-sounder looking down to tell us how far above the bottom we were, because we were working in this very tight situation. We were just 25 feet or so off the bottom, and knowing how far the ice was above us, so that we could check what we saw ahead against what we passed under when we got to it. We could continually check whether what we were seeing ahead of us was agreeing with what we saw when we went under it. This checking is essential at all times. We had good, precise knowledge of what we were going through, knowing what our sonar systems were giving us.

Q: Could the commanding officer read those, or did he have to have someone along?

Dr. L.: No. This, of course, was all new to all of us, except maybe Art Roshon and myself, who had been working with the diesel-submarines years ago in such a situation in <u>Redfish</u> or <u>Boarfish</u> or <u>Carp</u> through this same set of waters in the summertime in similar situations where we had avoided the ice with the diesel battery boats using the older scanning sonar. But the difference was, at that time we were running at perhaps two knots, very slow, now we were running at seven to ten knots in even a tighter situation with heavier ice than we had faced in the summer.

It was our previous experience combined with the Commanding officer and other senior officers in setting up the procedure for avoidance, interpreting the screens, making the decisions. The way we worked it was that we split up into three teams. Commander Nicholson, the commanding officer, and I took one team, and the executive officer and Art Roshon (the executive officer was Bill Yates), and then a third team was another engineer from NEL and one of the other senior officers — I think it was Ned Deitrich, but I'm not too sure now. In that way we had three separate teams, and we could split up the 24 hours: four on, eight off, type of watch, because it turned into a rather continuous nervous strain to watch. Four hours was quite long enough to hold such a watch with the decisions and course change and decisions to avoid the ice covers.

Q: A constant concentration! Couldn't relax for a moment, I would expect.

Dr. L.: Constant concentration, because we were passing or avoiding one ridge, and seeing more ridges coming up, and making decisions as to how to avoid those. So there was continual decision-making — choice of speed, choice of turns, choice of direction.

Q: Had the naval officers taken courses in the use of this equipment before the cruise started?

Dr. L.: No. We went through a test off Hawaii. The <u>Sargo</u> was a Hawaii-based boat. We did a couple of weeks of trials and tests off of Hawaii to simulate - using another submarine. It would act as a target and we avoided it and passed under it and checked out and that kind of thing. And then when we did get up into the Bering Sea, we had a partner, and the partner was the icebreaker, <u>Staten Island</u>, I believe - a Navy icebreaker to work with us. For the first two days we stayed near the edge of the ice where we still had some fairly deep water, maybe 300 feet, and we made many trials approaching the ice cover and moving to avoid ridges before we actually went into the shallow section. So we did have some trials and tests, before we got into the 150-foot water. It was not something we just suddenly got into with no trial. We were in deeper water which gradually became shallower and shallower. However we had to cross 950 miles or 1,000 miles of shallow water before we'd reach the Arctic Ocean deep water. Getting into shallow water, then, these watches became all-important, and four hours was quite long enough to handle a watch.

Q: Were you always telling the commanding officer what to do? You said there were three of you, was it a joint decision?

Dr. L.: A joint decision made - not really joint because, of course, the ship's officer was the decision-maker. The engineer watching with him was simply a sort of adviser, also watching to see whether he disagreed in any case with the interpretation that the officer was making of what he saw on the screen. We also kept an engineer there in case something happened with the particular equipment, because everything depended on that equipment at that point, so it was wise to have an engineer right there in case it didn't look right or the interpretation didn't seem right. And we'd help then in deciding what to do, whether to stop or what move to make. It also helped in memory, because one had to keep remembering all the ridges that one happened to see, so that it helped to have somebody else. Two people working together, just checking back and forth. We have just passed a ridge a few yards, or is there something to the left - trying to recall and keep in mind all the situations that were appearing.

Q: How long ahead would the sonar show you? How far?

Dr. L.: Probably 1,500 yards.

Q: That's not very far!

Dr. L.: No. We could keep looking ahead, and then bring the range in close to see what was near, and then look out ahead again. We were continually interpreting the situation. Of course, for many miles it might be very smooth, and we did not have any problems, and then we would get into a batch of ridges and turn and twist. At that point one person checking with the other was helpful. At the same time, the diving officer had the problem of avoiding any changes in the bottom, because we were moving through an area that had not been surveyed very carefully. Conventional ships don't much mind whether the bottom changes about 10 feet or 15 feet if one is on the surface, but when we are running 25 feet off the bottom, a 15-foot mound "shakes" anyone if suddenly come upon. So, the diving officer was on continual alert to watch for change in depth above the bottom, or change in bottom profile. Bottom in the Bering and Chukchi is flat, but in a couple of spots in the Bering Strait we did find these little hills of 10 to 15 feet, and they would "shake up" the diving officer. When he saw the bottom coming up, he would have to in a sense jump the boat up a little bit by blowing a bubble in so as to quickly come up a little bit, not knowing whether it was going to go higher, and as he starts to see the depth decrease he's not sure whether he's going to go to 15 feet above the bottom, or try 25 feet from the bottom. He had to play that game of watching the bottom, while the commanding officer was watching the ice, and had to be sure that he avoided ice ridges.

Q: As you look back on it, doesn't it almost seem incredible that it worked so well?

Dr. L.: Perhaps. *Sargo* was the outstanding ship of all the cruises, I think, without question. It was one of those cases where we had a superior commanding officer — Commander Nicholson had been the executive officer on the *Skate* in 1958, and a very outstanding one both for his engineering knowledge and his leadership. Then we had a group of men and officer that, as a whole, were outstanding. It showed up on this particular cruise. Maybe it was because of the tightness of the cruise that these people seemed greater, or maybe a whole lot of them were outstanding irrespective of the fact that they were on their highest mettle to get through this cruise. A combination made the most difficult come out a high success without any question.

The whole entrance from the Bering Sea into the Chukchi went without any effort, unusual stress or strain, and proceeded right according to the way it should. We surfaced a number of times without any difficulty through the ice cover. The equipment worked well, plus we had outstanding engineers with us, too. Art Roshon, the designer and builder of it, was there with us, which later proved extremely important, and he had one of his top assistant engineers with him. And I was handling the upward-looking profiling equipment, and we had two other people, Walt Wittman from the Oceanographic Office and also Art Molloy. Walt Wittman kept the story of the ice cover and oceanography, and Art Molloy the bathymetry. We had good engineers assigned to this cruise as well, that were old-timers with lots of experience.

Q: Not to mention yourself!

Dr. L.: Art Roshon and I, of course, knew this area from previous work, and that's important. It was not new. We knew what to expect.

Sargo got into deep water in the Chukchi Sea, and we did this time go by way of the valley that Harald Sverdrup had mentioned to me, near Harald Island. He said that was the easiest way to get across the Chukchi, and this was the firt time we tried it, and it did prove to be the case. We found a sea valley that gave us deeper water soon after we went through the Bering Strait.

Q: Is that to the west?

Dr. L.: That's to the west. One goes west from the U.S.S.R.-U.S.A. convention line. We turned west to go over to Harold Island, a small island, and right near it is a sea valley so one gets into deep water much quicker than if one stayed to the east and went past Point Barrow. It was an advantage in wintertime for a submarine in this kind of situation to try to get in deep water obviously as soon as possible. But then, when we did get into the deep Chukchi, what we had happen was this particular piece of scanning sonar equipment failed. It had a scanning motor in it, and the pressure-equalizing system which at that point either froze up or something happened and it failed, so we flooded the motor, and that meant we lost the scanning system which got us through the shallow water.

Q: But you were through the shallow water by that time?

Dr. L.: Yes, we were completely through it. It was when we went down deep that the compensating system put pressure on this motor and it failed. Something happened, and it didn't compensate for the pressure and, instead, the water ran into the case and flooded the motor, which meant it was shorted. I remember they tried to fix that. In fact, the ship spent 24 hours or 48 hours on the surface with fellows working in the sail in the bitter cold - 30° or 35° below zero. We'd thrown hatches open and, in fact, we froze buckets of water in the control room. It was cold going up and down the hatch, and the poor fellows trying to work in the ship's sail to get this training motor out and try to get it working again.

Q: You removed it, you say?

Dr. L.: We brought it down, took it all apart, and baked out the windings - did every possible thing to try to get it working again, but were not successful. So for the next two to three weeks while cruising around in the deep Arctic, we didn't have the scanning system, but we didn't need it. But all this time we were trying to figure - how do we get back out without it.

Q: Because were you going to go back the same way eventually?

Dr. L.: We were scheduled to return to the Pacific, so we had the decision to make - if we could not work our way back out through the Pacific, then we had to go through the Atlantic, but this obviously we did not want to do, that would be admitting defeat. The whole purpose of our cruise was working in shallow water. And while on this point, maybe jumping ahead a little bit, it was Art Roshon who came up with the very ingenious scheme of using two sonar systems on board, which was a very complicated engineering affair, but there was a standard equipment on Sargo, a listening array which extended around the bow of the ship and was for detection of other targets. So he could make a combination of that listening array with the parts and pieces that were still working on his scanning sonar projection system, so he was projecting with his scanning sonar system - projecting the beam - and then he was getting the echoes back on this other piece of equipment, this listening system. In processing he got a presentation on the scope which did give some picture of the ice targets ahead of us.

So this was all done on board between Art Roshon and the sonar men on board, wiring and thinking up ways to do it. So we did have a put-together system here —

Q: Jury-rigged?

Dr. L.: Jury-rigged, I guess, is the proper term — to get us out through this shallow water. And so we then proceeded to go out again to the Pacific by using this jury-rigged system.

Q: How far did you go east during this time? I was under the impression that you went into the McClure Strait?

Dr. L.: Right. While in the deep part we went from the west of the convention line, up to the pole, zigzaging to get the bathymetry north of the Chukchi Sea, to the pole, and surfaced there in the dark of the night. We were at the pole for a number of hours, then came south towards Nansen Sound in the Canadian Archipelago, and then into McClure Strait for a distance to get a few bathymetry lines on the entry to McClure. This was knowing that the Sea Dragon cruise was to come up later that spring - it was already scheduled, and we were in the process of planning for it while on this Sargo cruise. So this would give us an entrance line from McClure Strait because that's where the Sea Dragon was to come through later in the year. Then out of McClure and down towards the Alaskan coast, where the ice island T-3 was drifting again, and we approached it, and did some test runs with the sonar equipment which was mounted on the drifting ice station, and operated by the New London Underwater Sound Laboratory.

Then, after those tests, proceeded west towards Point Barrow and then began the exit, again through shallow water.

I think all of that deep-water operating was very straightforward, no particular situations or unusual things ~~that~~ occurred.

Q: Did you go back through the deep valley?

Dr. L.: No. This time we were coming from the Beaufort Sea, so we were coming towards the Barrow sea valley, off Point Barrow, whereas the Sverdrup sea valley was clear to the west on the other side of the Chukchi Sea.

Q: So you went one way and came back the other?

Dr. L.: Coming from the east side of the Chukchi Sea and now we were approaching again the shallow water problem of 150 feet of water, sometimes a little less, to get out across the Chukchi Sea down to the Bering Strait again. And now, keep in mind, we had this jury-rigged equipment which we weren't too sure just how it operated —

Q: If it would?

Dr. L.: Well, we tried it out, of course, under the ridges and it appeared to operate, but we didn't know all its characteristics, and that's what we soon found out because I think we had run for a number of hours – just how long I do not recall – in shallow water and seemed to be proceeding all right, but on, I think it was probably the 2000-watch, if my memory is correct, when Nicholson and I took over the command watch, it was somewhere after that that we slammed into a pressure ridge – not head-on, but a glancing blow which drove the ship down against the bottom, which was, of course, only 20 or 25 feet away.

Q: But you actually hit the bottom?

Dr. L.: Yes, and the sail struck the ridge on the side, and striking that ridge just pushed it right to the bottom. And, of course, that's quite a sensation when you have a collision with something! The ship operated extremely well in such an emergency. The alarm sounded, and everybody went through all their actions required, closing key valves and compartments, and operating everything according to a collision. We just stopped, and took note then of just what had happened, but after some time and no reports of any damage on board, we proceeded. But we had to understand, then, why did we hit when it appeared according to our sonar screen that we shouldn't have hit it. And what Art Roshon and the experts on the sonar scanning system finally worked out by looking at the various data on the sonar equipments that we were using -- they realized that the particular array of hydrophones that we were observing the echoes on had different response patterns than the equipment that was originally designed for our scanning system. What we had were what was called "side lobes" which means that you not only have the correct pattern looking straight ahead, but there's a side pattern, and the equipment can receive signals from the side of the main beam, which, if one has a very big target to the side, can respond from the side and look as though it's ahead. So there were problems on interpretation that we hadn't recognized until we banged into one. And this was particularly true when we were looking on very short-range scales, and these targets which were coming out of side patterns to give us false perspectives.

Apparently this is what happened. Nicholson and I shifted to short range and it looked as though there was a heavy target ahead of us, but it was probably to the side of us, and we made a turn too soon to avoid something that really wasn't there, and in turning, turned into the other one which was there and we thought had really passed us. Then we realized that we could not use this equipment at very short ranges. We always had to keep the range well out where these side lobe patterns on the equipment wouldn't disturb us. From then on we had no difficulty, and it never occurred again that we had any collision or misinterpretation of the patterns. We always had to be watching what was ahead of us maybe 400 yards or greater. This was a bigger strain on our memory then, because it meant that we couldn't look at anything inside of probably 400 yards, so once we saw a ridge coming in from 1,500 yards, perhaps tracking it down to 400 yards, then mentally we had to keep it in mind as we approached that particular ridge until we were sure that we were past it.

Q: Not only it was there, but its depth?

Dr. L.: Yes, if we saw it all the way into 400 yard range we felt that it was probably dangerous and would reach into our depth and we should avoid it. So anything inside 400 yards was really in our memory only. We just didn't look at it with this equipment because we could probably have false interpretations. So it meant that one kept watch of what was inside 400 yards and then watched what was ahead from the 400 yards or so out greater, and one had to make decisions remembering what's inside of 400 yards, and then deciding what he was going to do with what's coming up beyond the 400 yards. I think we both agreed that fortunately we never had two ridges in our memory and one coming up, otherwise we might not have been able to do it. But we could keep track of one in our memory and one coming up on the screen. If one ever had to try to keep two situations in his mind and was seeing one up ahead, he might pop a mental gasket or something.

Q: I think it's incredible that you did it anyway.

Dr. L.: Anyway, everybody turned a hand in the situation, and we were okay for the rest of the time because we had no more difficulties in coming out through the Chukchi and Bering Seas.

Q: How many days did that last?

Dr. L.: I suppose some ten days.

Q: That's 24 hours a day?

DR. L.: You're right. And we surfaced a number of times in coming out, but it's 900 miles or more, so it must have been certainly over a week.

Q: How did the personnel react to the impact?

Dr. L.: Of course, there's an immediate shock. After all, you don't run into thing every day, but the ship was well disciplined and made a recovery as soon as no report of internal damage, why, everybody proceeded and calmed down. There was no reaction, just sort of an initial nervous shock.

Q: Did Commander Nicholson attempt to explain to everyone aboard what had happened?

Dr. L.: Right. After we understood what had happened, then it was explained to everybody. The trouble was not understanding what the limitations were on this jury rig - why we had no further difficulty.

Q: It seems to me that people understand there's much less phasibility of hysteria than if they're kept in the dark and they don't know what's going on.

Dr. L.: Oh, right. This happened, of course, on the way back and when everyone had had a lot of experience, had surfaced, had looked at the ice, been in and out of the control room and knew how the ship was operated. As I say, this ship had an outstanding group of people, so that that was all taken in full stride, but it was a very long cruise, the longest up to that time. Actually days spent under ice and in the darkness in shallow water, so all of us suffered possible stress.

Q: Do people react differently when there's complete darkness?

Dr. L.: You can't be sure unless you took the same - those of us who'd been through both the darkness is to be expected, but it makes it more difficult to work. Of course, when you're down in the submarine the darkness doesn't make any difference, but it's when you surface and want to do things out on the ice cover, the darkness is troublesome then. You have to watch your footing, watch what you're doing very much more carefully than when you can see. The cold and the darkness together make it difficult to do things.

Q: The TV camera was on the Sargo, too, wasn't it?

Dr. L.: I don't think so. I don't recall actually using it -

Q: I was thinking in the dark it wouldn't be effective.

Dr. L.: No, it is not. I remember we tried lighting on the Sargo in the periscope and found that - that is, lights on the deck of the Sargo to try to help see the ice cover through the periscope, and found it was better to use whatever natural light we could get coming through the ice, rather than trying to illuminate it. Very similar problem to when you get in fog and try to use headlights and you find often that the headlights are directly into what you're trying to see and you get too much scatterback and can't see as well as if you lower the lights. It's a similar problem.

I thinktthat covers mainly the task of the Sargo. We learned how to go through shallow water with this scanning sonar system which did the job even though, of course, we had the difficulty, but that was just a mechanical problem which we solved.

Q: That was the crucial element, that particular piece of machinery?

Dr. L.: This is right and this was the purpose. Our purpose on that cruise was to see whether we could operate in shallow water. We learned the techniques and showed they were successful. We did do other things with communicating and found the usual problem of being surfaced and trying to communicate when there are no receiving stations nearby, just trying to break in on all the ship traffic in other parts of the world. This is just a plain old difficult problem when one is so far away from any receiving station. That's always been a problem and always will be when one is working without a nearby receiving station.

I think that should complete the Sargo.

Q: I'm sure you felt bad when the Sargo had its fire after it returned to Pearl Harbor!

Dr. L.: Oh, right, later that year there was that sad situation. Well, those things happen, then the technical procedures are corrected. That was an oxygen fire, and again the ship did an outstanding job of saving the ship, although one man gave his life to save the ship, the rest of the crew, in that particular fire, again showing the top performance of that particular group of men.

Well, Sargo ended and we almost immediately got into the Sea Dragon affair, because Sargo came back in March and Sea Dragon went in June. Anyway immediate preparation had to take place and again Sea Dragon had to have a special scanning sonar system because Sea Dragon was scheduled to go into iceberg country, the one remaining we had to see what we could do about. Sea Dragon was East Coast, at Portsmouth, so Art Rashon and his personnel were immediately involved in getting Sea Dragon lined up and all of its equipment on board. She was a new construction just out and this would be the first operation for Sea Dragon. And now we had the first commercially built scanning sonar system. The one on the Sargo was laboratory-built, now we had a commercially built boat type system on Sea Dragon. It was built by EDO Corporation.

So by the time that cruise left — and now I can't tell you the date —

Q: I have a date of August 1960. Does that seem correct?

Dr. L.: It could have left sometime in July. Yes, because I guess the actual operation part of it was during the month of August. It seemes to me we finally reached Nome on the 1st of September.

I'm not even sure of personnel now. The commanding officer was Commander George Steele, III (long Navy family). Then for the engineering staff, it seems to me we had Art Roshon along, I believe, and an engineer from EDO, and Art Molloy and Walt Wittmann again. I'm really depending on memory here. And we also took with us Commodore Robertson, RCN, who was the skipper of the Labrador back in the cruises of 1954 when we were doing icebreaker work. He was the Canadian attaché in Washington at this time, and a many-year operator, of course, in the Arctic, and keeping in mind we're going through Canadian waters. So we not only had him for — because it would be a U.S.-Canadian affair, plus his experience and being an old friend. This was a natural. He always wanted to go on the submarine cruises anyway, and this just fit together perfectly for having him go along. He had been on board Sargo briefly, because he was on the icebreaker earlier that year, but he had to stay on the icebreaker and couldn't stay on the Sargo. We had him on the Sargo for one day just to show him how the Sargo operated under the ice, then he had to return to the icebreaker across the ice by foot. We put him out of the hatch from the Sargo. Anyhow, he was on board Sea Dragon to take care of Canadian liaison and also for his knowledge of the Barrow Strait and Lancaster Sound where he had operated with the Labrador in 1954 and 1955.

The first part of the seagoing cruise, then, was the testing of the icebergs. We spent considerable time in Baffin Bay just trying out the sonar system against icebergs, to see whether the sonar system would present them properly, would detect them at good ranges, and if we could avoid icebergs, because icebergs extend very deep, much further than a submarine can dive - 1,400 to 1,500 or even greater depths. These are huge pieces of ice, of course, breaking off from ice caps. So an iceberg must be avoided, and this then was our first opportunity to try the scanning sonar system for going through Baffin Bay where great numbers of icebergs are located. We simply would look at them visually and go and check them out on the sonar to see if everything checked out as far as range and appearance, and if we could avoid icebergs in whatever sea we wished to cruise.

That was a straightforward demonstration, then, of being able to go at full speed through the area and avoid the icebergs. Having done that, then we turned into Lancaster Sound -

Q: I have a question. That had no relationship to going under the ice? You weren't under the ice?

Dr. L.: No, you're not under the ice, you're avoiding again, but in any area where icebergs are prevalant, which is primarily Baffin Bay, some of the East Caost of Greenland, if you approach it real close, is one continuing iceberg. Or, as I think we mentioned earlier, in some parts of the Kara and Laptev Seas there are some island with little ice caps which break off heavy ice, as well as along the northern coast of the U.S.S.R. where one can get into areas of calving of icebergs.

But you see in all of the work prior to this in the deep Arctic Ocean we always were on the premise that we would not see icebergs because we did not have the sonar equipment on our previous cruises to avoid icebergs. That's why we stayed out of Baffin Bay until this time when Sea Dragon was equipped to avoid icebergs and so we checked it out. Having demonstrated that, we really cleaned up all the remaining questions — shallow water, icebergs, breaking through the ice cover were all completed.

So, from then on, it was simply driving Sea Dragon through the Pacific and delivering her to the Pacific Fleet. Sea Dragon went through Lancaster Sound and Barrow Strait. We had to do a little bit of bathymetry work in there because a couple of islands at that time weren't too well located. We were looking for the best deep-water passage and that was found. From there on through Viscount Melville Sound, Barrow Strait, that had all been worked out pretty well by the icebreakers. So that cruise from that point of Barrow Strait west was very straightforward, out into the Arctic Ocean, through McClure Strait, up to the pole, then we began surveying. This was summertime now — no problem in surfacing, open-water whenever needed, no breaking through ice cover. And Sea Dragon came south again to drifting ice station T-3, which was somewhere near Point Barrow by this time. Did some sonar tests with the sonar equipment on the Ice Station, then out through the Bering Sea.

This was not a shallow-water transit now because it was open water. In summertime there's no problem of ice cover at all – just cruised on the surface south through the Chukchi and Bering Seas, and went into Nome for a celebration. An icebreaker was there and Sea Dragon tied up alongside the Northwind, I guess. We had a gala welcome at the city of Nome, and then went on to Honolulu.

Q: You'd really found a submerged northwest passage!

Dr. L.: Right. The first submarine through, and it was done very quickly and easily. So the real pay-off for Sea Dragon was the icebergs. All the rest of it was pretty straightforward.

Q: No problem at all with the sonar?

DR. L.: No problem at all with the sonar now. The problems we had had with the first one on Sargo had been corrected, and we didn't have that flooding problem. This prototype equipment was built and put on Sea Dragon, and we never had that kind of a problem since.

Q: Did you have to stand the same four off, four on, four hour watches?

Dr. L.: No. Maybe that's a good question, because what else we did with Sea Dragon was to let the ship do more and more of the decision and operating. And the engineers stayed out of the picture to see how the ship's crew and officers would handle the equipment, because, after all, the next step was to get this to be a complete Navy uniform operation.

Q: You couldn't go on every ship!

Dr. L.: No, and you shouldn't have the engineers there all the time. We had to get this over into a uniformed Navy operation, so we began to sort of wean the situation at that point. So part of it was where we were working with the icebergs, that was all new, and we had to get the information. The rest of the time the ship was operating all the equipment and making their own decisions. We were simply taking the data on oceanography on the ice cover, and so forth, for our own information, and the bathymetry and working out the passages, which is the responsibility of the scientist-engineer group.

Q: Have ships since that time been able to operate on their own?

Dr. L.: Right. Then the next cruise - the completion of Sea Dragon was kind of an end of chapter of all of the experimental cruises, because then we'd been through all these situations - shallow water, darkness, icebergs, breaking through the ice cover, had enough of the bathymetry to get various areas located, and so ships could operate. For example, after the Sargo cruise the Coast and Geodetic went into the Bering Sea and Chukchi Sea and made very close line surveys, so we know where all the little hills are. So we had that information. And information had been gathered from the submarine cruises also, and all put in the charts. So, really, with the close of Sea Dragon it was kind of close of chapter for the engineer experimental trial period, and the scanning sonar equipment then shifted from the experimental prototype into an actual production model. Commerical firms were building the equipment and it would come into ships just like any standard design accepted equipment on a ship in typical numbers and instructions and all of that sort of thing. It's standard gear now—

Q: I was going to ask you, do all submarine now have this?

Dr. L.: No. That would be another part of the story, so we're jumping ahead now because we're getting into the 1960s and this was a very strange period.

Q: You'll tell me then when we get there?

Dr. L.: Okay. Why don't we pick it up right now because 1960 was the close of the experimental era and we went into the decision then of what do we do now to get us from this experimental stage over to accepted standard procedure? What is to be expected of the Arctic as far as warfare is concerned? Well, we have the vehicle now, but what do we do with it? So the leading question came up what are the tactics, what are the weapons, and what you might expect in a warfare situation. And so the next plans then were for cruises to determine these things. The 1962 cruise was planned with its prime concern as weapons. So two submarines and an ice-breaker now went into operation where it would permit the submarines to play a war game type of thing to see what it would be like with another submarine that you had to detect and attack under the ice cover and what could be done in a military warfare sense. That was the prime purpose of the 1962 cruise, which had Skate, Sea Dragon, and Staten Island, the icebreaker, together, as well as aircraft. At this time, for this 1962 cruise, we shifted entirely to ship's officers and men operating everything. The Engineer-scientist group stayed back and watched. We made no comment unless we would recognize a dangerous situation. So that we'd get a picture of what training is required to indoctrinate people to handle this new situation - from an open-sea sailor to make him into an under-ice sailor. We wanted to train people - what training aids do we need to train people to go under ice and operate, use weapons, and all the rest of it, plus actually a number of weapons trials with the Mark-37 torpedo. Tests proved that the Mark-37 torpedo was the only one available at that time that could operate under ice, but that as a weapon it was a failure. This came out of the weapons tests we had. A submarine could operate under the ice cover, but we couldn't do anything with it in a military sense.

Q: Do you want to go back to 1960 than, and pick this up when we come to 1962?

Dr. L.: It may be well to keep this story running.

Q: All right, continue on then in its natural sequence.

Dr. L.: What came out of the 1962 cruise and the weapons trials - we had no weapons. So that began, then, with the R & D community and the torpedo people recognizing that they had a real problem as to what do you do - you detect a submarine on sonar; or that you've actually seen visually and you have no weapon to attack it

Q: What was the matter with it?

Dr. L.: The weapon is captured by the ice floes. It's an entirely different situation from the open sea. In the open sea, you have a submarine and it's the only target - maybe a big fish could be a false target - but when the submarine gets near the ice cover and all these pressure ridges, each pressure ridge, each piece of ice is a better acoustic sonar target than the submarine itself. So, what we found was the torpedo, which is an active, echo-ranging torpedo, would start out perhaps towards the submarine, but then it acoustically would see an ice ridge and just go over and attack the ice ridge.

Q: That must have been distressing!

DR. L.: If the submarine stayed well below the ice cover so it wasn't near it, then it became similar to an open-sea situation, but obviously a submarine would hide close to the ice. So these were the things we learned - that when you're in ice cover you stay as close to it as you can, you make the difficulties of detection and attack as great as possible.

Well, out of this cruise then this recognition of the problem of weapons. It's an entirely different warfare situation from the open sea. In the ice situation one can stay shallow, as close to the ice as possible, whereas in the open sea it's usually more beneficial in general terms to go deep as possible then there's depth to operate in. So Arctic ASW situation is very, very different from open ocean.

Q: Can you pursue the developments in the torpedo?

Dr. L.: The people concerned with the Mark-37 in 1963 until the next time we were able to test them, which was 1969, were very successful in correcting them to handle at least far better than the first, which was a complete failure. By 1969 trials, except when we made the effort to put the submarine near or into the ice cover, than I don't see how anyone's ever going to attack. When we gave the torpedo some chance, then the torpedo was successful in discriminating between the submarine and the ice. When the submarine gets right against the ice it's just an impossible situation for a torpedo or any kind of attacking weapon to pick out which is the submarine and which is the ice cover.

The 1962 cruise, then, was considered a high success, a high success in learning that we had problems. But then one must keep in mind that the Thresher loss took place in 1963, and this changed the entire submarine program for the Navy over-all. After 1962 we had a very elaborate plan or program for continuing to develop Arctic submarines, but that had to go by the boards like many programs did after the Thresher, because with the Thresher all effort within the Navy was to correct this problem of weakness from piping or in procedures to emergency surface in case of disasters taking place at depth, and it meant that every submarine went back into the yards for rebuilding, for checking - at least a great amount of work to correct for this recognition of the weakness all submarines had.

Prior to Thresher there had been a number of instances of flooding and casualties on board, but no losses, and the Thresher was lost, and that crystallized doing something right now about correcting the flooding weakness.

But it meant then that the available time for submarines to do work at sea was extremely limited, and so the Arctic program, being not of high priority or high emergency, had to step aside for all other ASW problems which had to use what available submarine time there was. So from 1963 until 1967 there certainly was not any time available for Arctic work. During this time, we were able to look at new constructions. So when the 637-class submarine, the Sturgeon class, which was being designed during this period - we were able to put into its equipment a sonar system capable of making a ship go under ice. So really the first class of submarines which are recognized to be Arctic-capable are the 637-class, which is a big class of submarines, and constitutes the United States Navy's effort or capability for operating in the Arctic.

Q: We have gone from the end of 1960 with the Sargo and the Sea Dragon, and then we did skip to 1962.

Dr. L.: There's nothing in between. In 1960 we went into planning for this major cruise, which was a very major cruise of 1962 - two submarines and the icebreaker, one submarine coming from the Pacific, the Sea Dragon from the Pacific Fleet, and one coming from the Atlantic, the Skate from the Atlantic Fleet, so we had a double fleet operation, plus the icebreaker coming from the Pacific.

Q: And you were on which submarine?

Dr. L.: I was on Skate. Walt Wittmann took the Sea Dragon.

Art Roshon was on board for a little while, but not all the time. This time we were using company engineers as riders just to check, but again there was the thing of making it entirely a full fleet service operation. Ship's personnel handled the sonar viewing, made all the interpretations, kept it running. It was a straightforward uniform operation. Then we simply recognized what problems we came up with. Those problems appeared in the weapons, as I said, and for us in ways of training, which are still major problems. How to train men to meet a situation of which they have had no daily experience. We also did a lot of survey work - we had the icebreaker doing survey work, we had electronic positioning equipment on the shore, very elaborate equipment to locate ships precisely and to handle these weapons tests. A very complicated operation, especially when two submarines are working together, which had to meet, one coming from the Pacific and one coming from the Atlantic, and they had to rendezvous somewhere north of the Kara Sea, as I recall. The rendezvous took place perfectly. Both ships arrived at point, at time, called up on the underwater telephone and there was the other.

Q: I was going to ask you how they communicated.

Dr. L.: It's all underwater telephone, UQC. This is standard equipment that we use at all times undersea anywhere, and it works very well. The two boats were in communication, both navigating separately and arriving at the point, good exercise in navigation. That went well, then the two proceeded together.

Then, 1963 was the <u>Thresher</u> and after 1963 we had planned ...

Q: I don't want to go past 1962 yet. I don't want to sound rude, but you're overlooking one important item in your own career, in that August the 7th 1962 you received some sort of award. Tell me about that and the circumstances.

Dr. L.: Oh, that was the presidential award from President Kennedy. That all took place while I was at sea so it seems a little unreal to me, and I got word of the whole affair while on board Skate. The presentation of the presidential award was to my family. They went to the White House to receive it. As far as I'm concerned it was ~~gafarobethe~~ *a far better* scheme of things than if I had been here, because it meant that my wife and both children and my mother went to the White House to receive the award. Four others from different departments of the government received awards that year.

Q: But I want to know for the record that it's the highest award that is given to a civilian.

Dr. L.: To a civilian employee of the government.

Q: And the award was for the pioneering development of the knowledge, techniques, and instruments that made it possible for a submarine to operate under the ice cap in the Arctic, a highly important contribution to the nation's security.

Dr. L.: Right. I must admit I was aware of the - it's almost a contest, really - because the laboratory that put in a bid for me and the fleet command pushed this and endorsed the bid for the award. I was aware of all this, but it still reminds me much of any contest. You don't know that you win the finals until you find out you made the final - until the final decision is in, because each time these awards are given there are many bids for them, of course, from all departments of government. So you're aware that it's going on, but then it's a complete surprise when you finally win the contest.

Q: I would have thought it pleased you.

Dr. L.: Oh, right. No question about that, but then again, you're in an entirely different world when you're out there. It seems very unreal, you're just dislocated from the world back here.

Q: Did you know it at the time? Did the word reach you while you were on Skate?

Dr. L.: Yes. It was sent by dispatch after the fact. I did receive a message I think from CNO or SubLant. Someone sent it that the award had been made. And then later, I guess when we got south to the icebreaker we were in contact again, and someone passed the information. That was when I learned that my wife and family had gone. I didn't know what the situation was - the fact that I was not there - how they would handle it in that case. And, really it was much better that way because I don't suspect that the Navy Department would have transported the entire family if I'd been around! To me, it was always a very unusual travel order to see the Bureau of Ships issue a travel order for my wife and two children and my mother to proceed to Washington.

Q: I'm sure that they were thrilled that your efforts were recognized.

Dr. L.: That was really the best thing that could have happened for them. They got far more out of it than I would have, actually.

Q: Well, you all got the benefit, in that case.

Dr. L.: For example, for my mother it was the only time she'd ever been in the Washington area. And, of course, to go to the White House, particularly with President Kennedy, is something she's never forgotten.

As I mentioned, training people to operate under ice is a major problem, because one just wouldn't have this daily experience in open seas. So, in 1960 and for a few years, I think, thereafter, we did succeed in having the SubLant forces each March take one or two boats into the Gulf of St. Lawrence where, for a few weeks, they find some ice. So this means that a very short distance from New London we can get a little practice in going under the ice and seeing what it looks like on the sonars, and recognizing what new problems there are when you operate under the ice cover, particularly how the sonar conditions change, and the fact that they got new targets on their screen due to the ice cover - how it looked to another submarine in such a situation.

So we did get a chance at low cost to get at least a few more submariners acquainted with what the ice problems are. Well, this went on again but it got into difficulty after the Thresher incident, because of the complete clamp-down on submarine time. It then disappeared as a training exercise for a number of years until it was picked up again by the 637-class and continued whenever possibl

Q: Do not leave the 1962 operations without giveing it proper attention. I wanted to ask you, if or Skate, on which you were present, had any narrow escapes?

Dr. L.: We had no narrow escapes relative to the ice cover, or again - see Skate went through iceberg country and there were no problems with icebergs. However, on the way up through Baffin Bay, somewhere off of Thule, we did have a flooding casualty, where a sea-water circulation line failed in one of the joints and the 4-inch sea-water line failed when we were down some 400 feet and sprayed sea water in and started to flood the engineroom, which was a major flooding casualty. In this case, we were able to surface, we didn't lose propulsion power, we were able to surface and also the engineroom crew got sea valves turned off very quickly so that the flooding was stopped. However, this was prior to the Thresher incident which probably was somewhat similar a year later, and of course Thresher was lost due to flooding. We note this at this point because there had been a number of these casualties reported through the preceding years, each case having been solved, and then came Thresher, where apparently the crew was unable to solve the problem and did not escape. That brought on, then, the corrections in the following number of years to all submarines to much improve the capability for surfacing and correcting any possibility of flooding problems. It's just one of those things that happen. The corrections are finally pressed to their ultimate when there's a loss, similar to aircraft.

Q: Do you know whether during this same period of time, say up to 1963 - I think that's where we are now - whether the Russians had done any work on under-ice experiments?

Dr. L.: I think it was - they were certainly active although I'm not in a position to know just how active or how well we knew what their activities were. They certainly had been moving in previous years up to 1963 and continued to move submarines back and forth between their Atlantic and Pacific fleets by way of the Arctic. And they did release the complete story on the submarine in 1962 for reaching the north pole - just newspaper stories with photographs of a Russian sub crossing the Arctic Ocean and reaching the north pole in that year. There had been previous various sightings and press releases, so I think we knew that they were quite active in Arctic operations, which they must be because their ports are right on the Arctic Ocean. Submarines must go in and out of the ice cover. It's very different from our situation.

Q: They have good training facilities, at least!

Dr. L.: That's right. We go to find it; they live in it.

Q: Did the Triton's voyage have any bearing on changing submarine construction, improvements to sonar?

Dr. L.: No, Triton did not, although part of the Triton story is that in 1963 the Triton was to be kept aside for Arctic research work. Then came Thresher, and then came all the changes in program and money et cetera, so Triton was lost to the Arctic program because of the reduction in available funds. She had to be laid up due to lack of funds. But it had originally been planned that she would be turned over to the Arctic research program. The plans for the cruises, the equipment, personnel, and everything else was set up and authorized until the Thresher incident came along and canceled all the plans to use Triton as the research vessel in the Arctic. She was a natural because she had two power plants, lots of room, could carry many personnel, and had a very thorough overhaul of special sonar equipment. She had space for installation of special research instrumentation, for example, an oceangraphic winch for operation while submerged under ice. Everybody's plans were changed.

Q: How long was that hiatus between the Thresher and when you picked up again ---?

Dr. L.: From 1963 till about 1968, some five years.

Q: I know that along with the submarine experiments there was much work being done in your laboratory which we have left to be a separate topic, and since we're in the interim between 1963 and 1967 perhaps this is a good place to go back and bring up to date on the laboratory aspect of your work. That begins with what year?

Dr. L.: We must return to 1950. If my memory serves me right, it was in 1950 that we recognized that we were doing this field work with the submarines, we were doing this survey work and oceanography, but that we had no place to do experiments either on learning what sea ice was or maybe doing engineering tests of equipment to put on our submarines back in the laboratory. There was just nowhere that we could test things that would be going on the submarines except to put them on a submarine. And, after all, that's the final test, but you've got to check many things. Also, our interest was in understanding sea ice which was the material that we were always contending with, it was that thing about the Arctic that was different from the open sea. And one way to learn something was to have it in the laboratory where you could study it. So we felt that if we could grow sea ice in the laboratory and work with it there, we could start to learn something about it.

So it was in 1950 that we proposed to the management of the Navy Electronics Laboratory that we should try to build a laboratory to study the Arctic problems. I remember presenting this to the management board - what did they call it then, the Scientific-Technical Board - of NEL, and the sort of reaction was, well, that's all very interesting but everybody immediately forgot it because, after all, in 1950, or even today, there wasn't too much high-priority interest in the problem and it certainly wasn't in 1950. So the technique used then was the next time we informed the technical board that we were going to go ahead and build this laboratory until somebody told us to stop. Well, of course, that was an easy way to proceed because nobody bothered about it anyway. We weren't told to stop, so we proceeded in any manner we could find to put together a laboratory.

The procedure was to find all the surplus equipment we could and adapt it as best we could. Then every year, at that time, the budgeting process in the laboratory was such that their major problems were financed in block. But usually at the end of the year, particularly in the Korean War period, there would be funds left in various projects at the end of the fiscal year that had not been committed to get the problem solved which they were trying to do, whether it be radio or communications or sonars or what. So we would stand by like a bunch of vultures waiting for the end of the year to come around and then we'd grab everybody's little pieces of money that they had left over from their problems and spend them on the Arctic pool for which we were buying equipment.

Q: You were scrounging at the end of the fiscal year!

Dr. L.: Scrounging on everybody's fiscal year, that's right. And we'd always pick up a little bit at the end of each fiscal year and then we'd buy compressors, or we'd buy pipe or we'd buy whatever we could that fiscal year to put together our Arctic pool, which was the main laboratory equipment that we required. It would be a large pool where we could refrigerate it simulating ice, then we could cover it with sea water, and then try to grow sea ice similar to the Arctic Ocean.

I should mentioned that no one had done this. Perhaps it was being done in the U.S.S.R. We learned later, I know, that the U.S.S.R. had a similar laboratory where they were studying the growth of sea ice by attempting to grow it in the laboratory.

We turned to a number of refrigeration companies. In fact, we tried to get a contract for design of it and found out that I knew more about refrigeration and the ideas involved here than any contractor. Obviously, because in industry there wasn't any need for growing sea ice! And it was an entirely different refrigeration problem than anyone faced in ice rinks or big refrigeration storage houses or any other industrial process. So we simply forgot about turning to industry for design, but we did turn to industry for engineering data on refrigeration plants. We used that. York Corporation helped out very much by providing engineering information

Lyon # 3 - 244

as well as the Kohlenberger Corporation and some other local refrigeration engineers - just their ideas. But we were on our own as far as the design, and as far as working out ideas of just how to build a place to grow sea ice.

So this was a long slow process from 1950 until we started to put the thing together and actually build a pool in 1956. It was a period of some five to six years that we were just gradually picking up the parts and pieces and laying out the design and ideas for the surplus and end-of-year fiscal money idea. I'm not sure, but I think maybe we mentioned earlier about the icebreaker cruises in the 1954-1955 period - 1955 was the last of the icebreaker survey cruises in the Beaufort Sea. Up until that time we had been funded by the Bureau of Ships. And I've forgotten for what reasons but there was a budget squeeze I think in 1956, at least there was a very close look at our financing at that time. That was the time of the DEW line being built in the Arctic, and in 1956, I know, we went through a very traumatic period because our budget was cut to zero by the Bureau of Ships for Arctic work and directing that NEL stop Arctic work. NEL's command decision kept the program going. I think I may have mentioned that we received the order from the Bureau of Ships to stop all Arctic work, and Franz Curie, the civilian director, and Captain Phelps, the military director, just lost the order for about six months, until we were able to build up the program again with the coming of _Nautilus_.

1956, the time we are now talking about, the laboratory was under construction - it was when we'd got all the material together. A very difficult year, the Navy cut back, we could not go on any cruises, we had no icebreakers. So all of us then turned to, i.e. my staff, we just became steelworkers and started the actual construction of the pool.

We didn't have any work to do in the field, and we didn't have any ships to operate. So that whole year, I remember, we were - okay, we've gotten all the stuff together, let's put it together. So we had a few welders, and we learned how to lay out steel and drive rivets and all kinds of things. We became steelworkers that year.

Q: They were your plans, according to your plans?

Dr.L.: Yes, that's right. We laid out the design and all, so we just began putting up steel girders, putting pipes together, and all the rest of it. So, all of us, the whole staff, except for the couple of people working at the field station on the Bering Strait, worked day in and day out as steel constructors. And by the end of 1956 and into early 1957 we had done a fair amount of the construction of the actual pool.

Well, then with the Nautilus situation coming in, and the whole pick-up again of the Arctic program, we got the recognition of the Arctic program. And it was then that Admiral Grenfell, who was ComSubPac, finally got the word through that he had been worried about icing of snorkel head valves on his submarines out in the Pacific, for I don't know how many years, and he finally got somebody to listen to him in the Bureau of Ships that he was having problems when he ran his diesel submarines up near the lower Bering Sea in winter and up around the Sea of Okhotsk in winter, the head valves would ice up due to low temperatures and a lot of moisture going into the head valves when they were running in rough seas. He wanted something done about it.

That came into the Bureau of Ships at the same time some of the submariners who knew of the problem were at the right spot in BuShips, and so we pointed out that we could probably do something about this problem if we had our pool finished. The submarine desk in the Bureau of Ships then took money from the construction of about four submarines -- took a little bit of money from each one's construction fund -- to give to us to complete the pool, so that we could try to do something about this icing of snorkel head valves.

So it was 1957, then, and 1958 that the Bureau of Ships then funded us from the submarine desk in BuShips, and this was Lieutenant Commander Carvel Blair, the same person who did so much on the provisioning of Nautilus during that period of getting ready for the crossing in 1958 took the funding from four different ships -- I remember one was Scorpion and one was Thresher, because they were both later lost and we've always been indebted for those funds for the completing of the pool. In fact, we have a plaque up on the pool now giving honor to the four submarines which contributed to the final construction of the pool. So in 1957-58 we had funds where we could bring in the -- what was it called then, the naval shipyard here in San Diego, the Naval Repair Facility. It's nonexistent now, it was existent then. It used to be the old destroyer base. We were able to bring their people in, some 10 to twelve shipfitters and welders and constructors and finish up the construction of the pool in 1957 and early 1958.

It was late 1957, early 1958 that we were able to get help from the Naval Repair Facility at 33rd Street here in San Diego to provide welders and shipfitters, metal workers, to finish construction of the Arctic pool. It was completed about the end of 1958. We had the pool about completed at the same time we were trying to put that cruise across the top of the Arctic Ocean by <u>Nautilus</u>, and immediately that the pool was finished and operating, although it was then I guess a very simple type of pool with cooling coils over the open sea water, and we had a big room in the floor of the pool which simulated a submarine. We had built into it a full-size head valve and snorkel mast, so that we could act as though it was a submarine with a snorkel head valve and an air suction equal to the engines on board the submarine. So we simulated then the problem of the Pacific submarines with the snorkel head valve coming up and down in cold sea water and blowing winds across it to see what was happening. And trying many ideas that had been put forth as to how to solve the icing of the snorkel head valve.

The pool immediately paid off because as soon as we could watch how the icing was taking place, it was recognized that the problem really was that not sufficient water was going into the head valve by the waves to keep the ice that was forming flushed out and down into the snorkel mast. But just enough spray was going in to actually freeze hard on little projections or on the lip of the head valve, and all the idea that had been put forward to heat the head valve by electrical heat really made the problem worse, because it melted the ice from the lip of the head valve, and would let it run about halfway down the mast and there it froze hard. We were able to show just by using hoses and sprays to simulate more water spraying the head valve than was going in normally in the cold air, that we could completely remove the freezing problem by spraying enough sea water in so that half of it was freezing, and when half the sea water froze we were equalizing the freezing process, and just enough to keep the rest from freezing, and let the whole thing slop down the head valve and into the snorkel mast as a slush, and then it could be pumped out at the bottom. The problem turned into a very simple answer, which was simply to put a hose on top of the head valve and squirt water into it. And within, I guess, six months this idea got out to the fleet, and from there on they never had any problem with head valves. Of course, that only lasted a few years and then nuclear power came in, so the problem had gone out of existence.

Anyway, it demonstrated what could be done in the laboratory when we were able to watch and see what causes the problem.

Q: Where did you put the pool?

Dr. L.: The pool was really just modifying a pool we had. We had a pool in our laboratory with fresh water in it for checking out sound heads, acoustical devices, and so forth - an open-water pool with no enclosure over it and no room in the floor. All we had to do was take this pool - in fact, we got a cesspool digger to come and dig a deep pit in the bottom of the pool, some 60 feet deep and 10 feet in diameter, to simulate a submarine. That was one thing to do, and then put a lid over it, and put periscopes in so it would look like - it had the devices of a submarine, and we fixed it so that we could enter from the outside. Then we had to enclose the pool with an overhead, and put the complete refrigeration coils and blowers in to simulate the cold Arctic sky. That's the way sea waters freeze up north — it's primarily the exchange with the cold air and cold Arctic sky. Then, we had to put in a sea-water line, which is over the west side of Point Loma, down to the ocean so we could get sea water, and we had to put in a method of pumping sea water up from below. The pool was sitting on the top of a hill, some 450 feet above the ocean. And then build the refrigeration plant with all the controls, insulate the pool, insulate the room so we could operate at 40 below zero in the air space above the pool.

Q: And did you grow sea ice?

DR. L.: Then, let's see, we left it in 1958. We had this problem with snorkel head valves and that was kind of a rush-push job. We finished that, then we in fact left the construction pool just to handle that particular problem. Then, from the cruises of the Sargo and the Skate and from the work we'd been doing at the field station on sea ice, we recognized that we didn't understand sea ice at all. We just didn't know anything about it. We didn't know how it was made or how it acted, its physical properties or chemical properties. So therefore after getting rid of the snorkel head valve, then we changed the pool again. By that, I mean we took out the snorkel head, mast, and all the stuff that had been put in just to take care of this simulation of the engines on board a submarine, scrapped the mast and the snorkel head in the bottom of the pool, changed it over (our submarine with a periscope, and having built into it a three-foot cylinder, thirty-seven feet long) to a gadget that could come up out of the floor of the pool and act like the sail of a submarine striking against the underside of the ice, like we did with the Skate and the Sargo.

It we grew sea ice in the pool, then we could simulate this breakthrough problem that we were doing with the sumarines. It took from 1959 till 1963 to make those changes, again limited for money, but primarily limited in how fast we could do the work just by the construction and the design required. And it was a major change, a major design job to make this change for simulating the sail of a submarine that could come up out of the floor of the pool at various speeds, and could be controlled to strike the underside of the ice in the pool. What we needed for the study of the breakthrough was a device that could come up at various speeds from the floor of the pool and strike against the ice to simulate the sail of a submarine striking the ice, and then we could study the way the ice broke under the impact, keeping in mind that we were successful in breaking through with submarines up north in an actual case. But we did not understand the forces that were involved, we had no quantitative measure of the pressures against the top of the sail in any of these breakthroughs. We did not know how to extend our capability, or really, what kind of risks we were taking, as far as quantitative measures and pressures were concerned in any of the breakthroughs we'd been doing.

It took us from 1959 till 1963 to complete this construction of a device for testing the impact on the undersurface – underside – of the ice, as well as learning, at least the first attempt, to grow sea ice. It sounds simple, but we found it was very complicated in controlling the sea water to grow the sea ice in an enclosed space. Mother Nature grows sea ice out in the great big wide open ocean, so when the sea ice grows the fact that some of the salt that's in the ice doesn't freeze and trickles out on the bottom and goes into the open ocean below doesn't bother the growth of sea ice. But when you're doing this in an enclosed pool the freezing process – that sea water that's in the ice and doesn't freeze and goes out to the bottom of your pool just keeps changing the salinity of the salt content in the water underneath and that completely changes the property of the sea ice. So, it's a chemical problem, keeping the mixing just correct. A very tight schedule, hour by hour, to simulate the wide open ocean in an enclosed pool. This becomes very tricky – to hold a body of water the size of a quarter of a million gallons of water, which the pool is, at just the right salinity, just the right temperature so there's always correct balance at the freezing temperature. And, as it freezes, it changes its salt content, so you're always escalating chemical problems – very complex.

Q: And you do that with instruments or with persons?

Dr. L.: We did it with people. It was too much for instrumentation. You use instruments, you continually monitor, and then you've got to make computations and change. It's not an automatic process. Even today we cannot do this as an automatic process.

In this first trial, this was in 1963 that started, we finally started to grow sea ice in our pool and get ready for the impact tests with the simulated sail. We ran a set of experiments from the fall of 1963 around to the spring of 1964. Keep in mind that when we set up one of these experiments we were on a twenty-four-hour continuous basis. You can't let go of anything at any moment, everybody is just living and sleeping almost in the laboratory. And we were running regular watches - night and day, weekends, continually, for that long period over all holidays, etc. So these experiments had to be set up and handled very carefully. We do not grow sea ice in a pool any faster than Mother Nature does up north. If we're going to grow ice three feet thick it usually takes on the order of a month to grow it that thick. It grows probably an inch on the first day, a foot in the first week, and about three feet in a month. That's about the rate we grow it. So, to do any one experiment just to break through three feet means that one spends a month growing it, and then runs the experiment to break it, and one breaks it up in a few seconds, and in a minute or so he starts all over again growing the next set of sea ice.

Q: This covered the entire pool, of course?

Dr. L.: It covered the entire pool, but we can only use really the center part because the ice that grows near the walls is different just because of the wall being near it. It would be as if it were out in the Arctic Ocean where there's no wall, and walls do affect the character of the ice. So that we only had really the use of the pool out near the center away from the walls. And once it's broken, we've got to clear it away and grow a new sheet.

Q: Clear the whole pool?

Dr. L.: Pretty much so, or at least clear a large section in the center.

Q: Well, that's a major job, isn't it?

Dr. L.: That's a major job.

Q: How do you do that — by melting or pulling it out?

Dr. L.: You just pull it out. To melt it takes about as long as it did to grow it, so one way to get rid of it is to pick it up and haul it out. What we'd normally do is to pick it up and stack it away in one corner, take out the center section and stack it around the edges. And we can do that about three times and then we've got such a large quantity of ice we would rather just stop and have it all carried out it truckloads. So, it's got its problems.

We were successful in running a set of experiments during that period, and it was the first time that we did see how we were actually breaking the ice. By that I mean we got a pattern of the way the cracks form, which tells a person a great deal about how the ice is breaking, and what forces are required to break it. Once one sees the crack pattern, one knows what sort of size pieces the thing is breaking into, and one can begin to calculate what forces are involved. This was the first instance where we could watch the whole procedure. When we are doing it with a submarine, all we see is what we hit before, and then when we get up and look at it we can't visualize what happened, due to the snow and the ice and everything lying all over the place. We can't find out how we broke through. But in the pool the cameras and observers, particularly cameras, get the whole picture of coming up, hitting it, watching the ice break. Of course, instruments on the ice tell us how much force was applied. It's quite a different story from doing things up north. It's a real laboratory experiment where we get numbers on things.

So, we were successful in breaking it in this pool but then we found that we were really not growing true sea ice like Mother Nature does. Any number of problems showed up. We had to circulate sea water very carefully in the pool to control the salinity and the temperature so that it was always at the freezing point, as I mentioned. This had a lot of piping, all kinds of heat exchangers and filters to keep the water clean, and all kinds of things. And we found that we were getting air bubbles into this system all the time. These air bubbles would come through the piping, would get in the pool, and they'd get into the sea ice. The sea ice was very bubbly, which is much different from true sea ice because it had so many air bubbles in it. The density was much lower than it should be. Normally sea ice weighs — had a density of about .93 and we were down to about .87, which is a very large change. And its having air bubbles means that it has a little hole where the air bubble is, and that weakens the ice greatly, so its strength properties are very different. And its salinity and salt content wasn't correct. The other things was it was completely full of rust particles because due to our lack of funds we had to use iron pipes. And sea water going round and round the same iron pipes for sixty days, we just got rust-out, so that our ice was actually red. We could see rust particles all the way through it. Now, that might not have been too serious, but we didn't really know how much that affected it. Certainly, the air bubbles were very serious, changing the properties of the sea ice. And the other thing was that we found the refrigeration system couldn't take care of the typical weather of the Arctic. By that, I mean that the typical weather is that first a cold front comes through and the temperature falls very low, that forms ice. Then comes a warm front and the temperature goes from well below zero Fahrenheit to 15 or 18 degrees above Fahrenheit. When that happens, the ice changes greatly because the unfrozen salt that's in little cells all through the ice – sea ice – when the temperature warms up, they enlarge and start draining through the ice and changing its properties. So, to have true sea ice you have to be able to match the weather of the Arctic, which is half cold fronts and half warm fronts and see how these things change it. Therefore, we had a major problem with the refrigeration plant. That had to be changed. So, recognizing all these problems if we were not going to be able to grow true sea ice until we changed them, it was in 1964 or 1965 that we started to modify the pool to make corrections, and this was major because it completely changed our refrigeration plant..

Q: Excuse me, but before you did that, had you learned something that would be of value, even though it might not be exactly accurate?

Dr. L.: Yes. The thing that we learned primarily was how we were breaking the ice and that was really the crack pattern, how the ice cracked and from that we were able to much more accurately estimate what sort of forces we were applying when we did break through with a submarine at various thicknesses, and we could use then the information which we got from measuring sea ice up north - actual sea ice in the Arctic - where you can go out on the sea ice and cut patterns of the ice and see what it takes to break it. We could translate that information through what we learned in the pool through the crack pattern to the actual case of a submarine breaking through.

So we were then at least much closer to knowing, although we still felt fairly large errors were possible - at least we were visualizing how we were breaking the sea ice and could make what I should call good guesses of the forces applied, even though we didn't have a complete understanding of the properties of sea ice - being able to extrapolate ourselves into unknown situations. WE could use the information from measuring a particular piece of sea ice and apply it across to a particular surface.

Q: In 1964 you said -

Dr. L.: In 1964, by then we really wanted to have an understanding and be able to meet any situation and to understand the material. Until you have a mathematical model that explains it, until you could predict its chemical critical properties, you really don't know it. One way to find out is to grow it. Of course, we had been growing something but it wasn't still like the good stuff. So the point was to change our pool so we could grow it - the correct stuff - knowing what errors we had made in the design of the pool.

So, starting in 1964, then we started to modify the pool and that was a major problem because we had to completely tear out the refrigeration plant and build a new kind of refrigeration plant. The prime change there for people who knew refrigeration was that our coils in the pool carried a primary refrigerant, which was ammonia, and we found that we could not control that primary refrigerant in the pool at exactly the right temperatures, which was the fine control that we required. So what we did was put a secondary refrigerant in the coils, really a heat fluid. We simply pumped methylene chloride through the coils which would not change its chemical phase with the temperature and we could either heat it or cool it without it changing in any way. It simply would take heat into the pool or take heat out and we could completely control it. So the main refrigeration ammonia plant we used then to cool down the methylene chloride in large tanks. The methylene chloride circulated through the coils in the pool and we could mix hot methylene chloride with cold methylene chloride in any mix we wanted to get any kind of temperature control we wanted. This gave us, then, very fine control either of warming the pool or cooling the pool, and we could simulate either warm fronts or cold fronts or any kind of a front going through the pool.

Then we changed all the piping of the sea water from steel to stainless steel, and we put in a system of taking the air bubbles out of the water, deaerating the sea water. So these were the three major things we found: control of the temperature of warmwitent, cold front was solved; the piping was changed to stainless steel to get rid of the rust; and the piping was changed so that we could control the amount of air in the water, get rid of the air bubbles.

This took from 1964 until 1966 - late 1966 - to do this.

Q: And where were the funds coming from at this time?

Dr. L.: Funds were coming from BuShips.

Q: They still wanted you to go ahead?

Dr. L.: That's correct. The Arctic program at that time was funded. Keep in mind now, they were not doing any submarine cruises whatsoever. All work was in the laboratories or in our field station at Cape Prince of Wales. So the funds we had available went into this correction of our pool.

We were just ready to start growing sea ice again for our breakthrough experiments in late 1966, 1967, when the Coast Guard came knocking at our door and said they had a problem, they'd had to design a new icebreaker because all the Wind-class icebreakers had been built way back in the 1940s and were very old and Congress, I think, had then promised funds for them to build new icebreakers and they wanted to make models of icebreakers, rather than just sitting down and trying to design one which everyone had been doing up to that time, and then building it full scale. Maybe they could do something with models first. So they wanted to use our pool as a model pool where they would come in with a model of the icebreaker and we would try to grow model sea ice, a very different problem from full-scale sea ice, and see whether they could do anything with making models and learning how the ships should be built, how many propellers it should have, and what the shape of the stern should be, by trying various models of icebreakers, which again was a whole new technology. This was not just growing sea ice, but modeling sea ice. The U.S.S.R. gave indication that they had done something with models in their sea ice tank.

This, then was using the pool very differently from what it was designed for. The suggestion was that - okay, we could use fresh water. We knew a lot about fresh water, and we could grow it in great thick sheets. Of course, the problem is now we want to grow very thin sheets because the scale, the thickness of that ice had to be to the same scale as the model of the ship, and a model of a ship, say, for example, the model scale could be 40 to 1 - a ship that's 300 feet long or so, comes out to be 7 or 8 feet or something like that. Then, the ice has to be to that same scale. That means the ice is down to the order of a quarter of an inch thickness for the ship to break through. And that has to be done very precisely because certainly on that small scale a sixteenth of an inch means a tremendous dimension on the scale factor.

Well, so then our problem was to have very precise control and try to grow very uniform thin sheets in which they could run their models. This became a priority problem for the U. S. government over-all. I mean, after all, the Navy had a stake in icebreakers, too, and anything that could be learned by models was going to be a great saving. We had a whole new problem now, the technology to try to develop models - which was a cooperative program with the

Coast Guard. So we took on the job of trying to grow model ice and the Coast Guard people did the work on the models of the ships. One of my staff was also a ship architect and he got very deeply involved with the problem, too. He had actually done some model work on icebreakers when he took his degree at the University of California.

We got deeply involved in this during 1967 and 1968. We'd just got started when along came this Manhattan Project for building a big ship for carrying oil to the Arctic, for carrying oil out of the Arctic, by Humble Oil Company and Atlantic Richfield. They had gone to the Coast Guard for their problem of how to change their big tankers for their tests, running tankers through the ice cover. So they wanted to do something by models. So, all of a sudden, we had not only the Coast Guard, but then we had the Humble Oil people mixed up with the Coast Guard coming with their models.

Q: It would seem that your pool met a need that it didn't all along?

Dr. L.: That's right. It suddenly became a very immediate need, but it should be pointed out that it was a very different kind of a problem than what we had designed everything for. It didn't have carriages for carrying models and all kinds of things had to be done on a crash basis by the Coast Guard and ourselves to try to handle these models, but we concentrated on trying to grow the ice. Well, we worked for a number of months on fresh water, but that very quickly showed although we were growing fresh-water ice very precisely, it was not breaking the way it should to simulate the problem. It would break up in great pieces. When the model hit the ice, a great crack would run across this thin sheet of fresh-water ice, and the pieces would break up which on the scale factor would be miles in size, rather than the way it does when watching it in real life. All of us had had long experience on icebreakers, and knew that when an icebreaker went through the ice it broke up into small pieces, and the pieces turned on edge and slid along the hull. That was the problem.

Modeling, then, had the problem that to model the ice we had to have - the ice had to break in small pieces, and be the same scale size as what would happen in a full case. That meant then that the thin sheet of ice had to have the same properties so that it broke up into little pieces, and those pieces then would scale right, and they would have the right friction on the surface to slide along the hull the way —

Q: It had no value?

Dr. L.: It wouldn't be valuable, although I should say that the model did work well in showing, even with the big pieces, how the pieces slid along the stern and got into the propellers. So we learned an awful lot, even on this first mock-up test, about what was happening at the stern.

The model work that was done for the <u>Manhattan</u> had almost no value as far as we were concerned, because it was done with fresh-water ice, the pieces were not breaking according to scale at all. They had a model of the <u>Manhattan</u>. The first of these tests we had not only a model of the icebreakers for the Coast Guard, we also had a model of the <u>Manhattan</u> provided by the Humble Oil Company and they ran the experiments. But these experiments were all done in fresh-water ice, and so they were not realistic because the ice sheet didn't break properly into the right sized pieces to simulate the full-scale operation. So that the result they got from running a model Manhattan really had no value. It could be discounted.

From all of this we recognized we had to do something. So then we got rid of the fresh water, filled the pool again with sea water, and started a set of experiments which went on for another year. Out of all of this we recognized that we were on the brink of a technology that could be very useful as far as models are concerned. By quickly freezing the sea water to a thin sheet it gets a very high salt content. By quickly freezing the sea water under good proper control, one is able to form a thin sheet with high salt content. And then by properly warming with control, one can change the strength properties of the sheet because of the high salt content. And if the model experiment is done at just the right time this high-salt-content sea ice seems to break up into pieces which are the right scale compared with a full-scale situation. Much has to be learned with this. All that we solved is that there is a real possibility of doing this, of using this technique for working up a whole model technology for sea ice and ships in sea ice, oil derricks in sea ice, any kind of a model problem one can attack. But it depends on being able to grow thin sea ice sheets, and control their friction properties and their strength properties, so that they are the right scale factor to the full-size situation.

Really, then, all we learned was here was a whole new field to undertake, but it was not for this pool that we had. The pool was a deep pool with a submarine in the floor, and certainly was not built correctly to attack this model problem. So we've kept that pool for growing sea ice in the full-scale normal, natural manner, as close as we can to the Arctic situation. When, we undertook the design and building right alongside another pool, which is for model work, and which we are now in the process of building. It's a pool similar, but it's a very shallow pool, and it has carriages on it for carrying models, and it has windows in it for looking from underneath, and all the things that we learned that we needed for doing model work, and the controls necessary to grow the thin sea-ice sheets, and to sweep them off the pool when finished with the sheet. All the things we learned about from the other pool were put into the design of this model pool. So, we'll have two pools - one for model technology, trying to work the whole thing out, and the other for studying submarines underneath the real sea ice.

Q: Is the new pool financed by BuShips?

Dr. L.: The new pool is financed partly by BuShips and partly by the Coast Guard in their funding of us during their big model problem. Everybody recognizing that we needed this kind of a facility so it would be usable by the ship industry, by us, and by everybody else, if we can work out the model technique. And that's an "if." We recognize that we have to work out a whole technology on model scale, but we can't do it without having a place to go and simply experiment until we learn how to do it.

Q: Was the technology for that pool as complicated as the big one?

Dr. L.: It is as complicated as the big one, but it has different requirements. It's not quite the same way. Now, we're using the same refrigeration plant and much of the same equipment is mutual to the two pools, but the controls are different, the techniques are different. The setups are different. The model pool grows the ice quickly and we get rid of it quickly and do another sheet, but in the big pool it takes all winter to grow sea ice. One is a very slow process, the other is a quick and precise-control process. That's why we had to have two pools. The two problems are just not compatible.

So, that's just about where we stand right as of 1971. It's the process of constructing a pool to attack the model technology program and that model technology will be both for surface ships and for submarines beneath the ice cover, and for piers, derricks, and anything else that has to be built to withstand sea ice pressing against it like would be on a warf in a harbor. All of these things we hope to attack with the model technique.

Q: And after you'd spent the money on the large pool to get the ice exactly the way you wanted it, were your experiments then satisfactory?

Dr. L.: We have not gone back to those. We were just ready to attack trying to see whether or not we could grow sea ice like it is done up in the Arctic when the model problems —

Q: You stopped the one then?

Dr. L.: Because we had to use that. That was the only pool we had.

Q: Of course.

Dr. L.: That was in early 1967, just after we had completed and we were ready to go, along came the Coast Guard and said - we've got a problem. And so we went into this model problem, and we thought - we'll solve this and get it out of the way. Instead, we got a whole new world to master. If we are successful in model techniques, then we have an extremely powerful tool to study all kinds of problems, not only in transportation, warfare, construction, and everything else that one really had in other fields. For instance, the Taylor Model Basin just handles ships in the open sea, waves, beaches, all kinds of things are modeled for the open sea, so this is really a corollary to that when you have ice. In other words, trying to do the same kind of model techniques that are used for the open ocean against beaches and against piers, against rivers, and all kinds of things, with sea ice.

Q: But until this new one is constructed you can't go back to the other at all?

Dr. L.: They're both so close to the same machinery that we can't do anything until the new pool is finished.

Q: When will the new one be constructed?

Dr. L.: We hope the construction finishes up this summer of 1971 and then we'll start the instrumentation and the trials and errors will go on for four years probably.

Q: Before you get back?

Dr. L.: Oh, no, we'll be back to growing sea ice in the other pool perhaps within the year, but I would say it's going to take us four years before we've completely solved the model techniques.

Q: And you can't do both at the same time?

Dr. L.: Oh, we'll be working on both at the same time, right. But the model techniques are going to take a long time. We're on our own, no one has solved any of these problems. We don't know what kind of carriages and gadgets, devices, are needed to handle models, how you build models, how you read them, how to measure them. None of these things have been worked out.

Q: What is the organizational change, if any, of the facilities since we last discussed them?

DR. L.: Organizational changes have been, of course, great, but they really don't influence what we do. We just sort of stand by in our laboratory there while all this management organization changes around us. Up until 1967 it was the Navy Electronics Laboratory which had been established in 1945. Then in 1967 management circles termed the word "centers" in the Navy, and so the idea was to combine those people who had been working under-water in one group, which became a center, and those people working above the water would be another center. This made a split down through the middle of NEL. NEL had been a combination of radio, radar, and sonar. So those people involved in sonar became associated with those involved in underwater weapons, which were part of the Inyokern Naval Ordnance Test Station, which became the Naval Weapons Center at Inyokern. So the people who were in Pasadena which had to do with underwater weapons were combined with the people at San Diego of Naval Electronics Laboratory and made the Underwater Warfare Center at that time. Then, that name got later changed to its present name of Naval Underseas Research and Development Center, a couple of years ago when "warfare" was considered a bad word.

We now have the Underseas R & D Center in which my group is located, and is the Arctic Submarine Laboratory.

Q: Was it not too recent that you became chief scientist? I got the impression from something Mr. Mason wrote that there had been some announcement of a change, of your changed position.

Dr. L.: No, that was just a change in name, no change in position. As I say, the Arctic Submarine Laboratory had been called originally under NEL the Submarine Research Facility under the Naval Electronics Laboratory. We couldn't be called a laboratory because that would have been a laboratory within a laboratory. And we were located right in the middle of the hill between what is now the Navy Electronics Laboratory Center on top of the hill and what is the Naval Underseas R & D Center at the bottom of it. We're right in the middle. We have so many pools and so many thousands of tons of steel, and we can't be moved anywhere, so we're just sort of sitting. Then when the Center got called the Center, why, then it was more appropriate to change our name to what we are, which is a laboratory, so then we became, two years ago, I guess, the Arctic

Submarine Laboratory of the Naval Underseas Research and Development Center.

Q: And you are the chief scientist?

Dr. L.: I am the director of the Arctic Submarine Laboratory.

Q: Director or chief scientist?

Dr. L.: I'm not anything as far as I know, but when you have a laboratory you have to have a director.

Q: I see. That would be organizationally and you are, in fact, the chief scientist in that organization?

Dr. L.: Well, the chief scientist term comes about really for these cruises, and it is also the proper name of the civil service position I hold.

Q: In any case, we are now up to the present day?

Dr. L.: As far as the laboratory is concerned - as far as the laboratory here on Point Lowman is concerned, that brings us up to date, but there are many other facilities around it, but the unique one is this pool. There are all kinds of other facility laboratories and equipments and whatnot associated with the pool for measurement of the properties of the ice, optically acoustically and so on and so forth, but all of those are just associated with the main element which now would be the two pools, the model pool and the big pool, the sea-ice pool. In addition to that, for laboratory work, since 1951 we maintain on a continual basis the field station up at Cape Prince of Wales in the BEring Strait, whose purpose has been to give us a field outlet where we can get sea ice, do sea-ice tests, where we can make oceanographic tests, ocean-acoustic tests, and that type of thing. This is a very small field station that's handled by one family on a year-round basis. One of the staff takes his family and goes there and stays maybe one year, two years, depending on how long he's interested in working in the area. And then perhaps for a few months out of a year, maybe three or four, other members of the staff will go and carry out measurements and then return. We've always run it on a one-family basis. It's a very small cost, but very highly successful way of handling a field station and getting information that we want, and has paid off greatly for monitoring the ocean at a very interesting point, because this is the Bering Strait where the exchange of ocean between the Pacific and the Arctic oceans takes place, and we've been monitoring the amount of water, heat, and ice that flows back and forth through this entrance over these many years. It is a long-term sea-ice oceanographic study point. I'd also consider that as part of our laboratory work really because of it being a fixed point where we can do these long-term tests.

That brings us up through the main part of our lab work, but in conjunction - to bring us right up to date - in conjunction with the work to try to understand the properties of sea ice about one-third of our staff has been continually involved in what we call basic research in the properties and physics chemistry of sea ice. And this has been the work that's been done in the laboratory, in the field station and, at the moment, this group is now out in the field on a drifting ice floe attempting to measure the exchange of energy from the ocean through the ice into the atmosphere, and vice versa, to understand how sea ice is formed in the natural state, and particularly to be able to get numbers on the heat exchange which takes place between the atmosphere through the sea ice because it is the main parameter that one must know to handle the whole weather system, to understand the exchange of heat between the atmosphere and the sea is the main factor, the driving function, what drives the weather drives the sea. And the Arctic Ocean, of course, is the heat sink where the cooling takes place. So this experiment is the joint work of the University of Washington, the Canadian research groups, and the oceanographic office and will take place during March and April on ice floes in the Beaufort Sea.

Q: Is that what's happening today with all the phone calls?

Dr. L.: That's what's happening with all the phone calls. The last of the party of people of eight men, the last four, are supposed to leave tomorrow morning to get up on the north coast of Canada and then go up on the aircraft to set up all the equipment that's necessary on a drifting ice floe. There'll be some 60 people total and a tremendous amount of equipment. We are sending up at least $900,000 worth of special equipment to make these measurements and eight men and their houses and everything else.

Q: That's a big logistic movement, isn't it?

Dr. L.: Oh, it is. A tremendous number of flights. We had to send a big C-141 with 41,000 pounds of equipment up to the north coast. All of this is done with automatic data processing that goes on tape. A tremendous amount of data must be measured continually as far as wind speed, wind direction, temperatures, humidity, moisture, and the amount of sun coming in and reflected by the ice, the temperature and the flow of the water underneath the ice, the flow of wind across the ice, the thickness of the ice, the temperatures in the ice, all of these things have to be measured at one time in order to get how the heat is being exchanged back and forth between the air flow and the water flow and the formation of the ice in between, and the sun's radiation coming in and being reflected back also contributes to this heat exchange. The heat exchange is the force that drives the atmosphere - drives the weather. And to understand it you've got to have these numbers of the heat exchange.

Q: That would be all related to your experiments here?

Dr. L.: Right.

Q: To your pool?

Dr. L.: In the pool it all has to fit together, because to run a pool and understand the same heat exchange process as we'd been doing in the pool. That's where we can study and change things. We can change it there under our control, but up north they're doing experiments on nature.

Q: Are all of those men doing the same problems, related problems?

Dr. L.: They're all on the same problem, but each one has got a different thing that they are measuring, or they're people that are expert in running these data-collecting devices, which are very elaborate, high-speed measuring devices. All the data have to be gathered on magnetic tapes and go through computers and be processed. One can't do this by pencil and paper. It's extremely complex.

Q: That's a story in itself.

Dr. L.: Oh, yes, that's a whole story in itself, a very complex story, and again one of the techniques of learning how to live and use these kind of things out on the ice. That is what this experiment we're involved in right now - it's the first time we've attempted to take such sophisticated, scientific equipment - this precise type of scientific equipment - out in the field and set up on a floating ice floe to try to do these measurements. We've never done that. We've always had it in vehicles, ships, or aircraft. But to go out and do it right where the ice is growing and forming and see whether we can do it - we're taking quite a gamble on this situation.

Q: I'd like to come back after you have the results of those and see what you found out! How long will it take?

Dr. L.: They will be out there from this week in March till probably the middle of April, about six weeks. It's really a pilot experiment. If we're going to do this we have to do these kind of things through a whole season to see what the fall situation is, what the freezing situation is, what the fog situation is in the spring in order to get the annual cycle.

Q: Well, we're going back now to 1967 to bring us up to date with the submarines, like we have with the laboratory.

DR. L.: We left the submarines which closed a chapter -- the Skate class and all of the trials and tests which showed what we could do. And then from 1963 to 1967 all the ideas for Arctic submarines and equipment moved into the standard, accepted military components for under-ice submarines, and contracts were let to buy the sonar system which we had developed for under-ice operations. This became then and with its regular number, for example, the BQS-8 sonar system which was built commercially as a unit and put on board the 637-class submarines as one of its regular pieces of equipment to permit its operation underneath the ice cover. It has a sonar scanning system for avoiding ice in front of the submarine, it has an upward-looking sound system for measuring the profiles under the ice, its' receiving and recording, it has a hardened sail for breaking through the ice cover. All of the masts and periscopes, et cetera, on the sail retract so that the submarine can break through ice, and it has the proper echo-sounders for measuring the ice thickness, and is recognized to be an under-ice operator. The Sturgeon class, the 637-class submarine, is the result of the experimental work done with the Skate class, and is the Navy's Arctic submarine capability.

Also from the period of 1962 to 1967, the torpedo people had worked on the Mark 37 torpedo and had corrected as much as possible its acoustic difficulties to meet the under-ice situation and greatly improved it, really as much as technology possibly could do for getting a torpedo that can discriminate against ice which is off to the side.

So we come to February of 1967 when the first 637-class submarine was available to try, and that was the Queenfish actually. The class is named Sturgeon class, which is the 637, but there was a little contest between the Electric Boat Company, New London and Newport News Shipbuilding in Virginia, and they got their boat out first, so we had the Queenfish instead of the Sturgeon, that being the first of the class. And so in February 1967, the Queenfish came out of the yard, and we were able to take her north for a very brief period before she proceeded west to become part of the SubPac Fleet. That was the first time, then, we got to try an entirely new boat built with equipment to go under the ice cover, and the big change between the 637-class and the Skate class is that the diving planes are in the sail, whereas the Skate class has its planes in the bow, and this means that when a ship breaks through ice the sail planes must come through the ice, and had been taken into account in designing the submarine.

Q: What's the advantage?

Dr. L.: In the stability in the handling of the ship. It had nothing to do with the ice cover, but the control of the ship. This is a whale-type rounded construction, very different from the ships of the Skate class. Of course, these are larger submarines, too - 4,500 tons - and they're single screw - quite different from the Skate class.

Q: How far did you go under the ice with the Queenfish?

Dr. L.: The Queenfish in the spring - we only had it for a very brief period with Commander Richard as the skipper and the exec was Commander McClaren. McClaren had been the photographer, photography officer, one of the junior officers, in the Sea Dragon in 1960, and he had been and continues to be one of the pushers for Arctic submarines. He was the exec. He had had some experience from the Sea Dragon, and Commander Richard was the commanding officer. I think three of us went from our laboratory. One person for the sonar system, the scanning system, and Dick Boyle and myself for the profilign and just the knowledge of how to handle submarines in the area. Dick Boyle joined my group in 1961, or 1960, maybe. He had been an officer on the Skate in 1958 and 1959, and then he resigned from the submarine force in uniform and went civilian and came to the laboratory and has been one of the main members of our staff ever since. He's the one person in the staff who has nuclear-power training, which is essential to our work with nuclear submarines in the ARctic environment. We got a chance, then, to see just how 637 operated and we took her into Baffin Bay, and so we got a chance to test it against icebergs, against the ice. It was just a few days to check out this equipment, because it was also a shake-down cruise for the submarine itself, a brand-new class, all kinds of new equipment, new designs, and those had to be all checked out, a shake-down for that plus this underice capability, the suit of equipment to handle the underice situation. That's what that particular cruise was used for, and it proved to be highly successful as far as a submarine operator under the ice was concerned, but all we did was go into the ice cover in February for a short period, break through some thin ice, check out against icebergs, see the profiling and everything worked right, found out a number of electronic problems that had to be changed and solved, which one always does the first time around, then came back and the Queenfish reported to the Pacific.

Then, we were followed by a number of cruises after that. In 1969, the Whale and the Pargo and the Skate went north, and we were back on a full-fledged complete submarine Arctic cruise again, and this time Whale went up to the north pole. And we got the first complete check-out on breaking through the ice cover in many different situations with these sail planes, and just see how the 637-class did handle breaking through pieces of ice, and it worked out very well. The techniques of handling a single-screw ship with sail planes, what the basic techniques are, whether the sonar system worked properly, learning a number of things that had to be corrected - these were electronics problems.

Q: Were you on the Whale?

Dr. L.: Yes. I was on Whale, Dick Boyle was on Whale. The Pargo was combined with the operation, and she went to the pole and carried out surveys of new areas, as well as break through experiments. Art Molloy of my group was on her, and Walt Wittman from Oceanographic Office. Pargo's a 637-class. Whale went earlier, so we found differences between the Arctic Ocean in April — I guess the Pargo came in May — the ice changed in just a month, and the two boats with Skate worked along the east coast of Greenland and did a lot of weapons testing.

Q: This was the same old Skate?

Dr. L.: That's the same old Skate. Her commanding officer was an old-timer who'd been a junior officer on one of the boats, but I can't tell you which one! So we had some experienced personnel. And Skate worked with one of the 637s, the Pargo, worked with both Whale and Pargo on these weapons tests.

Q: How did it happen in the scheme of things that made it possible now to have funds for the submarines to do Arctic work?

Dr. L.: It's difficult really to say. We had continued to be funded. Really, we were waiting for this class of submarines to come out, and once out, they are part of the submarine forces, Pacific and Atlantic, and one of our main responsibilities had always been to work and support directly these two force commanders. So, as soon as these submarines were available, then we were called upon by these forces to take part in trying them out.

Q: It wasn't anything that had to be forced, as did the original under-ice projects?

Dr. L.: No, not in this case at all because these boats were — And now, the situation is such that activities are taking place both by U.S.S.R. and U.S. along the marginal sea ice zone. Now it's a fleet operation confrontation. It's not just guessing what's going to happen. It's happening. That much has changed. Submarines now are using the edge of the ice as an operating area.

Q: Well, that was what my question was.

Dr. L.: It's from something that was just a hypothetical situation, something that we had to look for in the future as a possible fleet action area of interest, and something we had to be responsible for to one that is actually an area of action, and we must now train to use.

Q: In other words, am I interpreting it correctly, the Russian submarines under-ice capabilities are there -

DR. L.: Yes. Both parties now have the capabilities and are there. They are using the marginal edge of the ice area, which up until recent years they simply stayed away from.

Q: Is that in the Pacific?

Dr. L.: No, it's primarily the Atlantic. The Pacific, too, but the Atlantic is really the main one because there we have an ice edge and ice that extends clear from the U. S. right across Greenland clear over to Europe. So it's more an Atlantic area than a Pacific, but both are active. So, it changed from a problem of where it might happen some day to the problem for the fleets, but it's here. That makes quite a difference, and this 637-class submarine is made and recognized for this purpose. Now, that isn't saying that this is an area of high action, but it's a very small percentage, at least, of a total area that the two submarine forces are responsible for, so they've got to take that into account. It's part of their total area they must be accounting for all the time - this Arctic area. So these cruises - both force commanders are seeing that their people go to work, and these first ones, Pargo, Whale, and Queenfish last summer, and Hammerhead this past fall, they've all been of this type - to see what the 637 can do, and know her capabilities as a fleet operator. Keep in mind that this is different from when we were doing the Skate experiments, in which the civilians and the scientists had a big part in doing a lot of the things. These 637s are entirely a straightforward operation, although two or three of us are riding on board we are simply there to see what else is wrong - if there's something wrong, something that should be corrected on the equipment basis. We are not operating it in the same sense that we did -

Q: It is not experimental?

Dr. L.: No. We are not operating, the ship is operating itself, it's running the whole thing itself, and we're simply going along to pick up information. We came to see what kind of thing we can add for training, how we can help out, assisting in interpretation, and that kind of thing, to update and increase their capabilities. The Navy itself is operating them, the uniformed Navy.

Q: What did you say the Queenfish was - that you were on her first shake-down cruise?

Lyon # 3 - 280

Dr. L.: The first shake-down cruise of the Queenfish - that was 1967, February 1967. That was very brief and the real shake-downs and tests were Whale 1969.

Q: The one with these three?

Dr. L.: Yes, Whale and Pargo in spring 1969, and then followed by Queenfish in the summer of 1970.

Q: Were you aboard?

Dr. L.: No. Dick Boyle and Alan Beal from my group were aboard, getting the information and bringing back the data.

Q: That was just last year?

Dr. L.: That was last summer. And then this past fall, which just got through, the Hammerhead, another 637 class, in the Atlantic, which went clear up into the Arctic Ocean in the entire dark period. So we have had experience, you see, in spring, summer, and the deep winter.

Q: This new class of boats?

Dr. L.: These new class boats, to see if all of the things - whether she navigates right, whether she pilots under the ice right, whether she breaks through - all these things have been gone through.

Q: All the things that the other class you knew could do now the new class had —

Dr. L.: That's right, and on a fleet-operating capability. There was nothing special about it, no special interpretation, special people - it was recognized as standard procedure. So we've been through this now and in a sense have completed another chapter. As far as we're concerned the 637 class has been proven and ready to go and we know what we can do with her and she's had her weapons checked out, the Mark-37 at least has been brought up to the highest capability it possibly can as far as technology is concerned, and communications, all the things that a submarine needs to know and to do. They've been checked out.

Q: Are the Polaris submarines qualified to go under the ice?

Dr. L.: No. The Polaris submarine are not, they were never intended to be. They're open-water operators and keep in mind that the U.S. position by geography has no advantage for us to move weapons to the Arctic, whereas the U.S.S.R. is the opposite. That again is because we are a southern and they are northern and their ports come into the Arctic, so you should keep in mind the 637s are really the answer to their Polaris, but it's much more sensible for us to keep our Polaris - if we get into a confrontation with the U.S.S.R., we'd pull back. We don't go into the Arctic. That increases our resupply problems, all of our problems. We pull back and increase the range of our missiles. They have the opposite position. They are in the Arctic. They come out of the Arctic. They will use the Arctic. It's to their advantage. When they pull back, they pull back into the Arctic. We're the opposite. When we pull back because of confrontation, we are going into other areas. So we just don't think of Polaris having any advantage for us in the Arctic.

Q: Up until this new 637 you had been on every trip up to the pole except once, when one came from the Pacific and one from the Atlantic –

Dr. L.: Whenever there were two boats in at the same time, I was not on one.

Q: But other than that, you have been on every under the ice?

Dr. L.: Right. The ones I've missed now are the 637 class. Again we had two simultaneous, the one my group was on the Pargo and I was on the Whale. Then, this past summer I did not go on the Queenfish. Allan Beal and Dick Boyle went.

Q: Why didn't you go?

Dr. L.: I'm busy on the laboratory business with the pool, which is strictly my own engineering and design. I've had that ever since the beginning. It's essential that I stay with that, and I'm particularly trying to get other staff members to become the number one people on these cruises. We've got to keep coming up with change, with younger people coming up, and the only way you can break them in is to have them go out, just like this summer on the Hammerhead I had Dick Boyle, Allan Beal, and myself on that, because Dick Boyle and Allan Beal should be the two people for the submarine cruises. Allan Beal, particularly, to take my place as far as the field work is concerned.

Q: Now what happens, after the 637?

Dr. L.: Well, the 637 class, of course, will be the mainstay of the Navy for years. And so now we're back to what is the purpose of our whole laboratory setup and our models. If we solve the model technology, then we would be using that to try to design submarines that would be the next generation after this one. The idea would be here that - to develop or design a submarine that would defeat this class. Keeping in mind that the 637 class is really an open-sea operator. It's a submarine built for the open sea, and just given equipment and techniques for moving from the open sea under the ice cover. It is not a submarine designed for operating in the Arctic. Undoubtedly, we have many ideas and thoughts on what one would do if one designed a submarine for working in ice, using ice to the maximum tactical advantage of the submarine. It's an entirely different approach than taking a submarine that's designed for the open sea and adapting it to the Arctic. I know almost certainly that if one did this, and used such a submarine you could very easily surpass the 637 class submarine.

Q: Do you think that one such should be developed?

Dr. L.: That is the purpose of our whole program, and why we are so intent on solving a model technology, so we can use this for designing a submarine that works in the ice cover. Because we must use techniques of models to make these studies. We're not going to go out and build a full-scale submarine until we've tried this. It's too costly a procedure. We've got to get some ideas, and throw out those that are poor, and pick the best on how the hull should be designed and how the equipment should be designed with model techniques before we ever build the first experimental model.

Lyon # 3 - 284

Q: And is that a matter of years in the future?

Dr. L.: I would assume it's a matter of years. It's going to be a number of years just to work out the model technology, and it will take time to try different ideas, different schemes, as to how that should be designed with one or two models and come up with the best design that we can from the model technique, and then sell this to the right people, depending on what the military situation is at that time - either modify a present-day submarine or start from scratch and build one, according to what we learn from our laboratory studies. This all based on the belief that we must have control of the ice-covered seas just as well as the open seas. They're one and the same thing.

Q: Is your pool the only one, to your knowledge, leave out Russia, of its kind in the world?

Dr. L.: That is right. In the western nations - the only pool for this kind of work. There have been small pools important to some others, but nothing —

Q: You made a statement when I saw you before that the Navy still doesn't include the Arctic in its strategic plans. Could you amplify that?

Dr. L.: Well, this is typical, I think, of the thinking certainly on the whole over past years, and it still is very much the way of thinking. One just normally classifies operations or any of the thinking of our Navy immediately into no ice or open sea - that is no ice and open sea is one side, and ice on the sea is the other, and most people as soon as there's ice on the sea just say that is not a Navy problem. They then start to classify problem subjects after that, e.g. sonar, radio, communications, weapons, and so on and so forth. A typical mental approach is to classify ice on the sea as not an open sea, therefore not a Navy problem. And we're running into this all the time in management, money, and everything else. Few people have started to think of ice on the sea as still a sea, but a very different type of sea problem. It should be recognized as a naval problem. Unless they do that, why, then, they're just not considering a part of the ocean that truly is part of the ocean. So the Arctic isn't integrated.

This has been part of the -- well, now we get into something controversial. During the 1960s management in the Navy changed a lot, management throughout the whole DOD changed a lot. That, in addition to the _Thresher_ case when submarines were not available, management changes had impact on our Arctic program. As well as from 1962 until 1967 without any field work going on we lost the impact field work has on guiding a program. Then in 1967 taking _Queenfish_ into the ice in Baffin Bay, it struck home for me that there was a very real danger to the Navy in this interface between the open sea and the ice cover, which we call the marginal sea ice zone. All during the 1958-62 period we'd been using the _Skate_ class submarines we'd been busy running across the whole of the Arctic Ocean, and all the glory and bands playing and everything else and the excitement of exploring the Arctic Ocean. We had at that period almost lost sight of the real danger to Navy, which is not in the central part of the Arctic Ocean, but right where the open sea and the ice come together. This cruise by Queenfish, 637, brought this point home again — something that we learned way back with the Carp, that from the open sea and the first hundred miles or so of the ice cover is such a mixed-up, muddled, unpredictable ocean environment. It was the Queenfish cruise that brought back what we had learned many years earlier with the Carp, Boarfish, Redfish cruises that the marginal zone from the open sea and the first hundred miles or fifty miles is a mixed-up, messy muddle of ice — temperatures, salinity, waves — a very confused area, which means that the sonar conditions are extremely confused, and the submarines can be lost in these areas, in the sense of not being detectable by another submarine or by aircraft. It's the perfect place to hide and move where detection is extremely difficult. Or at least, we now know so little about the area that it appears that detection of a submarine is very difficult.

As a result of this, and then looking at the research and development program of the Navy, particularly with regard to the Arctic, I became very concerned that the Navy's Research and Development program had not in any way considered this problem. We also brought it to the attention, after this cruise, of the force commanders in the Pacific and Atlantic that their real danger areas, particularly as far as the north Atlantic was concerned, were along the marginal zone of the sea ice of the north Atlantic. The attention was called of SubLant to this area, and they took immediate interest to watch it from there on. And so the cruises that followed with the Whale, Pargo, Hammerhead, focused on the problem of the marginal zone, plus many other operations in the marginal zone of the North Atlantic were definitely within the purview of under their control. But the R & D community of the Navy still had not recognized the marginal sea ice zone as a problem, and the research community continued to pour their effort into the central Arctic. Looking over their programs, I was very much concerned that there was no interest, no attack, being given to the marginal zone. All interest was centered in the central Arctic or centered in those fields which were biological fields, geological fields, which just did not give data and interest direct to the problem that faced the Navy in operating submarines and detecting submarines along marginal areas. Those are the danger areas.

About this same time, I remember giving a talk to the Chief of Naval Operations and submarine warfare people about this matter, and at the same time there was much discussion of what the Arctic program should be for the Navy. And Robert Frosch, the Assistant Secretary for R & D of Navy, gave me the assignment of reviewing research and development programs of the Navy with regard to the Arctic. So I started out to do this - an attempt had been done to make this review a number of years earlier by Guy Harris at the Underwater Sound Laboratory. He had started the review, I guess two years earlier, but he died before it could be completed and so the whole study had been left for a year or two and not completed. Then this agitation all over to review the program, so I received the assignment to do it.

I first intended to go to all the laboratories and all the people involved in Arctic R & D and see what programs they had, and try to fit them together and see what was missing, and try to get an over-all program that the Navy should be undertaking in R & D for the Arctic. I went through all the programs and through all the laboratories, and interviewed all the people that were involved. And I had made the promise that I would write up the report and bring it round and let them check it over, and all of us would mutually agree on the report. But then Dr. Frosch changed the direction part of the assignment, which was the extremely difficult part, but made it extremely interesting, namely, that I could not change the total amount of money in the R & D program for the Arctic. I was given an assignment without an open-ended study. When you're not to increase the funding it makes it a very different study than when you are allowed to increase the funding. The change of the assignment was not readily understood by many people, and they didn't realize this in discussion which made it very difficult. I added up the total amount now given to the R & D community of the Navy in the Arctic; had to use that money only; must not increase it, then assign it to problems I believed had the highest priority and must be done. Now, that's very different than just putting down all the problems that ought to be solved and adding up what should be done in the way of manpower and money to solve them. This realistic constraint particularly made it tough, because it means that I am saying to some programs - you've got to stop this program and do something else or go into some other business, or you've got to start Arctic programs which are top priority. This became particularly difficult - that's why I say "controversial." Because this was right at the time in 1967 when we felt that we must do something about the study of the marginal zones. The total Arctic program was really in the central Arctic, and was not solving the submarines' problem at the edge of the Arctic.

So, as a result, believing what I did, I came up with a report which has never been released because as Robert Frosch said in a speech my report was like a grenade rolling down the halls of the Pentagon with the safety pin pulled because of the orientation that it demanded in changing programs, from what was now being funded and people doing to something else. I felt this had to be done to solve this marginal sea ice problem.

Q: Was any action taken on it?

Dr. L.: There's been all kinds of reaction. Reaction is still going on. That's why we can't finish the discussion. The whole picture is that what we've been saying about doing model work for the future generations of submarines, that is progressing — we're working on that part of it. Another part of it is the study of the acoustics of the marginal sea ice. And now, this year, in fiscal 1972 that is under way. These are the first years that the R & D community in the Navy are attacking these problems, and they are being attacked by people in the Naval Research Laboratory, by my group here managing the Applied Physics Laboratory, of the University of Washington, and General Motors group at Santa Barbara, some of the people in the Oceanographic Office. So there is that much under way now, field work to be done, and laboratory work, which is aimed at study of the marginal zone.

It certainly has been a lot of change and discussion on some of the much older programs which have been aimed at the central Arctic. I think a cry has definitely been heard, and the program is changing. Whether this has been the right decision, only the future will tell.

Q: But those are your recommendations?

Dr. L.: Those were the recommendations that were made, and they had certainly been controversial, and caused a lot of --

Q: I'm sure controversial by the people who had different ideas, of course!

Dr. L.: That's right, and if it's controversial maybe it isn't the right decision as to where the effort should be placed. Anyway, there has been a real shift in the R & D program to make an attempt to understand the marginal zone, and only the future will tell whether this was the correct thing to do or not. But we feel - at least it is my belief that the marginal zone is the area in which the submarine has a tremendous advantage, how much we don't know. Submarines will always be seeking out marginal zone areas to operate in, as opposed to the open sea, or as opposed to the more uniform under-ice environment well inside the Arctic Ocean. It is the marginal zone where this muddled, mixed-up affair of ice and water gives the submarine particular advantage to use the environment for hiding, for protected movement, a sanctuary from which to strike.

Q: It would seem to me that if we do not fully understand and are not able to combat some force might be there that is opposed to us, we're giving a natural sanctuary to an enemy. Is that going too far?

Dr. L.: No. I just sort of feel that "sanctuary" is exactly the word to use. It can be a sanctuary for submarines. You can't find him unless you bump into him.

Well, that brings us about right to where we stand now. So I can say that our program now is making its first attack since 195 on this marginal sea ice problem. We have finally returned to it, and on the submarine side of the picture we are definitely moving ahead, solving the model technology which should lead us to designing a generation of submarines for the Arctic, which would be an entirely new concept from that of taking one of our attack submarines and adapting from the open sea to sea ice situation.

Q: Is it necessary in the marginal zone to have nuclear submarines?

Dr. L.: No - well, a nuclear submarine has a terrific advantage in that you wouldn't have to worry about coming to the surface, but it's not as essential as it is in the central Arctic.

Q: Because ordinary submarines have gone in and out of that zone freely.

Dr. L.: That's right. You can get in and out, but again, assuming one is nuclear and the other is non-nuclear, the nuclear has an overwhelming advantage because she doesn't have to surface.

Q: I read some place that there is the possibility of the development of a tanker submarine to bring oil from offshore Alaska. Have you had any occasion to do exploration in that field?

Dr. L.: We've been in discussions, but the people who have done the most thinking on this are Electric Boat Company because they had to, in answer to the oil companies, go through the actual design exercises for such a vehicle. And it is perfectly feasible as far as the environment is concerned. Whether it's economical is an entirely different question. What the terminal facilities would be is an entirely different question. How do you land the submarine the oilfield and bring the oil from the oilfield by piping out to a facility which is under the ice cover and then bring the submarine in and load him - I'm not in any position to pass judgment. However, these are the kind of problems I think the model technology will be useful in solving. Bigger problems are just the economics of whether it pays to take oil out by such means, which is certainly far more expensive than getting oil in other areas and using standard steamers, tramp tankers, or any other kind of ships which are relatively low cost as a process. Once you combine nuclear power and the highly specialized personnel required to handle such tankers, the cost begins to rise, plus the terminal facilities required. It's hard for me to visualize the economics. In the immediate future or even in the fairly long future, whether the price of the oil would permit the higher costs. I don't see it. It just seems to me there are other fields, shale fields, other techniques available or can be developed that would underprice that oil, unless the pipeline can be solved.

Q: We haven't really talked much about you now, and this is your biography. So I am curious as to what kind of a person - how do you describe your own personality?

Dr. L.: How can I answer that!

Q: Maybe you could describe it this way. What kind of personality do you think a person should have in order to be successful in doing this type of exploration?

Dr. L.: Patience and persistance!

Q: I have one comment to throw in. You seem to like the cold weather. No matter what the temperature, you seem to enjoy being bare-footed and dressed - though I'm freezing, so you seem to be adapted to cold weather!

Dr. L.: Yes, maybe so. I've always been - I don't know whether the Arctic did that or whether it was like that before, because I've always lived in California which to most people is kind of cold anyway, and out of doors. So, I think that's where that comes from. I like the sunshine, I like to lie in the sun all the time.

Q: Let's go back to you   . You said patience and persistance. Can you amplify that a bit?

Dr. L.: Well, a lot of patience is required in attacking these kind of problems. I don't know that they're any different than any other kind of experimental problems. It's hard to judge because I've been in it so long and the challenge came way back when - the real challenge is when no one else is in it - in the field - and you've got the interest of using submarines in unusual situations, and then the challenge just stayed there, so I tried to follow this thing, and also always found at least a few people here and there - persons who were also interested. So the development of Arctic submarines never became an impersonalized management problem. It was always mixed up with people, individuals by name, which meant far more to me. I've never been able to fit into a management. I've always worked with people I knew by name anywhere in the Navy. Even today, the management process leaves me. I still feel influenced by people, know who I have to talk with even though we try to set up a management process which is more impersonalized, which is done by management processing rather than by people.

Q: They tell me you resent the socializing that comes from being such a prominent person in the field?

Dr. L.: Right, I've never shown any eager interest in that.

Q: Would you consider yourself or would you ever agree that someone called you rather cool and unflappable?

Dr. L.: Possibly. I don't know. Maybe so. Maybe I just don't react quickly, and that's what it is. You're asking about the socializing. I've always believed, even when I was in University of California, before I came here - I did not wish to make where I worked my social function. I kept this with the Navy, too. I just don't care to involve socially with the people I need to work. When I'm working with them, that's business, that's working, so I don't want to have any social responsibility to these people. I've avoided naval circles for this reason. I have no relationship there. So we've always tried to keep our social functions, like in badminton or handball or University women or the churches or somewhere else an entirely different relationship. When I go to work, there's no feeling that what you said at a cocktail party or what you did somewhere else together - the only social function once in a while is we have the staff people for a get-together, but that's just a small group then not related in any way to the total naval center or force commanders or anyone else of this sort.

Q: But you must have lots of demands on your time to speak?

Dr. L.: There have been. We mentioned that. After the Nautilus we had an awful lot of demand and then it started to get kind of nasty in some ways and I just refused. They kept me speaking only to technical groups where there would be some interchange of value, not just an entertainment.

Q: And for your recreation, what do you enjoy the most?

Dr. L.: For recreation now, I guess the last few years, has been badminton entirely, tournament play, and that takes probably eight hours a week and that's about all that can be given, and this is for a combination of staying in physical condition and good health and also complete mental relaxation. You can't be thinking about anything when you're playing a badminton game. It's just a complete break from whatever one is working on.

Q: If you were to stop and think of the things professionally that you'd be the proudest of, would you have a thought on that subject?

Dr. L.: I hadn't really thought of that, other than that -- I'm not quite sure what you mean, but it's bring this whole Arctic submarine from way back when it was nothing, just a trial, way back at the start to this 637 class, which is a full-fledged Arctic operation and watching other people use it.

Q: Without you it would have not occurred!

Dr. L.: Well, I don't know if that's quite true. There are a lot of people involved here. I'm really sort of the one that stayed with it from beginning to end. Now, whether that necessarily also means that without me they wouldn't have had them - I don't know.

Q: Didn't you start it? You were the initiator -

Dr. L.: I certainly was involved in the start, but other people had to assist, and I stayed with it to the end, so I'm the continuity. That's correct. And our group here in San Diego had - a few of us - have been together and have been the reason why it's gone from the beginning to the end. It hasn't been anywhere else, that's quite true. We started it and stayed with it and solved the problems and continued to provide all the information that we could find.

Q: Do you have a characteristic that you wish you didn't have, or that you'd say that's my weakness characteristic? Could you think of that point?

Dr. L.: Oh, perhaps it's not communicating more with people, instead of this don't bother!

Q: Well, I hope if you have any other ideas that you will think about them and when you get this manuscript, feel free to add them.

Dr. L.: Thank you very much.

Q: I hope I haven't overlooked any aspect of your career or the development of the under-ice submarine explorations or the laboratory itself that should be included in your biography. We haven't put in your wife's name or the names of your children.

Dr. L.: Virginia B. Lyon, wife. And my daughter is Lorraine Lyon Minning, living in Walnut Creek, California. My son is Russell Roy Lyon, and is here on Point Loma. My son is 27 and my daughter is 29 - in fact she's 29 today.

Q: Oh, my, you'd better do something about that!

Well, thank you, this is a different type interview than I've done, and I hope that you like the manuscript, and it sure will be a welcome addition to the library of the Institute.

Thank you very much.

Index

for series of interviews with

Dr. Waldo Lyon

Anderson, Captain William: skipper of NAUTILUS, 105, 111, 116-117; preparations for 1958 expedition, 126, 128, 134, 136, 140-143, 154, 163-165, 176

Antarctica: 15, 19-20, 26

Arctic Expedition of 1954: purpose of expedition, 81-84; expedition ends a period, 84

Arctic Exploratory Series with submarines: purely scientific series to the Arctic, 1949, 59-60; 1950-54, 61-65; conference in 1949 to chart future expeditions, 65; series comes to end with expedition of 1954, 84-85; order from BuShips to cease all Arctic work, 97-99; new series from Atlantic begins with NAUTILUS in 1957, 109 ff.; OPERATION SUNSHINE (expedition of NAUTILUS, 1958), 124 ff; duel purpose of 1958 voyage, 131 ff; aerial reconnaissance to determine ice cover in Chuckchi, 138; secrecy of NAUTILUS expedition, 141-146, 159-161 ff; 2nd trip, 1958, 164 ff; denouement, 176-178; SKATE expedition, 183 ff; SARGO expedition, 206, 224; SEA DRAGON expedition, 224 ff; deals with problem of icebergs in Baffin Bay - the last of remaining questions, 227; end of engineer experimental cruises came with SEA DRAGON, 228-229; a new series begins in 1962 - concerned with Arctic Warfare problems, 230-231; SKATE, SEA DRAGON and STATEN ISLAND participate, 230; what to do about weapons, 231; 1962 cruise points up the problems with weapons, 233

Arctic R and & programs: Lyon undertakes study of coordination and writes a report, 287-288; reactions to Lyon report, 289-290

Arctic Submarine Laboratory: origins in 1950, 89-90, 91-93; new designation, 267-268; current studies involving heat exchange, atmosphere and weather, 269-271; purpose of Laboratory, 283; discussion of Navy thinking as it pertains to ice-covered waters, 284-285; dangers in marginal sea-ice areas, 285-286

Arctic Warfare: after series of engineering, experimental journeys to Arctic, other cruises planned to explore warfare situations, 230, 281-282

Arctic Waters: discussion of entrance to from Atlantic in contrast with Pacific entrance, 109; discussion of varying depths in Pacific area (Bering Sea) and the Atlantic, 207

Arctic weather: conditions of, 255

Atomic bomb: reactions to, 13-14

USS ATULE, SS: used for experimental ice operations in 1946, 29, 43

Aurand, VADM Evan Peter: 123, 134

Baffin Bay: 29, 82; testing of icebergs and sonar system of SEA DRAGON in, 226

Banks Island: 83

Barnes, Clifford: Oceanographic Department, University of Washington, 63

Barrow Sea Valley: 169; SARGO uses this route to deep water of Chukchi, 214-215

Barrow Strait: 226-227

USS BAYA, SS: NEL experimental SS on 1949 Canadian expedition, 59, 65

Bayne, Comdr. Duke: 134, 163

Beal, Allan: Arctic SS Lab staff, 282

Beaufort Sea: 63, 65-66, 75, 78, 82, 170-171, 218

Beaufort Sea Expedition of 1952: 66-73

Bennett, Capt. Rawson: Commanding Officer of NEL, 28, 57, 91

Bering Sea: 27, 60, 81, 128, 168-169, 207, 213-214, 221

Bikini Atoll: 11

Blair, Captain Carvel Hall: responsible for preparation of NAUTILUS for Arctic Expedition, 105, 127, 246

USS BLOWER, SS: accompanied CARP on her 1948 Arctic expedition, 46

USS BOARFISH, SS: assigned as experimental SS with Navy Electronics Lab, 29; equipped with QLA scanning system, 32; echo sounder added to her equipment, 42; first dive under ice, 35-40

Boyd, Dave; 200-201

Boyle, Dick: with the Arctic SS Lab, 275; on 1969 cruise to Arctic, 276

Burke, Admiral Arleigh: 101, 134

USS BURTON ISLAND, icebreaker: participated in 1950 expedition to Arctic regions, 64; again in 1951 and 1952, 66, 70; expedition of 1953, 77-78, 80-81; expedition of 1954, 82-85

Byrd, RADM Richard E.: 15

Calvert, VADM James: skipper of SS SKATE, 183; 186; his description of Waldo Lyon, 190; 203

Cameron, Bill: Oceanographer at Nanaimo, B.C., 7, 14, 59

Canadian Archipelago: area of study for several scientific expeditions, 1950-54, 65, 77, 80-81; expedition of 1954 concentrated on oceanography and bathymetry in archipelago, 82, 217

Canadian Naval Laboratory: 65

Canadian Scientific efforts: 6-9, 59, 61-63

CANCOLIM: small Canadian vessel with 1952 Beaufort Sea Expedition, 67

Cape Lisburne: 158

Cape Prince of Wales: 60, 77, 80, 84; Arctic SS Lab maintains equipment there to measure ice passing through, 149-151; 196; 258; single family maintained on station for year-round observations, 269

USS CARP, SS: experimental ice SS, summer of 1948, 42; task assigned her, 45-46; 47-48; use of plane for spotting, 49-50; problems remaining after expedition, 51-52, 106, 108, 175

HMCS CEDARWOOD: Canadian oceanographic vessel used on 1949 expedition to Arctic, 59, 65

Christenson, Ralph: at Navy Electronics Lab, 56

Chuckchi Sea: 33, 41, 48, 50-51, 60, 126, 138, 152-153, 207, 213-215, 217, 219, 221

Cold water problems - with Echo Sounding gear: 6, 9

Combs, VADM Thomas S.: 134

Crary, Al: Chief Scientist on A/F Ice Station, Fletcher's Ice Island, 78

Cruzen, VADM Richard H.: task force commander, HIGH JUMP, 22

Curie, Franz: technical director of NEL, 97, 165

Daspit, RADM Lawrence R.: Chief of Staff to Admiral Momsen, 67, 164

Delsasso, Lt. Comdr. Leo: member of physics department at UCLA, 3, 191

DEW Line (Distance Early Warning System): 77-78; Canadian-U.S. Forces concentrate on and all other Arctic Expeditions come to an end, 85; description of forces involved, 85-89; 166

Echo-sounding systems: description of Lyon's work in this field, 5; work in cold, Canadian waters, 6, 9; use at Bikini Atoll, 12; system 'looking up' installed in BOARFISH, 33; work with 1949 expedition to Arctic, 60; only upward-looking echo sounding system available to NAUTILUS, 106, 108-109, 187

Electric Boat Company: installed equipment in NAUTILUS for 1958 expedition, 132-133; lost out in competition for contract on first of STURGEON class SSs, 274; has given some thought to construction of tanker submarines, 291-292

Esquimalt: 65

Fathometer: 5-6, 33, 187

Fields, Dr. George: Chief scientist, Defense Research Board of Canada, 65

Fletcher, Colonel Joe: 77-78

FRAM - Arctic exploratory ship, 1892-1896, 40, 52

Frosch, Robert: Assistant Secretary of the Navy for R&D, 287; asks Lyon to review R&D programs as they relate to Arctic, 287-288; places a limitation on funding for Arctic R&D, 288

Georgia Strait: 7

German submarines: WWII, 7-8; attack on Coast Guard icebreaker NORTHLAND, 8-9

Grenfell, VADM Elton W.: as ComSubPac raised question of icing of snorkels in diesel SSs, 168, 245-246

Gulf of St. Lawrence: 8

Gyro compass: ceased to function on NAUTILUS when near North Pole, 111

Haggerty, The Hon. James: White House aide to President Eisenhower, 124

USS HAMMERHEAD, SS: on Arctic cruise in complete darkness of December, 206; 279-280, 286

Harald Island: 214-216

Harbor Defense Systems: experiments on how to penetrate, 4; work with Canadians, 7; West Coast work sheds light on East Coast problems with German SSs, 7-8

Hayward, VADM John: conjecture about NAUTILUS and Arctic oceans, 144

Humble Oil Co.: uses NEL ice pool for testing models of AO MANHATTAN, 260

Hydrographic Office, U.S. Navy: 63

Inertial Navigating Equipment: installed on NAUTILUS for expedition of 1958, 127-128, 172

Inyokern: Naval Weapons Center, 267

Jackson, Senator Henry M.: attempt to interest him in Arctic SS program, 100-101

Kara and Laptev Seas: islands in this area responsible for calving of icebergs, 227; 235

Kennedy, President John F.: bestows Presidential award on Dr. Lyon for Arctic work, 236-237

Korean War: 96-97

Kotzebue, Alaska: 138

HMCS LABRADOR: Canadian icebreaker, 82; expedition of 1954, 84, 89; 225-226

LaFond, Gene: head of oceanographic section, NEL, 34; takes group of scientists on NEREUS to obtain multitudinous scientific data, 34; on BOARFISH for first dive under the ice, 35; on expedition of 1949, 59, 178

Lancaster Sound: 226-227

LITTLE AMERICA: 20-22

Lyon, Dr. Waldo: background information, education, 1-3; comprises in his person and his laboratory element of continuity in Arctic research, 95-96; receives Presidential award for Arctic work, 236-237; discussion of personal characteristics, etc., 292-294

Malloy, Art: represents Oceanographic Office on SARGO expedition, 214; on SEA DRAGON expedition, 225

Malmgren: early scientist working with ice chemistry, 51

MANHATTAN, tanker: Humble Oil tanker for use in Arctic, 260-262

Mark 37 torpedo: problems with torpedoes in Arctic resulted in new developments, 232-233

USS MARYSVILLE: NEL's surface ship for oceanographic work, 1949, 59, 65

MAUDE: Norwegian ice-strengthened ship, used in Amundsen Expedition in Arctic, 1919-1926, 40-41

McCann, VADM A. R.: 26-27, 33, 38-39, 42, 45

McClaren, Comdr.: executive on board QUEENFISH, 275

McClure Strait: 82-83; difficulties of McClure Expedition in Strait in 19th century, 84; 217, 227

McWethy, Robert: 64, 99, 102

Melville Sound: 82

USS MERRICK, AKA: 18, 20

Mercy Bay: 83

Momsen, VADM Charles Bowers: takes over as SubPac and cooperates with Beaufort Sea expedition of 1952, 66-67, 76, 94; 102-103

Morse, Leighton: on BOARFISH for first dive under Arctic ice, 35

USS MT. OLYMPUS: flagship for OPERATION HIGH JUMP, 20-21

Munk, Dr. Walter: on BOARFISH expedition, 34

Nanaimo, B. C.: 7, 14, 59

Nansen Sound: 217

NAUTILUS, SS: (ex-O-12), submarine used by Sir Hubert Wilkins in Arctic, 26-27; 115

USS NAUTILUS, SS: 99-101, 103-104; equipped for Arctic Expedition, 105-107; involved in expedition of 1957-58, 109; discussion of her accomplishments, 110-111; crew, 112-113; lessons learned from 1957 expedition, 114 ff; Arctic equipment removed in Scotland, 122-123; preparations for 1958 expedition, 126-128; changes made in her equipment, 127-131; dual purpose of her voyage, 131; turns back with first attempt, 136; new air breathing system installed, 137; encounters unusually deep draft ice on first attempt in Chuckchi, 150-156; need for decision to stay in area or retreat and return later, 153; security matters, 154 ff.; end of voyage, 176-178

NAVAJO Missile: inertial navigating equipment used for NAUTILUS, 128

USS NEREUS, SS: tender accompanies BOARFISH on Arctic expedition, 33, 40

Nicholson, Comdr.: skipper of SARGO (1960), 210, 213, 218, 220

Nome, Alaska: end of SEA DRAGON cruise, 228

NORTHLAND, USCG Icebreaker: German SS attack on from under the ice, 8-9

NORTHWIND, USCG Icebreaker: with operation HIGH JUMP, 22, 22; expedition of 1953 to Arctic waters, 77-78, 80; expedition of 1954, 81, 83, 85-86, 227

Office of Scientific Research and Development: national organization under Dr. Vannevar Bush, 10

OPERATION HIGH JUMP: inception of this project, 15; SS SENNET added to operation, 17-20; description of Antarctic ice, 21-26

OPERATION SUNSHIN: 125, 131; secrecy maintained on cruise of
    NAUTILUS, 133-134; 135; skipper returns her to Hawaii to await
    changes in icing conditions, 136; account of first attempt,
    148-149 ff; second attempt at North Pole, 164 ff; return home
    via England, 176-178; publicity, 179-182

OPERATION WONDERLAND: German efforts against Russian shipping
    in Barents Sea and Kara Sea, 9

Palmer, Comdr. J. H.: skipper of CARP, 45

USS PARGO, SS: Arctic Cruise of 1969, 276-277, 286

Phelps, Captain: NEL official, 97

Point Barrow, Alaska: 76, 78, 85, 169

Point Loma, California: 2, 9, 18-19

Polaris: 281

Polynya: Russian word for Open Spaces in ice cover, 48, 68, 76

Port Hueneme: 18

Pritchard, Don: on BOARFISH expedition, 34

Pro-Submarine Warfare: early work at Radio and Sound Lab, 3-4;
    continuous interchange with Fleet operators, 5

QLA System: definition of, 30-31; lack of such equipment on
    NAUTILUS expeditions, 108-109; similar equipment installed
    on SARGO, 207-209; system fails in SARGO, efforts to repair,
    215-216

USS QUEENFISH, SS: of STURGEON Class, built by Newport News Ship-
    building Co., 274; taken on brief expedition to Baffin Bay,
    275-276; 1969 expedition points up problems with marginal
    sea-ice areas, 286

Rashon, Art: originator of QLA system, 30; on BOARFISH for first

dive under the ice, 35; built sonar equipment needed for
SARGO cruise of 1960, 207-208; 210; 216-217; 219; 224-225; 234

USS REDFISH, SS: assigned by RADM Momsen to serve with 1952 Canadian-
U.S. Beaufort Sea expedition, 66-69; crucial test of Beaufort
Sea Expedition of 1952, 68-75, 77-78, 80; returned to ComSub-
Pac after expedition of 1953, 94-95; her equipment for
Arctic use transferred to NAUTILUS, 105-106; 159; 175

Revell, Dr. Roger: 11-12

Rickover, VADM Hyman G.: on sending SS NAUTILUS to Arctic, 104, 134

Robertson, Commodore: Commanding Officer of HMCS LABRADOR, 82, 89,
144; 225-226

ROWRY, Rex: 122, 130; on NAUTILUS Expedition of 1959, 140, 162,
164, 166, 178

Ruble, Wilbur J.: Commanding Officer, Radio and Sound Laboratory, 191

Russian Submarine activities: 239-240; 277-278; 281-282

St. Lawrence Island: 158

Sanders, Fred: Canadian Scientist - head of Canadian Naval Laboratory in Esquimalt, 65

USS SARGO, SS: used in Arctic expedition of 1960, 109-193; planning
for shallow water experiment in Arctic waters, 206-207;
description of sonar equipment designed for expedition of 1960,
207-209; problems encountered, 210-213; judged outstanding
ship of all Arctic cruises, 213; reaches North Pole, 217;
make-shift sonar equipment causes problems, 218-221; summary
of expedition, 223-224; 225; contrasted with STURGEON Class
of SSs in some ice equipment details, 274; Arctic cruise of
1969, 276

Schatzberg, Walter: 188, 203

Scientists and Naval Officers, cooperation of: 43-44

Scripps Institute: 27

USS SEADRAGON: submarine makes McClure strait transit in 1960, 84; getting ready for expedition of June 1960, 217; testing sonar with icebergs in Baffin Bay, 226; ends cruise at Nome, 228; participates with SKATE and STATEN ISLAND in expedition of 1962, 230 ff

Sea Ice: growing of ice in laboratory (NEL), 242-245; study of sea ice properties, etc., 249-258; study of technology of sea ice and ships in sea ice, 262

Sea of Othotsk: 246

SEDOV: ship used by Russians in 1936-37 in polar expedition, 52

USS SENNET, SS: becomes part of OPERATION HIGH JUMP, 17-18; description of her equipment for HIGH JUMP, 18-19; problems in ice of Antarctica, 22-25

Service Squadron #1: controlled icebreakers used in Arctic expeditions, 1950-54, 61-62, 67

USS SKATE: SS used in Arctic explorations of 1958 and 1959, 109, 129, 131-132, 161, 164, 166, 172; carries out quite different assignment from NAUTILUS, 178-179; a winter expedition planned, 183; depth-sensing system designed and installed for winter expedition, 184-185; other installations, 186-188; new problems for winter cruise, 189-190; uneventful cruise but much knowledge gained of winter ice, 193-195; discussions of calculations on necessary upward pressure of SS to break ice surface, 197-198; frogmen and scuba divers, 200; problems with sea-water circulating pump, 201-202; use of flood lights and TV, 204; distance travelled, 205-206; participates with SS SEA DRAGON and STATEN ISLAND in expedition of 1962, 230 ff; problem of flooding while submerged, 239; summary description of SKATE Class as it was equipped for Arctic work, 273

SLOT - between Greeland and Svalsbard: used as escape route by NAUTILUS, 115-116

Sputnik: 123

USS STATEN ISLAND: Icebreaker with DEW Line operation of 1955, 85; participates in Arctic expedition of 1962, 230

Steele, Comdr. George, III: skipper of SEA DRAGON, 225

STURGEON Class, SSs (637); first of Arctic-capable submarines, 234; 273-274

Submarines vs icebreakers: lessons learned on Beaufort Sea Expedition of 1952, 73-75; evidence of ice piling up due to winds, expedition of 1953, 78-80

Submarine Signal Co. (Raytheon): 187

Sverdrup, Harald: Norwegian oceanographer, 27, 40; scientist in MAUDE, 40-41; 115-117, 121-122; 152; 214

Swartz, Comdr. John: skipper of BURTON ISLAND, expedition of 1950, 64

Tacoma, Washington: Lyon hides out until NAUTILUS sails from Seattle, 141-142

Taylor Model Basin: NEL sea ice pool are corollary in that they handle similar problems with ice, 265

USS THRESHER, SS: loss of causes Arctic program to halt temporarily, 233-234; 239

Torpedoes, Mark 37: 273

USS TRIGGER: diesel-powered SS accompanies NAUTILUS, 119

USS TRITON, SS: 240, 241

Tully, Jack: Oceanographer at Nanaimo, B.C., 7, 14, 59, 65

Turner, Jack: Commanding Officer of BOARFISH, 39

UCLA: Dr. Lyon returns to teach in physics department, 1948-49, 55-56; course in spectroscopy, 56

UQC, underwater telephone: standard equipment on submarines, 235

T-3, Drifting Ice Station: 227

U. S. Coast and Geodetic Survey: 83; after cruise of SARGO sent party into Bering and Chuckchi Seas for close line surveys of sea bottom, 229

U. S. Coast Guard: uses models of icebreaker designs in pool at NEL, 258-259; helping in financing of 2nd pool at NEL for work with models, 263

U. S. Navy Electronics Laboratory: 10, 15; Division of Marine Research, 15-16; permission given by CNO to send SS on OPERATION HIGH JUMP, 17; freedom to develop projects within purview of laboratory, 28; reorganization, 56-59; 97; special research division sponsors Arctic expeditions, 50-54; 97; possesses a betatron for X-ray work on steel castings, 100; not made aware of 1958 expedition of NAUTILUS, 133, 165; review of laboratory work in preparation for Arctic explorations from 1950 on, 241 ff; growing sea ice in laboratory, 242-245; building pool for sea ice, 244-247; early solution found to snorkel icing problem, 247-249; from 1959-63 pool redesigned for study of sea ice, 249; study of sea ice, 249-258;

study of technology of sea ice and ships in sea ice, 262; use of pool in helping Coast Guard with icebreaker models, 258-259; assists Humble Oil with models for MANHATTAN, 260; a second pool for work with models being constructed, 263-264; organization changes come to NEL, 266-267

U. S. Navy Radio and Sound Laboratory: 2-3, 9, 11; administrative set-up in WW II, 16; 191

Vancouver: 46

Viscount Melville Sound: 227

Walker, Archie: on NAUTILUS expedition of 1958, 131, 134, 166-167, 170

War Research Division, UCLA: 9-10, 15, 18

USS WHALE, SS: Arctic cruise of 1969, 276-277, 286

Wilkins, Sir Hubert: 9, 27, 115; burial service from SKATE in Arctic waters, 199-200

Wilkinson, VADM Eugene P.: (Dennis): Commanding Officer of NAUTILUS, 99-100; 103-104

Wittmann, Walter: representative of Oceanographic office on SKATE winter cruise, 188; on SARGO expedition, 214; on SEA DRAGON expedition, 225, 234

USS YANCEY, AKA: on OPERATION HIGH JUMP, 20

www.ingramcontent.com/pod-product-compliance
Lightning Source LLC
Chambersburg PA
CBHW082150070526
44585CB00020B/2158